Inference and Persuasion

Leslie Armour & Richard Feist

Fernwood Publishing • Halifax

BC
71
.A76
2005

Editing: Jane Butler
Printed and bound in Canada by: Hignell Printing Limited

A publication of:
Fernwood Publishing
Site 2A, Box 5, 32 Oceanvista Lane
Black Point, Nova Scotia, B0J 1B0
and 324 Clare Avenue
Winnipeg, Manitoba, R3L 1S3
www.fernwoodbooks.ca

Fernwood Publishing Company Limited gratefully acknowledges
the financial support of the Department of Canadian Heritage,
the Nova Scotia Department of Tourism and Culture
and the Canada Council for the Arts for our publishing program.

Library and Archives Canada Cataloguing in Publication

Armour, Leslie, 1931-
Inference and persuasion : an introduction to logic and critical
reasoning / Leslie Armour and Richard Feist.

Includes bibliographical references and index.
ISBN 1-55266-158-X

1. Logic. 2. Reasoning. I. Feist, Richard, 1964- II. Title.

BC71.A76 2005   160   C2005-901602-7

CONTENTS

Chapter 4

Chapter 5

Part III: Belief and the Fallacies

Chapter 6

Part IV: Logic and Knowledge

PREFACE

THIS IS A DIFFERENT SORT OF LOGIC BOOK. It might even be described as a book for people who like to think but don't like logic books. Logic texts offered to undergraduates and those few books that seek to address the small part of the general public curious about logic frequently, at least in the English-speaking world, have three properties I find very odd: They proceed with great self-assurance as if the basic questions of logical theory were long ago settled; they avoid disputed theoretical questions; and they concentrate almost exclusively on the logics associated with philosophers like Russell, Frege and Quine, logics much favoured by thinkers in what is usually called the "analytic tradition." Not only do they ignore the logics of Hegel, Bradley, Bosanquet and other idealistic thinkers and the dialectical logics offered by Marx, they also have little to say about the logics derived from John Dewey and others like him.

This is currently a serious problem. The logics most favoured in text books were designed to talk about the world as a collection of bits and pieces of things, a world composed of individual things, some concrete (like humans, mountains and pigs) and others abstract (like classes or sets). Most people in the environmental movement now insist that the world must be seen as a whole and that a radical reconceptualization is required. If this notion can work at all, it will certainly require rethinking basic logical notions, and philosophers like Dewey as well as philosophers in the Hegelian tradition (which includes Marxists) have made contributions to this. Thus there are obvious uses for dialectical logics and for logics like those of John Dewey. This book is not, however, written in a missionary spirit, for I certainly do not believe that all the problems associated with a rethinking have been addressed, much less solved. The book poses problems and makes suggestions, but it does not, of course, seek to ignore or to denigrate the logics widely regarded as "standard," unless arguments to the effect that standard logics do not contain all that is interesting by way of logic are taken to be denigration.

Behind its order and approach, there is, though, a well-known philosophical story—about which we can form our own judgements. Immanuel Kant, whose ideas and problems have never been far from the minds of serious philosophers since he published his *Critique of Pure Reason* in 1781 and 1787, claimed to have discovered something very important: Reason, left to itself and without reference to experience, ends in paradox. Unrestrained, it can support *both* members of pairs of contradictory propositions, and itself generate contradictions. Experience, by contrast, if we simply think of its content, is anchored in individual perception or "intuition" and is, therefore, subjective. Only bringing reason and experience together will enable us to reason successfully.[1]

The order of exposition here begins with those logics (especially the modern ones in the tradition of Russell and Frege) which take themselves to be independent of experience. The paradoxes produced by logics—particularly the central paradox developed by Russell himself—form a major part of the theme. It then proceeds to John Dewey's logic, which incorporates empirical elements and asks how well Dewey succeeded in overcoming the subjectivity in such ideas. Dialectical logics, in a tradition associated with Hegel, are then explored to see whether they provide the basis for some effective integration that will not (or, at least, need not) end in paradox or subjectivity.

Even apart from such theoretical concerns, however, the exclusion of various interesting "logics" is another reason that undergraduates not infrequently find the standard logic books arrogant and uninformative and wish they were enrolled in other courses, while the general public ignores them more often than one would wish. (How often does one find a logic book reviewed in a daily newspaper or a periodical for general readers?)

Ultimately, however, this book is predicated on the belief that a knowledge of logic is an important element of human freedom in the kind of society in which we live—one in which information and argument are crucial to one's understanding and survival. One must be able to assess the claims of politicians, bureaucrats, scientists, manufacturers, used car salespeople, editorial writers and even the clergy who enter our homes every day via television. If we cannot defend ourselves against them and make up our own minds, we become victims.

This book is also predicated on the belief that many of the most central issues in dispute in logical theory can be stated simply so that any serious person can understand them. It is not, to be sure, meant to perform all the tasks that other books address. For particular courses, books that offer more details about the calculus of propositions or moral or scientific reasoning can easily be used as additional materials.

For the general reader, though, it should be possible to read this book through and to follow, from the footnotes, only those issues of particular interest.

I have tried everywhere to indicate doubts where doubts ought to be indicated, to allow such expressions as "perhaps," "maybe" and "it is possible that," which one finds all too seldom in logic books. The reader is invited to argue with the authors and with all the others mentioned in the book.

Curiously, for two thousand years, despite important writings to the contrary, many people thought that Aristotle had settled the most important questions in logic. In fact, whenever a system of logic has been laid out, it has enabled us to see beyond its limits, and so to ask new questions. In logic, nothing is settled. Perhaps it is the very nature of the human spirit, as R.G. Collingwood thought, that it no sooner lays out a system than it has, by its very nature, transcended it.

The origins of this book are in the complaints that my students in Cleveland and Ottawa raised against the logic books they had been given to read. I therefore owe thanks to students at the University of Ottawa and at Cleveland State University who took part in courses in which these questions were raised. I also owe thanks to Cindy Bellinger, who struggled to decipher and get straight some early drafts, and to Diana Armour, without whose editorial work this would have been a much worse book.

More recently, Richard Feist has used it in several of *his* classes. Significant improvements—and some simplifications—are the result of his knowledge of mathematics and logic while others stem from the reactions of his classes.

Leslie Armour,
The Dominican College of Philosophy and Theology,
Ottawa, October, 2004

THE HISTORY OF MATHEMATICS AND LOGIC demonstrates an interesting combination. Although the truths of mathematics and logic never really change, they are constantly susceptible to new and deeper understandings and interpretations. This text, in my opinion, is the only one that has managed to encapsulate this combination and portray it in an accessible manner. I am pleased to have played a role in this text's development.

Richard Feist,
Saint Paul University,
Ottawa, October, 2004

Note

1. Immanuel Kant, *Kritik der reinen Vernunft,* Riga: Johann Friedrich Hartknock, 1781, 1787. The translation as *Critique of Pure Reason* by Norman Kemp Smith, London: Macmillan, 1929 is standard in English. Kant also wrote his own *Logic*, Konigsburg: Friedrich Nicolovius, 1800, tr. Robert Hartman and Wolfgang Schwartz, Indianapolis: Bobbs-Merrill, 1974. Though the edition of the *Logic* regarded as standard dates from 1782 (a year after the first version of the *Critique*), it only partially covers the ideas in Kant's major works.

Chapter 1

INFERENCE, LANGUAGE AND FREEDOM

1. Freedom and the Idea of Inference

What is "thinking"? It can consist either of random and open mental acts like daydreaming or of directed and focused mental acts like problem solving. We are concerned with focused acts.

Problem solving begins when one encounters a situation and wishes to change it. Suppose that one is in Canada and wants to travel to England. To do so, one needs a plan; one's thoughts must be connected. One asks: given where I am in Canada, which means of transportation should I use to get to England? If one were in a hurry, one would also be concerned with finding the quickest way.

The solutions will depend on *factual* things like how one gets to the airport and one's time restrictions and so on. One learns these factual things by observing the world—reading maps, plane schedules and clocks. But some factual things, like planetary positions or the water levels of the St. Lawrence River, one dismisses as irrelevant to achieving one's goal. So, one considers only some factual things while making one's travel decisions. However, it is difficult sometimes to decide what is relevant to achieving a goal.

One links thoughts in a pattern so that if one follows the pattern, one achieves the desired result. To link thoughts together, basing one thought on the previous thought, is to make an inference. For instance, on the basis of being in Canada and desiring to be in England, plus all the possible routes and time considerations, one might infer that taking flight X would be the best choice.

A more precise but more abstract definition would be: inference is a human act—the act of passing from one belief, judgement or proposition to another according to some rule. Without inferences we would all be prisoners of our immediate associations of ideas, creatures of whim or slaves to our instincts, biological drives, conditioned reflexes and habitual pattern of thoughts.

Is there a connection between inference and freedom? When we claim to be free, we are claiming that *we*, not our passions or habits, make our choices. Someone who chooses haphazardly or habitually is not making free choices and so is not making inferences. Hence, the claim to freedom is at least the claim that we can infer, and that, since we can infer, we can get from one

1

proposition to another according to a rule of our own choosing. *It is important to recognize here* the claim that we can move from proposition to proposition according to a *rule* of our own choosing. If we could only move from proposition to proposition on a whim or in response to immediate feelings, we could never tell whether or not we were free. It is only the introduction of a rule that enables us to check the grounds for our acceptance or rejection. In this sense, one is free if one can adopt one rule or another and then check to see whether this rule or some other has been applied.

We are enquiring into the nature of inference and persuasion to set ourselves free. It is partly a matter of intellectual self-defence for we are constantly exposed to flawed and dishonest arguments. They are in the advertisements, political speeches, scientific journals and *even* writings of philosophers! To be free we need to understand how arguments should work. It is also partly a matter of expanding our knowledge—of getting from what we know or think we know to what we want to know.

2. Freedom and Argument

Some say that humans are not free, that they are always prisoners of some conditioning force. But if that were true, one could not truly examine one's arguments. One would always come to the conclusion to which one in fact did. One could not have *chosen* a different argument or conclusion. For example, suppose that when Joe is presented with proposition X, he is determined to conclude proposition Y. Hence, Joe could not truly question the link between X and Y. It would be beyond his capabilities even to ask whether moving from X to Y is a good inference.

It also appears that the way in which we accept conclusions by applying rules to premises differs from the way in which one physical event determines another. If two billiard balls collide, their initial velocities and masses determine their resulting trajectories. But it seems that when we set out to make an inference, we come to one conclusion or another depending upon the rules we choose and how we apply them. Thus, when we talk about arguments, we can distinguish between acting on rules and acting otherwise. We can choose our rules, make changes in them and see what happens. We can set ourselves goals and discover whether we have met them.

3. Aristotle, Aquinas, Lonergan and Kenny

In ancient Greece, Aristotle claimed that there is a connection between being able to reason and being free. Moreover, our ability to discuss the issues intelligently is evidence of the connection. In the Middle Ages, St. Thomas Aquinas developed Aristotle's claim: the intellect abstracts characteristics from reality and receives them by its capacity as "the passive intellect." But there is also an "active intellect" that thinks and reflects. When the intellect has knowledge, it is also aware of its power to choose and thus to act. Clearly knowledge exists, so choice exists. Human beings have knowledge, so they are free to act.

The contemporary philosopher Bernard Lonergan has also developed this claim.[1] He agreed with Aristotle that knowledge often entails choice.[2] Knowledge produces choices insofar as knowledge is the cause of an action. For instance, a doctor's medical knowledge *could* be used either to save or kill a patient. The doctor has to make a choice. Lonergan conceded that various forces might still govern our choices. Developing Aquinas's notions, he distinguished between the will's "essential freedom" and its "effective freedom." The essential freedom of the will is its capacity to know and the necessity of making choices.

Effective freedom is that which influences the choices. Lonergan argued that one's character determines one's choices and that one's choices modify one's character. Consider lazy Joe. His character may lead him to read Lonergan because Lonergan is easier to read than, say, this book. Through his lazy choice of reading materials, Joe may come to realize his own free will. Knowing that he is really free, his laziness may not influence his decision making as much. So, Joe has begun to modify his character.

Behind this is a traditional philosophical view that knowledge exists in a different way than things exist. For instance, suppose that Joe has a particular upbringing. Joe's "upbringing" is a set of concrete situations, the actions of his parents, grandparents and so on. We would admit that Joe's current actions are governed or determined by these previous situations. But we also think that after Joe has become aware of or knows about these previous situations, something changes. That is, we now say that he is responsible for his own actions. But Joe is only responsible if he is in some sense free. We could say that freedom begins with knowledge.

Lonergan's discussion of freedom is complicated, involving difficult ideas like knowledge, choice, the nature of reality and so on. Moreover, when Lonergan said that "one who knows *must* choose," what does "must" mean? Is it also necessary that one knows? Does one have a choice about what one might or might not know?

Fortunately, another contemporary philosopher, Anthony Kenny, had a simpler discussion of freedom.[3] Kenny's discussion did not involve ideas about *the* nature of reality at all. He held that freedom of the will is a direct consequence of our ability to do practical reasoning. But to understand Kenny's view, we must understand the basics of theoretical reasoning.

QUICK QUIZ #1

1. Are there readily identifiable differences between reasoned arguments and simple chains of assertions? Can we tell if someone is giving reasons? Is inference necessary for reasoning?
2. If we couldn't reason, could we be free? If we can reason, must we be free? Could there be an *argument* that proves determinism?

3. Did Aristotle, Aquinas and Kenny make a plausible connection between freedom and argument? Does the possession of practical reason force us to make choices?
4. Do we need Lonergan's distinction between essential and effective freedom? Is that distinction of moral, social and political significance?

4. Theoretical Reasoning

The first term to examine is argument. For now, an argument is simply a list of sentences. One of these sentences is called the conclusion; the others are called the premises. In general, an argument can be represented as follows:

> Premise 1
> Premise 2
> *Premise n*
> Conclusion

On this scheme, there are three types of sentences that we allow into arguments.

1. Contingencies:
   > e.g., The cat is on the mat. Joe received an A in his critical thinking course.
   > A contingency *could* be true or it *could* be false. To know what it actually is, one needs to look at the world.
2. Tautologies:
   > e.g., The red car is red. A tree is a tree.
   > A tautology *must* be true. One does not need to look at the world.
3. Contradictions:
   > e.g., The red car is not red. A hat is not a hat.
   > A contradiction *must* be false. One does not need to look at the world.

Other types of sentences, like commands and questions such as "close the door" and "is it raining?" are not allowed into arguments. It makes no sense to ask whether commands or questions are true or false. We only allow sentences capable of being true or false. Such sentences are called statements.

QUICK QUIZ #2

For each of the following sentences, explain whether it is a contingency, contradiction or tautology, or something else.
1. The moon is made of cheese.
2. Look out below!
3. The statue in the garden is made of stone.
4. Joe thinks that the statue in the garden is made of stone.

5. The sun rises in the east and sets in the west.
6. A rose is a rose.
7. A human being needs three meals a day.
8. The red hat is not red.
9. Did you know that 2 + 2 = 4?
10. You ought to visit your friend.

The most important term in critical thinking is validity. Consider the following arguments.

Argument 1:

> Santa brought presents to all the good kids last Christmas.
> *Billy was a good kid.*
> Santa brought Billy a present.

Each statement is a contingency, but based on our knowledge of the world, we would say that the first premise and the conclusion are *in fact* false. However, just imagine that the first and second premises are true. You would then have to accept that the conclusion is also true. So, if you accept that the premises are true but claim that the conclusion is false, you would be contradicting yourself. *It is crucial to understand that an argument can be valid even if its premises and conclusion are false.*

Argument 2:

> Sally is taller than Steve.
> *Steve is taller than Jim.*
> Sally is taller than Jim.

Each statement is a contingency. But you may not know whether the premises are true or false. However, if you accept that the premises are true, you must accept that the conclusion is true. If you try to say that the conclusion is false you are contradicting yourself.

Argument 3:

> Canada is north of the USA.
> *The USA is north of Mexico.*
> Canada is north of Mexico.

Each sentence is a contingency. Based on geography, one would say that the premises are in fact true. Again, if you accept the truth of the premises, you must accept that the conclusion is true. In general, an argument is valid provided that:

If you agree that the premises are true, you must agree that the conclusion is true.

This definition asserts the following about valid arguments.

A valid argument cannot have BOTH (1) all of its premises true AND (2) its conclusion false.

With this in mind, consider the following valid argument:

Argument 4.

> Drinking milk leads to healthy bones.
> *Drinking milk does not lead to healthy bones.*
> Drinking milk is harmless.

This is valid because the premises contradict one another. If one premise is true, the other must be false. So Argument 4 could never have "all true premises" and thus it could never have "all true premises and a false conclusion."

Consider the following argument:

Argument 5.

> The earth has water on its surface.
> *The planet earth is not a planet.*
> The earth has unicorns.

This is valid because the second premise is a contradiction. It cannot possibly be true. So this argument could never have "all true premises" and thus could never have "all true premises and a false conclusion."

Consider the following argument:

Argument 6.

> The sun is hot.
> *There is water on the surface of Mars.*
> A rose is a rose.

This is valid because the conclusion is a tautology. It cannot possibly be false. So this argument can never have "a false conclusion" and thus could never have "all true premises and a false conclusion."

Arguments that are valid simply because they have a contradiction in the premises or a tautology for a conclusion will be called trivially valid.

QUICK QUIZ #3

Explain whether the following arguments are valid or trivially valid.

1. Joe ran faster than Jim.
   Jim ran faster than Ted.
   Joe ran faster than Ted.
2. Alan has a new car.
   His new car is red.
   A hat is a hat.
3. My dog ate my Frisbee.
   My Frisbee was made of iron.
   My dog ate some iron.
4. Alice bought new golf clubs.
   Alice did not buy new golf clubs.
   Alice plays golf.

Consider the following argument. Before reading on, try to explain why it is NOT valid:

Argument 7.

> Earth is further from the sun than Venus.
> *Venus is further from the sun than Mercury.*
> Apples ripen in the sun.

All the statements here are contingencies and are in fact true. To check for validity, consider the premises. If you accept them as true, you do not then have to accept the conclusion as true. That is, you could accept that the premises are true and then deny the conclusion without contradicting yourself.

Now explain why the following argument is valid:

Argument 8.

> Earth is further from the sun than Venus.
> *Venus is further from the sun than Mercury.*
> Earth is further from the sun than Mercury.

All the statements here are contingencies and are in fact true. To check for validity, consider the premises. If you accept them as true, you must accept the conclusion as true. If you accepted the premises and denied the conclusion, you would be contradicting yourself. Argument 8 is a valid argument with factually true premises. A valid argument whose premises are in fact true is called a sound argument.

Explain why the following is a sound argument:

Argument 9.

Tyrannosaurus Rex was the largest carnosaur in North America.[4]
Albertosaurus was a North American carnosaur.
Tyrannosaurus Rex was larger than Albertosaurus.

First check for validity: if you accept that the premises are true, you must accept the conclusion as true. If you accept that the premises are true and deny the conclusion, you are contradicting yourself. So it is valid. To check for soundness, one has to know that these premises are *in fact* true. So one would have to know some facts about these dinosaurs. In most cases, to determine when a valid argument is a sound argument, one has to know something about the world.

Explain why the following is valid but not sound:

Argument 10.

Ottawa is south of Toronto.
Toronto is south of Miami.
Ottawa is south of Miami.

First, explain the validity by considering the premises. If you accept them as true, you cannot deny the conclusion without contradicting yourself. So it is indeed a valid argument, but the premises are false. So the argument is not sound.

QUICK QUIZ #4

For each of the following arguments, explain whether or not it is invalid, valid or sound.

1. Mars is further from the sun than Pluto.
   Pluto is further from the sun than earth.
   Mars is further from the sun than earth.
2. Pluto is further from the sun than Mars.
   Mars is further from the sun than earth.
   Pluto is further from the sun than Mars.
3. A yellow hat is yellow.
   Today is sunny unless it is not sunny.
   A dog is a dog.
4. Albert Einstein rode a bicycle.
   Albert Einstein could tie his shoes.
   Albert Einstein was a genius.
5. Albert Einstein discovered the theory of relativity.

Albert Einstein worked on the theory of Quantum Mechanics.
Albert Einstein was a genius.

6.   Albert Einstein discovered the theory of relativity.
Only a genius could have discovered the theory of relativity.
Albert Einstein was a genius.

So far we have learned the types of sentences that go into arguments (contingencies, tautologies and contradictions) and the types of arguments (invalid, valid and sound). The last term of theoretical reasoning (for now) is logical form. To begin with, let us separate logical form and grammatical form. Consider the following discussion between Alice and the King taken from Lewis Carrol's *Through the Looking Glass.*[5]

> "I see nobody on the road," said Alice.
> "I only wish *I* had such eyes," the King remarked in a fretful tone. "To be able to see Nobody! And at that distance too! Why, it's as much as *I* can do to see real people, by this light!"

The King has confused the distinction between grammatical form and logical form. For instance, both "I see nobody on the road" and "I see somebody on the road" have the same *grammatical* form:

Subject + *verb*	+	*object*	+ *prepositional phrase*
("I") ("see")		("nobody" or "somebody")	("on the road")

But these sentences have different *logical* forms. "I see nobody on the road" really says "It is not the case that I see somebody on the road." So, "I see nobody on the road" is the denial of "I see somebody on the road."

But we still have not stated what the logical forms of these sentences are. Think of logic as a special kind of language. The logical form of a sentence is displayed in the translation of that sentence into the particular logical language. And as we shall see, since there are different kinds of logical languages, a given sentence will have different translations. In the following we shall simply introduce one type of logical translation and will go into more detail later.

Consider the following valid (but not sound) argument:

Argument 11.

> If cats have five legs then cats run very quickly.
> *Cats have five legs.*
> Therefore cats run very quickly.

Notice that there are only two phrases in this argument: "cats have five legs" and "cats run very quickly." A very simple logical translation would replace these phrases with letters:

> P: "cats have five legs"
> Q: "cats run very quickly"

Form of Argument 11.

> If P then Q
> *P*
> Therefore Q

This form is called *modus ponens*. Lots of arguments have this form.

For example:

Argument 12.

> If Joe is paying attention in class then he will pass his philosophy course.
> *Joe is paying attention in class*
> Therefore Joe will pass his philosophy course.

You can substitute any sentence you like for P and Q into this form and you will always get a valid argument. So *modus ponens* is called a valid argument form.

There is one last thing to note about validity. Let us modify Argument 11 by adding more premises:

Argument 11.

> If cats have five legs then cats run very quickly.
> Cats have five legs.
> It is raining.
> *Two plus two is four.*
> Therefore cats run very quickly.

Note that the argument stays valid and will remain so no matter what sentences we add to it. *In theoretical reasoning a valid argument cannot be rendered invalid by adding new premises.*

QUICK QUIZ #5

Using the letters P and Q, write the forms for the following arguments:
1. If Joe eats pizza, then he likes cheese.
   Joe eats pizza.
   Joe likes cheese.

2. If Sally wins the first, second and third parts of the contest then she'll win the vacation prize.
   She won all the parts of the contest.
   She won it all.
3. If Riemannian geometry is empirically adequate to the ontological structure of space-time, Relativity Theory is at least corroborated.
   The adequacy of Riemannian geometry has been confirmed.
   Relativity Theory has been corroborated.
4. If Gary eats ice-cream then he isn't lactose intolerant.
   Gary is lactose intolerant.
   He doesn't eat ice-cream.
5. Either you study philosophy or history.
   You do not study philosophy.
   You study history.

---

5. Practical Reasoning

Look at the following is argument. Ask yourself why it is *invalid* and try to ascertain its form.

> If it is raining then the sidewalks are wet.
> *The sidewalks are wet.*
> Therefore it is raining.

You could admit that the premises are true and deny that the conclusion is true without contradicting yourself. You could simply say that the sidewalks are wet because someone left a sprinkler on or a firefighter opened a hydrant. This argument has the following theoretically *invalid* form.

> If P then Q
> *Q*
> Therefore P

However, according to Kenny this form is valid in *practical* reasoning. Consider his example.[6]

> If I catch the 2:30 train, I'll be in London at 4:15.
> *I'm to be (i.e., in some sense of "I have to be") in London at 4:15*
> Therefore I'll catch the 2:30 train.

This argument is about how I am to fulfil what Kenny called a "fiat." The fiat here is "I have to be in London at 4:15." "Have to" does NOT express any kind of necessity. It just means that "to fulfil my aims, I need to be in London at 4:15." If the way to do it is to catch the 2:30 train, then to fulfil my aims, I'll catch the 2:30 train.

It seems that there are missing premises here such as that "Any way of getting to London by 4:15 is OK." Kenny's point is that the conclusion is valid in practical reasoning even though not necessary. In practical reasoning one has done a good enough job if one has a conclusion that ensures reaching the goal—subject to the usual caveats, of course. (The premise that the train will get there by 4:15 may be false, as may any premise in any valid argument.)

Kenny stresses that since we *can* reason this way, it is clear that we have choices—for the choices we make yield valid practical arguments about the real world. Nothing stops us from *deciding* what will make the conditions of validity. For instance, suppose that we add the premise: "it is against my religion to ride trains." The conclusion no longer follows. If my religion is more important to me than getting to London, then I should *not* catch the train. So adding a new premise can invalidate the argument. In general, we can always add a new premise that may be something that we *choose*, like religion.

In sum: theoretical and practical reasoning have different notions of validity. First, an argument form valid in practical reasoning is not valid in theoretical reasoning. Second, practical validity is affected by human choice whereas theoretical validity is not. Practical reasoning does not involve necessities of any kind. Kenny is concerned with the freedom in the human world—the "lived world"—of speaking and acting. Some might argue that this freedom is illusionary since the "lived world" is ultimately governed by the "world in itself," which does contain necessities (i.e., biological or physical laws). This may be true. But some would reply that the idea of a "world in itself," beyond perspective and language, is a nonsense notion.

If the notion of a wholly independent world is not nonsense, then determinism might be true of some world outside our discourse. However, we would still be free to act on the conclusion of a valid practical argument. Kenny expressed an uncertainty about whether determinism was true and also about how this issue of whether or not the world is deterministic could ever be settled.

When we say we can make choices, we mean, at least, that we can do reasoning of this kind. Now this is like the Lonergan argument except that it doesn't talk about the metaphysics of knowledge. Probably something like Lonergan's argument is necessary if we are to understand the difference between the realm in which practical reasoning takes place and the realm of knowledge. And probably something like Lonergan's distinction between essential and effective freedom is needed to make Kenny's thesis interesting, for Kenny was really talking about what Lonergan called "essential freedom." But essential freedom is surely of much less interest if it is not accompanied by effective freedom.

Later we will need to talk more about the distinction between practical and theoretical reason. Meanwhile, we can see that freedom is inherent in our ability to engage in practical discourse—if we can manage to gain control of the process of inference. The pressing questions are really about whether discourse, which involves reasoning, can theoretically be developed so as to be comprehensible in a way that would give us practical freedom, and about whether or not, if the theory exists, we can actually manage to apply it.

QUICK QUIZ #6

1. Explain the difference between theoretical validity and practical validity.
2. What is the "fiat" in the following practical argument? How would one invalidate such an argument in the practical sense?

   If I do my shopping, then I will be able to buy that present.
   I have to get that present.
   I'll be doing some shopping.

---

6. Meaning and Language

Consider the valid argument form *modus tollens*:

> If P then Q
> *Not Q*
> Therefore Not P

To apply this form, the meaning of P (and Q) must not change. If it did, then P in the conclusion could mean something different from P in the first premise. Consequently, we could substitute anything we wanted in the conclusion. In general, any proposition could lead to any conclusion.

Here is a simple example of what could happen when meanings are not held constant.

> I keep my money in a bank.
> *A rabbit hole is in a bank.*
> My money is in the same place as a rabbit hole.

Clearly "bank" has changed its meaning from one premise to another.

But what is this thing we call "meaning"? This is an old and difficult question. Basically, meanings are only possible where there are options. Consider a simple example of a railway signal, a red light. If it is *always* on (or off), it will not tell us whether the train is coming. If it is on when the train is coming and off when it isn't, then the signal will tell us about the train. However, someone has to ensure that correlation holds between the signal light and our intentions (to know what the train is doing). *Meaning* (in this sense) *is a matter of correlation of signals with intentions.*

When we made an inference involving Ps and Qs, we had to hold meanings constant through the argument. Our freedom to infer depended upon our ability to do this. Indeed, throughout language, it is invariably the possibility of establishing options and of correlating them (by rules) with intentions that sustains this notion of freedom. The real question, then, is whether we can make good this claim to freedom by understanding the ways in which this rule-making process occurs and whether we can put it to use by justifying certain rules and not others. There are, evidently, a number of factors involved—the assignment of meanings, the making of rules, the granting and withholding of belief, and the correlation of belief with action. This book is about all these processes—and about the ways in which they could be misunderstood, corrupted, and blocked so that we would lose our freedom.

Inference is intended to lead to belief. Someone who succeeds in making his or her own inferences controls beliefs and governs life in such a way that some of the events in his or her life may be said to be actions (and not just reactions, reflexes or whatever). An "action" in this sense should have about it an element of freedom. One whose rules are imposed, whose inferences reflect the intentions of others and whose beliefs do not follow from actions in some way, is in a kind of bondage.

We all attempt to make inferences. Without them, we have suggested, our lives would be very different. Throughout any language, meanings flow in a coherent way so as to make a single system. Every assignment of meaning has both a positive and a negative outcome. Positively, a meaning assignment identifies something—for instance "cat" signifies a small, furry animal or a certain sort of person or something else. We must decide exactly what it signifies. Negatively, a meaning assignment excludes everything else, all the functions of the rest of our language. The assignment of meaning is not done in a single, simple way.

The expression itself, the context of surrounding expressions, the drift of the conversation or the text in which it appears all have their influences on meaning. But because, to get *a* meaning, we must exclude all other meanings, the ultimate context must be a system as wide as the language in all its moods and functions. We cannot achieve this without inference, and thus we cannot claim knowledge and meaning for mere isolated propositions.

Behind language, perhaps, lies thought—whatever it is that is expressed through the language. But thought is subject to the constraints of language insofar, at least, as it expresses intentions and it, too, is therefore bound by inference.

The system is too vast to be wholly under our control. It is also, because of its complex inter-relations, peculiarly open to corruption. One who debases some part of it will lay waste to huge surrounding tracts of meaning. Let us consider two examples of such debasement. Ordinarily, to say that one "loves" X is to lead others to suppose that X is intended for approval. People could use "love" to get others to make certain inferences. Suppose a beer company claims to "love" its beer. So it would use only the best ingredients and so on. Clearly the intention is to have us infer that the company makes good beer. This will not convince us but it does introduce confusion about the use of "love." When others use the term we do not know if they are using it like the beer company does or as we normally do. The process, with respect to "love" is, of course, very old. Value expressions are consistently open to appropriation and are usually drafted into someone's army of words. As corrupt conscripts, they become increasingly useless to everyone.

Second, consider the term "freedom." Politicians often claim that we live in "the free world." So "free acts" are those of which we approve, and one who argues against us is not "exercising freedom" but performing a wicked act. This muddles the language of political dissent by associating the word "free" with a political viewpoint. There is nothing new about this: language is constantly changing. But if, as we suggested, human freedom is most crucially the freedom to determine meaning and inference, it seems evident that some procedure for its management is to be much desired.

QUICK QUIZ #7

1. Why is it so important to "hold meanings constant"?
2. What would life be like without inferences?
3. Do we really need a theory of "meaning?" Or is the meaning of "meaning" something that everyone already knows about?

---

7. Can Language be Policed?

Talking may be the oldest really human activity. Policing language is likely only a little younger. Language control probably began with religious authorities trying to control the means by which people "communicated" with the gods. It is an old view that the mysteries of human life are connected to language and its integrity.

Inference, if left to itself, follows the natural contours of language. When those routes from expression to expression become blocked or confused, attempts are made to straighten them out or to forge new routes. Priests, grammarians and logicians have all stepped in to perform these functions.

Language changes since no one owns it. Each time a word is used, its meaning changes slightly because every context is slightly different. This is like the law: each time someone is convicted of stealing, the meaning of "larceny" changes a little because it now contains the specific deed specified in the charge, which is never exactly like preceding deeds.

But institutions nonetheless try to control language. Religious bodies have laws against heresy, schools for teaching orthodoxy and so on. Secular authorities have laws for proper usage, schools for teaching such usage and so on. Even "society" at large has codes about polite usage.

In our time, religious bodies have mostly abandoned these practices, often expressing their messages through popular usages. Sermons rarely involve technical theological problems and few church-goers could discuss the Trinity. Televangelists speak in the language of the boardroom: God and Jesus seem to be the "Chairman of the Board" and the "Chief Executive Officer."

Grammarians once held that their task was to maintain traditional usages and to show that these usages were the truly rational uses of language. Most grammarians now hold that spoken language has precedence over traditional usage, that correct usage is simply what people actually use. The grammarian's job is only to *report*—not determine—how people use language.

A language, with its plans and patterns of natural inference, is like a vast system of canals. Traditional grammarians endeavoured to keep the system open for traffic by stabilizing it. They brought in standard usages, standard notions of syntax and spelling. To some degree, in the eighteenth century, any educated person could understand the writings of any other educated person. Such people could and often did read philosophy, such as Newton's works on physics, and did not require English professors to interpret works of literature.

But there is a paradox here. On the one hand, grammar had been extended beyond the church's concern with ecclesiastical language to all language. Education, which ran strongly to ancient languages and to the extension of their grammar to the vernacular languages, was a rather dreary and formal affair. In essence, the way *literate* people used language was held as the correct form of language. On the other hand, this policing of language, this high degree of order imposed on language provided a marked degree of freedom. For one could understand and be understood. The channels *were* open.

8. Languages and World Pictures

In the nineteenth century, the order that produced the freedom of understanding began to break down. For one thing, the conflict between rival world pictures has been intensifying since the end of the Middle Ages. Christianity's world picture and science's world picture were further apart than ever. These were rival claimants on words and on the relations between words and the world. Physicists were developing their own language and by the end of the nineteenth century, it was no longer true that just any educated person could understand it. The growth in specialized languages and their associated world pictures is characteristic of knowledge in the twentieth and twenty-first centuries.

Control of language by specialized interests differs in principle from the control of language by grammarians, who had only a small personal interest in the matter. Moreover, their power was limited since all they really did was keep the channels of communication open. However, specialized interests use *their* control of language to create an elite that has knowledge which no one else can share unless the price for initiation into the caste is paid. Even the English professor has a vested interest in obscurity. There is no need for grammarians if everyone can understand what is being said without help.

There was another tendency that we have already mentioned—the tendency for people with something to sell to make their case by moving around pieces of language. To a degree, an educational system that insisted on a standard usage was a defence against this process. But the growing view that knowledge was objective and independent of value judgements countered the view of traditional grammarians, who preserved traditional uses of language as intrinsically *the* rational ones. But grammarians were told that their view was not objective; rather, it contained value judgements about how the language *ought* to be used. Again, most grammarians began simply to report on how people actually used language.

How then was the freedom of movement to be maintained? Beyond the tactics of the grammarians there had always been, at least since Aristotle, the tactics of the logicians. Logicians sought general principles of inference—not just those that expressed the natural connections within language as we know it, but connections that would hold any time and could be expressed in any language.

But there is the possibility of confusing the development of an unambiguous logical language and the development of devices for controlling ordinary language. Traditionally logicians spoke as though they were simply "cleaning up" ordinary language when, in fact, they were really creating a specialized *logical* language. Instead of tidying up ordinary language, they were really translating it into a logical language. So one might ask: is something lost in the translation?

9. Material Content, Logical Form and Translation

To answer this question, let us start with the following argument.

> *Smith is mortal*
> Therefore, Smith is sometimes afraid.

This argument turns on the material content of the concepts of "mortality" and "fear," suggesting that there is an *experiential* connection between them. For example, we often become fearful upon realizing our own mortality—say in a near miss by a speeding bus. This ordinary inference is valid *because* it is *true* that mortality and fear are linked. Hence, in an ordinary inference there is no distinction between soundness and validity.

However, in logic we make this distinction. But to do so, some modification of the argument is required. A logician would claim that the argument's validity is independent of content, depending only on form. Let us see what the above argument looks like when it is translated into traditional logic, often referred to as Aristotle's logic.

Aristotle's logical language, which we explore more deeply in Chapter 3, deals with classes or collections of things and how these classes relate to one another. So, all sentences in Aristotelian logic *must* talk about classes. Here is a simple example:

> Ducks have wings.

In Aristotle's logic this would translate as:

> All creatures that are ducks are creatures with wings.

The class of ducks is related to the class of winged-creatures. Here is another simple example:

> No dogs have wings.

In Aristotle's logic this would translate as:

> No creature that is a dog is a creature with wings.

However, the first sentence in our ordinary argument is about a single thing (the person "Smith") and not about a class. So, we would have to translate it as follows:

> All people who are identical to Smith are people who are mortal.

Now, in order to have the validity of the argument turn on its form and not its material content, Aristotle would say that there is, in fact, a hidden premise in the ordinary argument:

> All people who are mortal are people who are sometimes afraid.

So, the ordinary argument now looks like this in Aristotle's logic:

> All people who are identical to Smith are people who are mortal.
> *All people who are mortal are people who are sometimes afraid.*
> All people who are identical to Smith are people who are sometimes afraid.

Arguments like this—that depend on relations of class inclusion and exclusion that relate their premises to their conclusions by calling attention to class inclusions and overlaps—are called syllogisms. (The classical ones in the textbooks are usually like the one above and have two premises, and conclusions; longer arguments called sorites, can be constructed.)

So, to translate an ordinary language argument into Aristotle's logical language, one first translates one's sentences into a form that speaks about classes. The argument we stated above about fear and mortality consists entirely of propositions of the form "All S is P"—of what are called universal affirmative propositions. (We shall see that there are four forms of statements.) Aristotle believed that everything sayable about a matter of fact or a state of affairs would have to be stateable in not more than one of these forms if all our arguments were to become syllogisms. Then the validity of the argument will depend simply on its *form*.

There is much that might be said about this process, but only part is immediately relevant. Recall that in the ordinary language argument, the distinction between truth and formal validity does not arise. The argument persuades because it links concepts that have roots in experience, or it does not persuade at all. In its translation, the form ensures that it is a valid argument. But the conclusion is known to be true only if the premises are known to be true. (The conclusion could be true even if the premises were false.) So the argument can be valid even though the premises are false. There is a persuasive element in the argument form but it is quite different from the kind of persuasion one would need if one wanted to believe that the conclusion were *true*.

So here we have a formal structure for arguing. One might think it could be applied to any language and any subject matter. We simply take ordinary language sentences and translate them into one of the forms that express relations between classes. The argument will be valid provided that the *form* of the premises is related to the *form* of the conclusion in a special way.

But note that translating the original propositions into standard Aristotelian propositions really creates a new language. First, instead of the many forms of declarative sentences that we might have in English, German or Chinese, we now have only four. (All As are Bs, Some As are Bs, No As are Bs, Some As are not Bs.) Second, we have introduced a new subject matter. Every sentence is now about two things—about what it seems to be about (fear, mortality and humans), and about the relations between classes, or predicate sets, or whatever it is that one happens to take as the reading for the "logic." If we introduce this subject matter, we shall then have to know what the relation is between being a human and being a member of the class "man."

So we may quote the logician as follows:

> I can rescue you from all the confusions of language. But you first must accept my translations of your sentences. Afterwards you can easily tell how one proposition follows, or fails to follow, from another.

Should we accept this offer? Even though philosophers and logicians are the same people, they don't seem to accept it. Aristotle did not write his philosophy in standard-form propositions suitable for syllogisms. Bertrand Russell did not write his philosophy in the logical language he used to reform Aristotle's logic. Perhaps this offer is not quite what it seems.

Notice that one would have to give up saying whatever cannot be said in the standard forms of propositions. Then one must give up arguments that might otherwise be convincing if they could not be made to fit the inference forms. Finally—and this may be most important—one will find oneself committed to accepting the consequences of the new subject matters demanded by the logic one adopts.

Let us illustrate what is at stake with a simple example. Suppose you promise us that you will be at the coffee shop today at lunch. But shortly before our lunch you say that you cannot make it. Suppose that we reply by saying: "You promised. And people ought to keep their promises."

Let us translate this response into Aristotle's logical language:

> All acts that are promised are acts that ought to be performed.
> *All acts that are identical to your act are acts that are promised.*
> All acts that are identical to your act are acts that ought to be performed.

Something has been lost in the translation. We understand the act of promising as the giving of one's word to another. It is meaningful provided that the one who promises performs. If one usually breaks one's promises, one's promises will be meaningless. If most people usually break their promises, promising itself will become meaningless.

The translated argument, that is the formalized argument, makes it seem as if the soundness of the argument depends upon two independent considerations—the formal validity of the argument and the truth of the premises. But the first premise is not *simply* just true or false.

We are often concerned with whether we have good reasons for breaking a promise. If you broke your promise to be at the coffee shop because you were busy saving a life, most would say that you were right to do so. If you broke your promise simply because you felt like it, most people would say that you were wrong to do so.

The formalized argument neither distinguishes between premises of various kinds nor between "All S is P" and "All S is P (presumptively)." Certainly, we can make modifications to the formal scheme—people have been doing it since Aristotle, hoping to get a more neutral formalization, a formalization that will not lead us astray, and one that will not prevent us from saying what we wanted to say. Translation problems are not limited to Aristotle's logic. In fact, one could say that the problem of translating ordinary language into a logical language has led to a profusion of the study of logic.

QUICK QUIZ #8

1. Why do meanings of words change over time?
2. How has the role of the Grammarian changed over time?
3. What have logicians often claimed to be doing? What are they most likely doing?
4. Translate the following argument into Aristotle's logical language.

Sally is often happy.
Therefore, Sally often smiles.

5. Can everything be defined? Why or why not? Why are definitions important? Can a true statement about something be a bad definition of it?

6. Logicians have sometimes dreamed of an ideal unambiguous language. Is this a logical possibility? Can language be controlled?

7. How does language influence what we can think about the world? How can we argue about different linguistic world pictures?

Notes

1. *Understanding and Being,* Toronto and New York: Edwin Mellen Press, 1980.
2. *Understanding and Being,* p. 279 ff.
3. *Will, Freedom and Power,* Oxford: Basil Blackwell, 1975.
4. At least as far as we know, at the time of writing.
5. Lewis Carroll, *The Complete Works of Lewis Carroll,* New York: Vintage, 1976, p. 223.
6. *Will, Freedom and Power,* p. 70.

Chapter 2

JUSTIFYING A "LOGIC"

1. Formal Logic

We have seen the advantages of formalizing arguments. After translating arguments into the forms of a logical language, we can see whether or not a conclusion follows from the premises. Since we decide which forms to use, we regain control over a language whose naturally determined inference-lines often become distorted as the language evolves. Formalizing arguments enables us to focus on either the argument's validity or its soundness. Finally, two "formalized" arguments can be closely compared. Sometimes we accept an argument because it has the same form as an argument we have already accepted.

We have also seen the disadvantages of formalizing arguments. What if some desirable statements are not translatable into these standard forms of our logic? Should we abandon such statements and keep the forms? Or should we keep such statements and look for new forms? Suppose that we think that a particular argument is good, but when formalized, it turns out to be invalid according to the logic's inference rules. Again, we are faced with choices and it is not clear how we should make them. Finally, there will be problems in determining the equivalence of the formalized argument and the original argument. How can we be sure that we have not lost or added things in our translations?

Such questions are difficult to answer. Suppose we ask a logician to argue for her particular logic. She will argue using that particular logic, some other logic, or just ordinary language. Whatever choice is made, problems follow. If the logician argues in the logic she wants to justify, the argument is circular. The argument is valid by the rules the logician is trying to impose. If she uses another logic, she appears suspicious. For the logician ought, one would think, to prefer the logic in which she made her case.

Here is the more general problem that faces us. We want to think of logic as an instrument of our freedom, as a defence against those who would impose their special interests upon us. But it seems that we are already prisoners of whatever special interests the logician may have in mind. Let us now look at three responses to this problem.

2. Quine's Response and its Problems[1]

The great logician W.V.O. Quine was, at least at one time, impatient of attempts to define logic and, presumably, of attempts to justify logic. He held that logic involved "basic particles," such as: "not," "and," "or," "unless," "if," "then," "neither," "nor," "some," and "all."[2] The subject matter of logic consists of statements such that these particles "occur in them in such a way that the statement(s) (are) true independent of (their) other ingredients."

Consider the statements, "Socrates is mortal" and "Socrates is not mortal." These are both contingencies. To know which is true we have to check the facts of the world. Now let us connect these statements with the particle "or." We get: "Socrates is mortal or Socrates is not mortal." This statement is different in that it is not a contingency. It seems to be obviously true. We do not need to check it against the world to know this. It is true because the logical particles "or" and "not" are located where they are. This statement is a tautology, or a logical truth.

We combined two contingencies to get a logical truth. It would seem to be true that the combination of *two* statements, *either* of which might, independently, have been *true or false*, into *one* statement that is *true* is the result of a logical operation. It also seems that we could extend the "principle" embodied here so as to get a traditional and acceptable pattern of inference. Consider the following argument:

> Either Socrates is mortal or Socrates is not-mortal.
> *Socrates is not not-mortal.*
> Therefore, Socrates is mortal.

Let us symbolize this argument as follows:

> Either S or not-S
> *Not not-S*
> Therefore S

Recall that a valid argument is such that *if* its premises are true then its conclusion must be true. The first premise here is logically true; it has to be true. The second premise and the conclusion are contingencies; they could be true or false. Let us now see what happens if we accept the second premise as true.

Consider the logical "not" in front of the "not-S" in the second premise. This logical "not" cancels out the first premise's "not-S," leaving just "S." So to accept the second premise as true is the same as asserting the truth of "S."

To assert now that the conclusion is false, to deny the truth of "S," clearly is to contradict oneself. More generally, we could say that it is just obvious that if you accept that the premises are true then you must accept that the conclusion is true. In sum: this is an obviously valid argument.

History, however, has taught us that it is dangerous to think that anything is "obvious." (Is it not "obvious" that the sun rises and sets?) Let us now look at what could be considered controversial in our above attempt to provide an obviously valid argument. It turns out that there are three problematic issues. The first involves the relationship between the two predicates "mortal" and "not-mortal." The second involves the problem of negation. The third involves the problem of self-contradiction.

Problem 1: The Predicates

Consider the statement "Socrates is mortal." If "Socrates" is the name of a single, atomic entity, then it follows that, on ordinary usage, Socrates cannot be both mortal and immortal. But no one supposes this. "Socrates" may be the name of a collection of physical particles in space and time. Perhaps, however, the ultimate particles are "immortal" ("not-mortal"), though Socrates is mortal. Or "Socrates" may be the name of a certain pattern or arrangement of those particles. That pattern certainly is mortal. But that is not, usually, what we mean by "Socrates." We usually mean to refer to a certain moral agent, a certain kind of mental activity and so on. And we do not know, immediately, what to say if we are asked if those are immortal or not. But since "Socrates" is the name of many things, it may be quite possible to say that Socrates is *both* mortal and immortal. Perhaps his body dies and his mind lives on. To reach Quine's simple truth, we would have to be able to substitute for "Socrates" the names of atomic entities that could not be the bearers of both these predicates. But how do we know when we are there?

"P is Q" or "P is not-Q" only holds for some values of Q. We would require a new rule about what could be substituted for Q. And there is no *obvious* rule. The proposal represents an ideal situation that can be translated into some *ideal* language. It is widely believed that we do *not* have such a language.

Problem 2: The Law of Bivalence

One might agree that we may not *know* when we have the names of atomic entities that we could substitute for "Socrates." But one might insist that there must *be* such entities since a statement must be either true or false. There is nothing in between. The logic of two truth values (bivalence) is often referred to as a "standard" logic.

The law of bivalence is assumed in the above argument, which says that "not not-S" is the same as "S." If "S" is true, "not-S" will be false. So it seems obvious that "not not-S" will bring us back to true again, that is, back to "S."

Now suppose that statements could be either true, false or a third possibility, say *indeterminate*. With these three possibilities, let us re-examine our second assumption. If "S" is true, "not-S" could be false or indeterminate. We cannot immediately say which. If "not-S" is in fact false, "not not-S" could be true or indeterminate. We cannot immediately say which. The point is this: "not not-S" cannot simply be *assumed* to be the same as "S." In sum, what first seemed so obvious may really be rather problematic.

Aristotle provided us with an example of a statement whose truth value is indeterminate: "there will be a sea battle tomorrow." Such statements (future contingencies) are neither true nor false. So the law of bivalence fails for future contingencies. Centuries later, the logician Jan Lukasiewicz[3] read Aristotle as having proposed that we need a third truth value to deal with future statements. Lukasiewicz went on to develop a non-standard logic with at least three "truth" values, "true," "false" and "indeterminate."

To say that the law of bivalence fails for future statements is to say that statements regarding the future are undetermined. "There will be a sea-battle tomorrow," being neither true nor false *now*, means that whether or not a battle happens tomorrow is not determined *now*. But given that a battle *must* either happen or not happen, what influences the world so that one of these alternatives happens? This is a huge and difficult question, one that we cannot enter into here.

Thus, it is controversial to say that the law of bivalence is obvious. To reject it leads to problems and to accept it seems to lead to fatalism, the view that we are not free but destined to do things. Suppose we dig in our heels and assert that bivalence holds unconditionally for all statements. We can then use it to construct our obviously valid form of inference. However, we are using a law that denies our freedom to argue for a rule of inference that is supposed, as we said in chapter one, to preserve our freedom. Are we not contradicting ourselves? If we say that it holds only for certain propositions and not others, then we are back to the same old questions. Which propositions? Why some and not others? All claims to obviousness seem to go by the boards.

Problem 3: Self-Contradiction

Quine also suggested that we cannot adopt "deviant" logics; there is no choice. Consider the principle of non-contradiction, which says that P and not-P cannot both be true. Suppose a deviant logician wants to deny this rule. Orthodoxy has it that if both P and not-P are true, then *every* imaginable statement is true. Simply put, if one has a statement P, then not-P refers to everything that is not P. So, P and not-P together will refer to everything. If P and not-P are true, every statement is true. No deviant logician would accept this. So, the deviant logician is not really denying the principle, but changing the meaning of negation. As Quine said, "Here, evidently, is the deviant logician's predicament: when he tries to deny the doctrine, he only changes the subject."[4]

Based on Quine's talk about logical particles and statements, we might think that he was simply talking about language. But he claimed to argue "against the view that the logical truths are true because of grammar, or because of language."[5] And later on he insisted that his "most general definition of truth [rests] on two things, grammar, which is a purely linguistic affair and truth, which is not."[6]

Quine seemed to say that there are limits to how we can talk about things. The limits are not a result of language or grammar rules, but of *negation* itself. If we understand what negation really is, then we must accept the principle of non-contradiction. Quine does not tell us what negation really is, but it remains an issue. Indeed, is there something called "nothing," something that would be left if everything were negated? If so, would this tell us what negation is?

The twentieth century German philosopher Martin Heidegger once suggested that there is, after all, one subject that science never discusses: Nothing. And he believed that it was very important. Understanding it, he thought, is the clue to getting beyond the limitations of science.[7] Quine would react to such assertions with a look that one might give to the certifiably mad. Yet the problem remains. Even Quine's later suggestion was not without problems.

Indeed, such questions quickly become very complex. People impressed by the fact that statements asserting logical truths *are* really *true* yet do not seem to state facts about our world sometimes suggest that logical truths are true for all possible worlds, whereas contingent truths are true only here and now in our world or in some other world. But this poses difficult questions: How does one know what worlds are possible? How is finding truths about every possible world different from finding "logical truths"? If there is no difference, what is gained by talking about possible worlds? If there is a difference, must there not still be something else special about logical truths?

QUICK QUIZ #1

1. What difficulties are involved in trying to justify a logic?
2. Suppose someone tried to justify his/her logic as follows:
   "I am not going to *argue* for my logic; rather, I will simply say that my logic is extremely useful and doesn't lead me into problems with the world. What more do you need?"
   How could you respond to this?
3. In Quine's construction of an "obviously valid" argument, what are the three presuppositions?
4. Why are each of these presuppositions problematic?

---

3. Inclusion as a Response

Consider the following syllogism:

> All people are biteable by mosquitoes.
> *All things biteable by mosquitoes are animals*
> Therefore, all people are animals.

The first statement says that the class of people is contained within the class of things bitten by mosquitoes. One could draw a circle for "people" and another surrounding it for the class of things bitten by mosquitoes. The second premise says that mosquitoes bite only animals. So we can draw a third circle enclosing the other two. The conclusion states that the innermost circle is contained in the outer most.

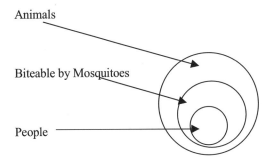

Animals

Biteable by Mosquitoes

People

Consider the following syllogism:

> All baseball players are creatures that chew tobacco.
> *Some people are not creatures that chew tobacco.*
> Therefore, some people are not baseball players.

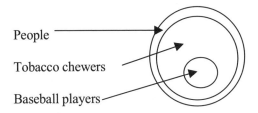

People

Tobacco chewers

Baseball players

We might think that the validity of the arguments depends simply on the fact that the premises include the conclusion. The argument must be valid because the conclusion adds nothing new to the diagram of the premises. This kind of argument is often called deduction and it amounts, on *this* view, to the literal "drawing out" of the conclusion from the premises. Let us apply this to the "either/or" argument. Consider the following:

> Either Joe is drunk or Joe is sober.
> *Joe isn't drunk.*
> Therefore, Joe is sober.

In the Socrates argument our first premise was a logical truth. Here we may doubt our first premise. (Joe may only be slightly buzzed.) But "either/or" *arguments* can be valid (supposedly) even if the premises are only contingently true.

Either Beatrice will work hard or Beatrice will fail.
Beatrice won't work hard.
Therefore, Beatrice will fail.

The first premise states that one of two statements is true. The second says that a specific one is false. The conclusion merely asserts the one remaining. You can write the first premise as two propositions and write the second premise as a line striking out one of them. The conclusion is the remaining one. Once again, the validity seems to depend upon the fact that the conclusion, in fact, is given by the premises.

This, however, is problematic. The nineteenth century English philosopher John Stuart Mill complained that syllogisms cannot take one beyond one's premises. Furthermore, the price is high. We have already seen that translating all our arguments into the appropriate forms exacts much from us in the way of changing language and in the way of introducing new and difficult subject matters (such as, perhaps, talk about classes, problems about predication, problems about atomic reference units and so on).

4. Truth Tables as a Response

Let us now consider simple formal arguments that are not explained by drawing circles within circles. Consider for instance:

P implies Q
Not Q
Therefore, Not-P

This argument hinges on the way we define "implies." If we adopt the law of bivalence, make P and Q to be statements, we can define implication by truth tables. (T – true and F – false.)

The truth table for P is just:

P
T
F

The truth table for Q is identical. But, the truth table for *both* P and Q is:

P	Q
T	T
T	F
F	T
F	F

We have four possibilities. The convention is that the relation "implies" holds for each case, *except* the one in which P is true and Q is false. The above argument states that P implies Q and that Q is false. Therefore, the result is that P must be false also, for if we are given P, *and* P implies Q, then Q. (The convention has it that *P and Q* holds for the case in which they are both true and that *P or Q* holds for the cases in which at least one is true. But "implies," "and" and "or" are normally replaced by logical symbols to indicate that *just* these relations hold. "And" is often replaced by a dot; "or" by a v; and "implies" by a horseshoe on its side.)

Now we may question the definitions and the use of truth tables, but that is not the point. The point is that the argument depends upon a certain decision regarding the notion of implication and not on some general rule about including the conclusion in the premises. This is an arbitrary notion of implication yet we may need to decide whether or not to accept it. But how are we to make such a decision?

The remaining simple thesis is just that some principles are *intuitively* true. We have seen, for instance, that another way of characterizing the arguments is by showing that they all depend upon our use of the principle of non-contradiction. When one rejects them, one contradicts himself, and utters a formal inconsistency. Some people, George Boole amongst them, have urged that one can tell whether a logical principle is acceptable by inspecting it.[8] Indeed, he claimed that logic is, in this sense, empirical.

One might *think* that principles like "A is A" (the law of identity), "not both A and not-A" (the law of non-contradiction) and "A is either B or not-B" (excluded middle) are "intuitively" true and readily applied to arguments to determine validity. Yet logicians have had different intuitions. Not everyone has had the same understanding of the principle of non-contradiction; some have found the law of excluded middle most unlikely.

The claim is not that they are obvious, but that they correspond to the basic conditions under which we would accept the conclusion of an argument. But what are they about? Are they conditions for the world, as logical realists have thought? Are they necessary conditions for the maintenance of symbol systems—essentially rules about propositions? Or are they accounts of the ways in which propositions are associated with their truth values?

5. Summary of the Problems of Justifying a Logic

I

Perhaps some arguments are simply intuitively valid. Everyone who understands the words and is of sound mind sees that if P implies Q and P is true then Q must be true also, or that if all baseball players chew tobacco and Jones is a baseball player, he chews tobacco. But we have also seen that this may not be true, for difficult logical notions underlie all such discussions.

II

It might be that we could draw pictures of valid arguments and show that if all baseball players are included in a circle that is inside the circle that represents tobacco chewers, and Smith is within the circle of baseball players, then he is within the circle of tobacco chewers. But what do these circles represent? Perhaps they represent classes. But we shall see that there are difficulties with the notion of a "class."

III

It might be, as Professor Quine suggests, that there are some "logical particles"—like "and," "or," "if then," "some," "all" and "not," which, if they are distributed correctly in the sentence make the sentence express a necessary truth, no matter what it is about. "If Socrates is either mortal or not-mortal and he is not not-mortal, then he is mortal" seems to be such a sentence. But this creates difficulties. What does "Socrates" mean? Perhaps the man is mortal and his electrons are not.

IV

One might, finally, suggest that logic depends on some undeniable principles.

- Either P or not-P is true {law of *non-contradiction*}
- Either P is true or P is false {law of *bivalence*}
- A is A {law of *identity*}

One likely has to accept the law of non-contradiction. Otherwise one would not be saying anything at all. Furthermore, the most important thing to know is always what a proposition excludes—what would falsify it. We may not know how to prove that the law of gravitation is true, but we all know what would falsify it. But as we shall see in the next chapter, some philosophers propose that the law of non-contradiction can, in some cases, fail.

As for the law of bivalence, alas, it seems false. The sentence "Pamela Jones will be prime minister of Canada in 2012" is neither true nor false in 2005. As we shall see in the next chapter, some people do flatly deny this law and construct a perfectly good logic anyway.

And as for identity, it has problems. What sorts of things have identities? We saw that whether Socrates is mortal or immortal may depend on what one thinks Socrates is. Bishop Butler is supposed to have said "each thing is what it is and not another thing," but if that is literally true, nothing much can be said about anything. Words, other than proper names, potentially always refer to more than one thing. A sentence full of proper names would convey nothing. Is the law of non-contradiction enough?

It is true that when we argue, whether in science or morals or logic, we can do so on a number of levels. We start off with facts, cases or single propositions and if we can't agree about them, we can move to laws, hypotheses, rules, or logical laws. If you don't know whether this apple is likely to fall or not, you appeal to the law of gravitation. If you wonder about the law of gravitation, you point out that three-dimensional non-interfering, homogenous spaces provide a limited and determinate set of directions within which forces can disperse. So you expect to get lots of inverse square laws in three-dimensional spaces, and you would get inverse cube laws if you had four-dimensional spaces. This is a "principle." So in morals, if you don't know if those who buy chests of drawers with hidden packets of money in them should keep the money, you appeal to a law—to the legal notion of stealing by finding, perhaps. If you can't tell whether that law fits, you appeal to the notion that property should revert to whomever has the best claim to have made the thing, or to have acquired it by fair trade. This is a principle. If you don't know if an argument is valid, you appeal to some rule or law, like the rules for syllogisms. If you still can't tell if the case fits, you begin to look at the underlying principles. And that will bring you to the law of non-contradiction.

In the end, perhaps, there must be only one moral principle from which all the others follow. Otherwise there would be irresolvable conflicts. Is this true either of physics or of logic? We shall learn more as we go along. Principles differ from rules or laws in that principles are ultimate in the sense that there is nothing to refer to beyond them. But principles, since they are more general than rules and laws, most likely require more interpretation. Much can be said about non-contradiction, but non-contradiction does seem a little thin as the foundation for a whole logic.

These are all complex notions and we must then ask ourselves if we have intuitions about these secondary questions as well. Somewhere, it seems, we will have to justify our choices. The next chapter, therefore, will be concerned with attempts to get out of the circle of "justification" problems. We will consider some more formal aspects of logic.

QUICK QUIZ #2

1. In what sense is "the law of bivalence" a law? What would happen if we denied it? Why does Quine think we cannot adopt "deviant" logics? Is he right?
2. Is "nothing" a possible subject matter?
3. What is the central logical principle of the "syllogism?" Why is "deduction" so highly thought of? Should it be?
4. Why is the truth table thought to be a useful device? Discuss the truth table definitions of "implies," "and," and "or."

Notes

1. Quine urged us to keep the obvious. Logical truths will qualify as obvious. But he added that they are obvious "in a behavioural sense"—i.e., people will agree to them. (See *Philosophy of Logic,* Cambridge, MA: Harvard University Press, 1970,

1986, p. 102).

2. *Mathematical Logic,* second edition, revised, Cambridge, MA: Harvard University Press, 1951, p. 1. For a longer discussion see Leslie Armour, *Logic and Reality,* Assen: Van Gorcum; and New York: Humanities Press, 1972, p. 6–7.

3. Jan Lukasiewicz (1878–1956) was a Polish logician, recognized as the father of "multi-valued" logics. They play an important part in electronics.

4. *Philosophy of Logic,* Cambridge, Mass.: Harvard University Press, second edition, 1986, p. 81.

5. *Op. cit.,* p. vii.

6. *op. cit.,* p. 95. We shall return to the problem of the nature of truth later on.

7. See "What is Metaphysics?" his inaugural lecture at Freiburg University, given July 24, 1929, in David Farrell Krell, ed. and tr. *Martin Heidegger Basic Writings,* New York: Harper, 1977, p. 95–112.

8. George Boole (1815–1864) was an English mathematician and one of the pioneers of modern logic. See his *Investigation into the Laws of Thought,* 1854, reprinted, New York: Dover, n.d.

Chapter 3

ARISTOTLE'S LOGIC, MODERN LOGIC AND GÖDEL'S RESULTS

1. Aristotle's Logic

Aristotle's logic deals with statements called *categorical propositions*. The following table summarizes the four types.

Categorical Proposition	Logical Form	Name
All philosophers are people.	All S are P	A (Universal Affirmative)
No philosopher are people.	No S are P	E (Universal Negative)
Some philosophers are people.	Some S are P	I (Particular Affirmative)
Some philosophers are not people.	Some S are not P	O (Particular Negative)

Note: A, E, I, O are the traditional names, derived from the vowels of the Latin words designating them.

Since ordinary language statements rarely look like categorical propositions, we often have to rewrite them as categorical propositions. But doing this can be tricky since ordinary language is full of different ways to say the same things.

Consider the following A categorical proposition: All pigs are mammals. Here are a few of the ways that ordinary language might express this:

Each and every pig is a mammal. Pigs are mammals. If it's a pig, it's a mammal. There aren't any pigs that aren't mammals. Pigs are exclusively mammals. If it's not a mammal, then it's not a pig.

Consider the following O categorical proposition: Some animals are not carnivores. Here are a few of the ways that ordinary language might say this.

Not all animals are carnivores. There are a few animals that don't eat meat. Most animals don't eat meat.

QUICK QUIZ #1

Identify each as A, E, I or O. Then, rewrite it as a categorical proposition.
1. Every crustacean lives in water.
2. There are no intelligent chickens.
3. Some federal politicians are not Tories.
4. There is a federal politician who is a Tory.
5. Not all apples are red.
6. Most chickens lay eggs.
7. Joe likes cheese.

Given a categorical proposition of a certain type, we can change it in *three* ways.

Categorical proposition A	All pigs are mammals.
Converse of A	
(Switch S and P)	All mammals are pigs.
Contrapositive of A	
(Switch and negate S and P)	No pig is a non-mammal.
Obverse of A (Negate P and change	
from affirmative to negative)	No pig is a non-mammal.

Note: All E and I propositions (but not all A and O) are equivalent to their converses.
All A and O propositions (but not all E and I) are equivalent to their contrapositives.
All propositions are equivalent to their obverses.

The following table summarizes the changes in our four types of propositions.

Proposition	Converse	Contrapositive	Obverse
A All S are P	All P are S	All non-P are non-S	No S are non-P
E No S are P	No P are S	No non-P are non-S	All S are non-P
I Some S are P	Some P are S	Some non-P are non-S	Some S are not non-P
O Some S are not P	Some P are not S	Some non-P are not non-S	Some S are non-P

QUICK QUIZ #2

For each of the following, construct its converse, contrapositive and obverse. Explain whether or not the resulting categorical propositions are equivalent to the original.
1. All cats are mammals.
2. No dogs are reptiles.

3. Some pigs are pink.
4. Some computers are not steam-powered.

As we have seen, Aristotle's logic formalizes arguments in terms of *syllogisms*. Once one has translated everything into the syllogistic format, there are four rules that one can apply to check whether or not the argument is valid. Consider the following syllogism:

> All dogs are mammals.
> *All mammals are warm-blooded creatures.*
> All dogs are warm-blooded creatures.

Major term: the predicate of the conclusion ("warm-blooded creatures").
Minor term: the subject of the conclusion ("dogs").
Middle term: found in both premises but not in the conclusion ("mammals").

We say that a term is *distributed* when it refers to all the members in the class. For instance, in the proposition "All dogs are mammals," the term "dog" is distributed while "mammals" is not. The proposition tells us something about *all* dogs (that they are mammals). However, the proposition *itself* does not tell us anything about *all* mammals. (We may already know that some mammals aren't dogs, but the proposition *itself* does not tell us this.)
We can now state the four rules for testing whether or not a syllogism is valid:

1. The middle term must be distributed at least once.
2. Any term distributed in the conclusion must be distributed in a premise.
3. There must be at least one affirmative premise.
4. If the conclusion is negative, exactly one premise must be negative.

QUICK QUIZ #3

Identify the major and minor terms of the following syllogisms and explain whether or not they are distributed. Also, apply the four rules of syllogisms to see whether they are valid.

1. All students are taxpayers.
   Some taxpayers are people in debt.
   Therefore, some students are in debt.
2. Every smoker is a nicotine addict.
   Every nicotine addict is a tobacco user.
   Therefore, every tobacco user is a smoker.
3. Every computer is a perfect logician.
   Every computer is a thinking machine.
   Therefore, some thinking machine is a perfect logician.
4. No mechanic is a vegetarian.

> *Every philosopher is a vegetarian.*
> Some philosopher is not a mechanic.

2. Towards Modern Logic: Frege, Russell and Whitehead

Logic had been changing in the middle of the nineteenth century through the work of George Boole and W. S. Jevons,[1] and it had caught the attention of thinkers like Cardinal Newman.[2] But it is Gottlob Frege (1848–1922) who is often called the father of modern logic.[3] After him, it was Bertrand Russell (1872–1970), with Alfred North Whitehead (1861–1947), who developed its foundations in a way now deemed to be standard.

The issues are most easily approached through the work of Russell and Whitehead. When they wrote *Principia Mathematica*,[4] they made the rather simple claim that they were looking for a logic that would systematize and formalize some basic requirements of elementary arithmetic.

Two things are certainly true: we do, as a matter of fact, accept the kind of reasoning characterized by arithmetic, and there are common properties between arithmeticizing a given subject matter and talking about it clearly. Very simply: we have a concern with associating properties of things with numbers so as to render them discrete, comparable, measurable and so on. We can, then, reason in a way characteristic of arithmetic, so as to determine whether or not sets or classes of them are equal or unequal, and, if unequal, whether one is greater than another and so on.

More important, however, logicians like Russell appear to have had a certain notion of what it would mean to formalize a system to make it "adequate" to elementary arithmetic. These logicians meant to adopt a procedure much like the one we saw advanced for cases like the notion of "implication." They meant, that is, to lay down some simple and obvious axioms and rules of inference and to show that every case of a valid inference in the relevant area would turn out to be a substitution instance[5] for those axioms and principles. Indeed, the rules of inference were simply to be devices for allowing one to make the substitutions. Therefore, there are two different sorts of crucial considerations: should one accept the original axioms, and can the task of substitution be carried out?

In fact, for various reasons, some quite old and others relatively new, the association of logic with arithmetic posed grave difficulties.[6] The logic of Russell and Whitehead, as we just suggested, proposed in effect to reduce arithmetical statements to tautologies—propositions, roughly, true by definition in much the same way that it was thought to be true that Socrates is either mortal or not-mortal, or in the way which we saw earlier was justified by the classical argument form "P implies Q. Not Q. Therefore not P." In that case, we exhibited its validity as a property of our understanding of the relation of implication.

Since Aristotle's logic deals with classes, we had to translate ordinary statements about individuals into rather clumsy categorical propositions about classes. Modern logic is more basic than Aristotle's since it can directly deal with individuals. Modern logic is also broader since it can deal with statements that resist translation into categorical propositions.

But modern logic does not simply *add* to Aristotle's logic. It introduces a major change. Like most ancient philosophers, Aristotle thought it absurd to speak and reason about non-existent objects. So, Aristotle's logic always deals with things that exist. For example:

> All dogs are mammals.

This proposition is making a claim about existing things, that is, real dogs. Aristotle's logic embraces an *existential* view of *all* categorical propositions.

With the existential interpretation the following argument is valid:

> *All dogs are mammals.*
> Some dogs are mammals.

This, we suggest, would appear to be a reasonable inference for most people. However, modern logic accepts the existentialist interpretation only for I and O propositions, *not* for A and E propositions. Now "All dogs are mammals" does not talk about existing dogs, but says that "IF something is a dog, then that something is a mammal." Consequently, modern logic does not regard the above argument as valid. No doubt many would regard this as rather strange. Why drop the existential assumption for A and E propositions?

Modern logic allows *universal* reasoning about non-existent objects. Suppose that we say to the class at the beginning of an exam:

> All cheaters will be expelled.

This does not mean that there really are cheaters, just that *if* one cheats, then one will be expelled. Indeed, scientific statements often talk about things that may or may not exist. So logic does feel pressure from the concerns of life.

3. Modern Logic

Modern logic has many divisions, far beyond what we can cover here. We will concentrate, therefore, on what is called "modern elementary logic," which divides into two parts, sentential and predicate logic.

Sentential Logic

Sentential logic treats each statement as a whole; each statement is translated as a letter. For example, "It is raining" could be translated as P. "Joe is late today" might be Q. A more complex statement like "It is raining and my knee hurts a lot" could be P and Q. ("P" and "Q," like many such symbols, are just proper *names* like "Suzie" or "Harry." They are picked arbitrarily. There might be—but there doesn't have to be—a reason that Suzie was not called Harriet. We have the names our parents gave us unless we decide to change them. Similarly, propositions have the names that logicians give them. Pairs of propositions in sentential logics are usually called P and Q, but they can be called R and S or Y and Z—or anything else.)

There are four operators in sentential logic. Basically, operators hook statements together or negate them.

1. Negation: negates a statement
   Example: "The earth is round." This is true.
   Its negation is N (not) "The earth is round." This is false.
2. And: connects statements
   Example: "The earth is round," "The floor is flat."
   "The earth is round and the floor is flat."
3. Or: connects statements
   Example: "The earth is round," "The floor is flat."
   "The earth is round or the floor is flat."
4. If–then: connects sentences
   Example: "The earth is round," "The floor is flat."
   "If the earth is round then the floor is flat."

(If–then is usually represented with a dash to show that something generally comes between them. Sometimes it is represented as "If, then.")

One can build up more and more complicated compounds by combining more and more sentences. So one can translate ordinary statements into logical symbols and then work with the logical symbols themselves. Here are a few examples.

Natural Language	**Sentential Logic**
It is a sunny day	P
It is a sunny day and my knee hurts	P and Q
If you study you will pass the course	If R then S

QUICK QUIZ #4

Translate the following into sentential logic.
   1. Ottawa is a city.
   2. Joe is happy and he is living in Ottawa.
   3. Sally is wearing a hat and Ottawa is a city.
   4. Either Montreal is north of Ottawa or Montreal is south of Ottawa.
   5. Two is greater than one.
   6. Ottawa is between Toronto and Montreal.
   7. All birds have wings.
   8. Some elephants have four legs.

Here is a simple, valid inference we might make in everyday language.

> If it is raining then the sidewalks are wet.
> *It is raining.*
> Therefore the sidewalks are wet.

Here is a translation of it into sentential logic.

> If A then B
> *A*
> Therefore B

The translation into sentential logic preserved the validity of the argument in ordinary language. But consider the following valid argument:

> All philosophers think clearly.
> *Buffy is a philosopher.*
> Buffy thinks clearly.

Here is its translation into sentential logic.

> P
> *B*
> F

This is *not* valid. (We could say that P and B are both true while F is false.) So, the translation lost the original validity. Why? Because we treated the original statements as wholes. We did not try to open them up and translate each of their parts.

Consider the second premise. It just talks about Buffy—a single person. But the first premise is different in that it contains the word "all." This part was skipped over in our translation and as a result we lost the validity of the argument. To preserve the validity in our translations, we have to start translating the *parts* of sentences. Now we have to use what is called predicate logic.

Predicate Logic

Predicate logic does not treat statements as wholes, although it does use the connectives of sentential logic. Predicate logic translates parts of statements by introducing a few more logical devices: terms, predicates, variables and quantifiers.

Terms and Predicates

Consider the following sentences:

> Barbara is smart.
> 5 is greater than 3.
> Red Deer is between Calgary and Edmonton.

These are all singular simple sentences. A singular simple sentence asserts:

Either:

> an individual object possesses a property
> (Barbara possesses "smartness")

Or:

> a certain relation linking two or more objects in a particular way
> ("greater than" links 5 and 3 in a particular order)
> ("between" links Red Deer, Calgary and Edmonton in a particular order)

TERM: an expression that names or describes individual objects ("Joe," "2")
PREDICATE: an expression that stands for a property or relation ("smart," "between")

Predicate logic uses upper case letters to symbolize predicates and lower case for terms. For example: "Barbara is smart" becomes Sb in predicate logic. It would simply be P in sentential logic. Another example: "Red Deer is between Calgary and Edmonton" becomes Brdce in predicate logic. It would simply be Q in sentential logic. So we can see that predicate logic is closer than sentential logic to reflecting the complexity of ordinary language.

Consider this example: "Fanny is taller than Alphonse and Sam is taller than Beatrice." In sentential logic it might look like Q and P. But in predicate logic it would look like Tfa and Tsb. The point is that predicate logic links symbolized sentences using the same connectives as sentential logic. However, predicate logic's symbolized sentences themselves are more complex than those of sentential logic.

Variables and Quantifiers

Consider the sentences: "Everything is red." "Something is red." Notice that they do NOT contain any names. So, they are not singular like the sentences just discussed. To open these sentences up we need variables. Variables in predicate logic work much like pronouns do in ordinary language. That is, they stand for many things. Perhaps it is easiest to simply open up these sentences and look at how they work.

Let us begin with "Everything is red." Now, suppose that x stands for any object. It could be a pig or an airplane or a dream; it does not matter. The x is a variable. "Everything is red" could be *temporarily* translated as the following two-part expression: "for every x, x is red." Consider the second part. It has a predicate expression, "Red," which we symbolize by R. We could symbolize the second part as "Rx." But of course, we are not quite done. Now the new machinery of predicate logic comes in. To symbolize "for every x" we need what is called a quantifier. There are two types of quantifiers in predicate logic. Since our sentence talks about all x's we need a universal quantifier. "For every x" is translated as ∀x. Putting both translations together we get:

Natural Language: **Predicate Logic:**
Everything is red   ∀xRx
(The symbol "∀" stands for "every" or "any." You will sometimes see "∀x" written simply as "(x).")

Now let us open up "Something is red." This is fairly similar only now, instead of speaking about everything, it says that "there is an x such that x is red." So, we do not need the universal but the existential quantifier. The existential quantifier captures the part, "there is an x." So our translation looks like:

Natural Language: **Predicate Logic:**
Something is red   ∃xRx
(The symbol "∃" just stands for "something" or "there is a"—something is red, there is a red thing.)

Let us look at a slightly more complex sentence. "Someone took the pizza and everyone is upset." Let us now compare translations into sentential and predicate logic.

Natural Language: **Sentential Logic:**   **Predicate Logic:**
Someone took the pizza   P and Q   ∃xTxp and ∀yU
and everyone is upset

Recall the *valid* argument that sentential logic *cannot* handle.

> All philosophers think clearly.
> *Buffy is a philosopher.*
> Buffy thinks clearly.

Predicate logic would symbolize it like:

> ∀x(If Px then Tx)
> *Pb*
> Tb

The first premise says that *for any x whatever*, if x is a philosopher then x thinks clearly. So the first premise could be thought of as a summary of sentences like:

> If Alan is a philosopher then Alan thinks clearly.
> If Skippy is a philosopher then Skippy thinks clearly.
> If Buffy is a philosopher then Buffy thinks clearly.

And so on for any name that you care to mention. The only rule is that in a given sentence the name cannot change. You cannot include "If Tommy is a philosopher then Bonita thinks clearly" in the list of sentences summarized by our first premise. So, let us return to the argument and fill in this step.

> ∀x(If Px then Tx)
> If Pb then Tb
> *Pb*
> Tb

The second premise here is simply the first premise minus its universal quantifier and Buffy's name (symbolized by "b") inserted for x.

But now look at the second and third premise. These, plus the inference rule *modus ponens*, lets us conclude Tb. This translation preserves the original argument's validity.

QUICK QUIZ #5

1. Translate the statements of the previous *Quick Quiz* into predicate logic.
2. Translate the following valid argument into sentential logic. Explain why it loses its validity when translated into sentential logic. Now translate it into predicate logic. Explain why it regains its validity: My dog Rex certainly chases cats. Without exception, dogs do that.

---

4. The Notion of a Formal System, Consistency and Completeness

To keep things simple and yet be able to achieve our goals, we shall only discuss the formalization of sentential logic. We begin by describing a *formal language*, a language in which *everything* is firmly nailed down. (There are lots of formal languages.) Ours will be a formal language for sentential logic. We call our language FLSL.

FLSL consists of two types of symbols and a couple of formation rules. The symbols are the vocabulary of FLSL and the formation rules are its grammar rules.

FLSL:
1. Symbols:
     a.   Variables: P, Q, R,...
     b.   Logical constants: "and," "not," "or," "if...then"
     c.   Grouping indicators: "(" and ")"

2.   Formation or Grammar Rules:
    a.   Any variable standing alone is grammatically acceptable. Example: P
    b.   For any two acceptable formulas, P and Q, the following are acceptable:
        Not P, P or Q, P and Q, if P then Q
    c. Nothing else is grammatically acceptable.

With FLSL we are almost ready to formalize sentential logic.[7] We have to add two more things: axioms and inference rules. Let us call the system of formalized sentential logic FSL.

Axioms[8]
1.   If P then (If Q then P)
2.   If (If P then (If Q then R)) then (If ((If P then Q) then (If P then R))

Inference Rules
The single inference rule is *modus ponens*. Suppose that ¥ and š stand for grammatically acceptable sentences. The rule is simply:

> If ¥ then š
> ¥
> š.

(Once again "¥ and š" are just arbitrary symbols. Greek letters are often used. We have chosen ¥ and _ to make clear the arbitrariness.)

A proof is simply a sequence of grammatically acceptable sentences of FLSL where some (the premises) are axioms and one (the conclusion) follows from the premises using *modus ponens*. A theorem is simply a grammatically acceptable sentence of FLSL that is the conclusion of a proof.

Now we can *state* Kurt Gödel's[9] completeness theorem for sentential logic. This theorem says two things:

1.   Any sentence S that you can derive in SLF is a tautology.
2.   Any tautology that you can write using the language of SLF you can also derive in SLF.

These statements tell us that the concepts of "provability" and "tautology" coincide in SLF. If a sentence is a tautology, then we can prove it. Also, if we can prove a sentence, then it must be a tautology. Now, if all that we can derive are tautologies, then we certainly cannot derive a contradiction. If we cannot derive a contradiction from a system, we say that that system is consistent. We also say that sentential logic is complete, but we have to consider this term extremely carefully since it has more than one meaning.

Gödel showed that sentential logic is complete in the sense that it can derive *any* tautology that can be expressed using the language of sentential logic. In other words, use the symbols of sentential logic and write down any particular tautology. You will be able to prove it.

Now, let us consider a different sense of completeness. We will try to illustrate it first with an example. Suppose we use the symbols of sentential logic and write a statement like "P or Q." This is not a tautology and so we could not prove it using sentential logic. (Remember, sentential logic only lets us prove tautologies.) "P or Q" is a contingent statement; it might be true or it might be false. Sentential logic cannot prove either way. So, sentential logic is incomplete in that it cannot prove (or disprove) any sentence that can be formulated in its language. Conversely, sentential logic is complete in that it can prove all the tautologies that can be formulated in its language.

There is a lot more that one could say about consistency and completeness in logic. The previous discussion is sufficient for our purposes here. Let us now return to Gödel.

5. Gödel's Results: A Slightly More Formal Discussion

But we want logic to talk about more than tautologies. So, let us see what follows when we ask logic to talk about the natural numbers, i.e., the series, 1,2,3,... The branch of mathematics that deals with the natural numbers is called *elementary arithmetic*, which consists of addition, subtraction, and related notions. To proceed in a rigorous fashion, we have to *formalize* arithmetic. We will call our formal system, which tries to capture all the truths pertaining to numbers, FA (for formalized arithmetic).

Within FA we can prove many statements about the natural numbers. The first question we might ask is: "Can we can prove *all* the truths about the natural numbers"? But, before we ask this, let us consider whether FA is consistent. That is, could we use FA to prove some statement, Q, and its negation? Could we use FA to derive the contradiction, "Q and not Q"? The consistency of the system is important. If FA were *inconsistent*, it would indeed be able to prove all the truths of the natural numbers, but it would prove falsities as well. This would not be a very useful system.[10]

We might just insist that FA is consistent. However, simply *insisting* that FA is consistent does not cut much ice. Can we *prove* the consistency of FA? Remember that a proof, so to speak, is something that lives inside a formal system. There are many technical details that we have to gloss over here but the basic answer is this: we simply *claimed* that FA talks about the natural numbers 1,2,3,..., but does it really? That is, maybe we *could* interpret the symbols of FA in different ways. For instance, FA could be read as talking about the integers 0,1,2,..., so which series is FA *really* talking about, the natural numbers or the integers?

The answer: FA *can* be read as talking about all sorts of different series, not just the natural numbers and the integers. But we can prove that it is perfectly legitimate to read FA as talking about 1,2,3,..., and since there are no inconsistencies with the natural numbers, FA must be consistent as well.[11] But, again, remember that a proof lives inside a formal system. Which formal system do we use to prove that FA can be read as talking about natural numbers (and so be considered consistent)? It turns out that we would have to build assumptions into the formal system that are stronger than the axioms of FA itself. Think of it this way: to prove the consistency of FA we need a more powerful formal system than FA. Is this more powerful system consistent? How do we prove that it is? To do so we would need an even more powerful system. The problem just goes on and on.[12]

So we accept, like Gödel did, that our formalization is consistent. Let us now return to the first question we asked about FA: can it capture all the truths about natural numbers? Simply put, no. So, FA is incomplete. Now, recall our discussion of sentential logic and completeness. We said that sentential logic is complete in that it can prove all the tautologies that can be formulated in the language of sentential logic. But it cannot prove (or disprove) every statement that we can form using the language of sentential logic. Some of these statements are true (but of course they are not tautologies). It is the second type of incompleteness that Gödel showed applies to FA.

Unfortunately (or fortunately depending on your tastes and patience) we must bypass just how Gödel actually proved all that we discuss. In other words, we will be explaining only his results.[13] However, these results are about as secure as any piece of mathematics can be.

Gödel constructed a sentence, G, with some remarkable properties. First, G is expressed in the language of FA. So G is a statement involving the natural numbers.[14] Second, FA cannot prove that G is true nor can it prove that G is false. But this is the interesting point: G is a true statement. G is a *true* statement in the language of FA but G cannot be proven within FA. In sum, if FA is consistent then it is incomplete. This combination of consistency and incompleteness is the essence of Gödel's first incompleteness theorem.

Before stating the second incompleteness theorem, we should note a couple of things. First, we cannot complete FA just by adding G. If we do this, then another sentence within FA + G, say G', could be formed that could not be proven. So, FA is *essentially incomplete*. Second, although G may not be provable within FA, that does not mean that G cannot be proven in any formalization of arithmetic. In other words, Gödel's work does not show that there are absolutely unprovable statements about the natural numbers. Our G might be proved within a different system. It is just that no one particular formalization can prove all the truths of arithmetic.

The second incompleteness theorem has already been touched upon. Essentially, Gödel showed that we cannot prove the consistency of FA within FA itself. We cannot be absolutely certain that FA is consistent, but since the axioms of FA formally state the arithmetic operations that we do every day, and we know that these everyday operations give good results, we have good reason to think that FA is consistent. But again, we cannot be absolutely certain. We have to settle for what is often called "relative consistency."

6. What are Numbers?

Beyond these logics are fundamental questions leading up to central difficulties associated with "Russell's Paradox." Russell had been impressed by Giuseppe Peano's work,[15] but he also had an itch to generalize the principles involved in it. To do this, he needed to discover some properties of the most crucial ingredients in the structure. The most obvious of these was the notion of number. Numbers were postulated in Peano's axioms—the concept was simply taken as "primitive" and therefore undefined, though, of course, some properties of numbers were given in the successor relations. Frege and others had made important suggestions about the nature of numbers and Russell adopted these, essentially making numbers classes of a certain sort. He defined number, most simply, in his *Introduction to Mathematical Philosophy,* as "anything which is the number of some class" and "the number of a class" as "the class of all those classes which are similar to it." He was aware that this seemed to be circular, but since he was able to define the "number of a class" without reference to number *in general,* it was not, technically, circular.

This requires explanation. What Russell was doing, by his own account of the matter, was simply deciding that he would take the class of all couples *as* the number two, the class of all triples *as* the number three and so on. He admitted that this might seem odd, but in fact, such a notion would do all the work required within the domain that most interested him.

More importantly, it has an obvious connection with the easiest reading of an important part of the traditional Aristotelian logic. For it makes numbers into classes, and propositions which figured in Aristotle's logic can, if they are read as propositions about relations between classes, be systematized rather simply in such a way as to make the inference relations fairly clear and even diagrammable.

Thus we might link a good and clear kind of reasoning (the sort having to do with numbers) with some very general notions about inference. Russell had it in mind, in any case, to generalize and extend Aristotle's logic, applying to it the model that he could derive from a logic adequate to arithmetic.

7. Russell's Paradox

Russell's difficulty was that he quickly discovered that there are paradoxes about classes. To make notions about classes work in a logical structure of a rather formal kind, one has to be able to make statements about them consistent with one another. The larger question of what consistency *is* can be left untouched for the moment. Suffice it to say, at least, that it entails that the same statement should not be both true and false. (A statement that is both true and false is consistent with everything and, in a sense, everything follows from it. It thus destroys the structure of any inference pool into which it falls.)

Now it turned out that there are inconsistent statements to be made about classes[16]—and no apparent way to avoid them. In one form, the problem had been discovered by a mathematician called Cantor, and Russell had discovered it, in another form, in the logic he most admired, that of Frege. We have come to know it as "Russell's paradox."

It begins, innocently enough, with the notion that some classes are members of themselves, and some are not. The class of all yellow things is not, for instance, a yellow thing. For classes are not "things" in space and time and have no colour. The class of all unitary things may, however, be a unitary thing—for it is one class, not many. If, as Russell once thought, numbers can be defined so that the number two is the class of all couples and the number three is the class of all triples and so on, then the class of all numbers is itself a number, some kind of infinite number. At any rate, if some classes are members of themselves and some are not, there are some rather general classes—the class of all classes and the class of all classes that are not members of themselves. Now the class of all classes that are not members of themselves is either a member of itself or it is not. But if it is a member of itself, then it is not a member of itself—it is not one of those classes that are not members of themselves. But if it is not a member of itself, then it *is* a member of itself—it *is* one of those classes that are not members of themselves.

Now this may seem rather silly to you and, in fact, Russell realised that it is a version of the ancient paradox of the liar. (If the liar says "everything I say is a lie" then, if what he says is true, it is false, and if it is false it is true.) But the difficulty is that Russell had opted for an arithmetic and a logic of *classes* and, for this position to be consistent, the classes must stand to each other in certain determinate relations.

Behind this is a larger question. In *Principia Mathematica,* Russell and Whitehead realized that these paradoxes were basically paradoxes about totalities. And though they don't dwell on the matter very much perhaps, it is clear that problems about totalities were quite vital to their concerns. For theirs is a logic of determinate entities whose descriptions depend upon one another in a certain way. A good example is the series of natural numbers that must form a single system with certain uniform properties throughout. It must be possible to say certain things *(notice Peano's* LAST *axiom)* about the whole system. (It does not matter, for this purpose, that the system is infinite as long as certain properties are distributed throughout it in a certain way.) Failing that possibility, the system breaks down in such a way that we cannot determine what place anything has in it. (Suppose it was possible that there was *no* number 9—what then would be the significance of its present predecessor and successor?)

In general, however, any system that works by imposing general requirements that systematize the whole of a domain of discourse into discrete logical atoms (whether it is the simple either/or propositions we met earlier or something rather elaborate like a number system), will require one to be able to make some general statements about the totality of that system.

What is more (and worse), as people like Frege and Russell began to wrestle with the contradiction about the classes, it began to look as though the problem would spread through any such totality whether or not one used the notion of classes. Suppose we were to decide not to talk about classes, but to talk about *anything* else. Suppose we call that something else a property. But properties, whatever they are, have something in common with classes. Just as classes are either members of themselves or not members of themselves, so properties either exemplify themselves or they do not.

If we have this distinction, then, of course, it turns out that the property of being a non-self-exemplifying property is either a self-exemplifying property or it is not. (It is *exactly* like the class of all classes which are not members of themselves, for it is the property of being the property of non-self-exemplification. Such a totality of exclusion either excludes itself or it does not. If it does not exclude itself, then it is self-excluding and if it does exclude itself, then it is not self-excluding.)

That may make our heads spin a little, but it was a serious matter to Russell. For it meant that the solution did not lie in redefining the concept of classes. It ran through a very large set of discrete distinctions with self-excluding properties, whatever one chose to call them and however one chose to exemplify them.

Russell's solution was to develop what he called the "theory of types." This solved the problem by dividing discourse into types that one can think of as strata or layers. The solution invoked a rule that every proposition must refer to a level below itself and never to the level on which it, itself, belonged. Thus the example of the liar in the liar's paradox would exclude the proposition in which he uttered his statement "everything I say is a lie" and apply his saying *only* to the next level of statements—those about which the statement was made. The class of all classes not members of themselves would, then, exclude itself from its reference and so on.

This would seem to deal with the issue, but Quine, in his *New Foundations for Mathematical Logic,* points out that it creates another problem. There has to be a way of coping with everything in the system and this requires what Quine calls a universal class. But, if discourse always refers to a stratum which does not include itself, then there must be infinitely many such levels. "The universal class ... gives way to an infinite series of quasi-universal classes, one for each level. The negation 'not-x' ceases to comprise all non-members of x and comes to comprise only those non-members of x which are next lower in type than x."[17]

Such a notion will get in the way of even quite simple arguments that depend upon general exclusions, but the point, again, is that we need some general way of speaking of properties that apply to the system as a *totality*, and we seem to get a fragmented result instead.

Quine's solution was, in effect, pragmatic; he simply defined a membership rule that prevented the generation, in his system, of classes that proved offensive in Russell's system but still allowed one to talk about "the universal class" and associated notions.

But will that work? Well, we are now in the position of saying that we put items in our logic just because they make that logic work and keep us out of contradiction. Quine's invention of a rule to do this is not to be taken lightly as an intellectual achievement, but it now puts us back where we were before we discovered the virtues of arithmetic. We are left with the notion that we simply enjoy our logic and find it tolerably obvious.

In any case, we doubt that Quine's proposal will actually work *if* the problem is really to enable us to talk about totalities. For we think totalities conceived as collections of discrete things actually result in a necessarily self-contradictory concept. Consider: as a rule, we can talk about discrete things because we can mark them out from their neighbours against some background. It makes sense to talk about France as a distinct geographical entity only because France does not occupy the whole domain under discussion. If "France" were simply the name of the whole of space, there would be no point in using it. "France" would be the name of everything and we already have a name for that—"everything." There is a point to talking about France because we can contrast it with Belgium, Germany, Italy, Luxembourg and so on. But this contrast is possible because France has boundaries. To know those boundaries is to know something about the boundaries of Germany, Switzerland, and Belgium. Discrete entities are only possible objects of discourse because they form parts of systems.

But what shall we say of any such system? It is apt to have a name, in this case "Earth." Is the totality another "thing" or not? The answer is usually "yes" and "no." The totality is not another member of the same class of things. There is not France, Germany, Canada, Tanzania, China *and* Earth. But it is something that can be talked about—though only because there are other members of the class of things to which *it* belongs. We have Mars, Venus, Pluto and Mercury.

In the end, however, we either come or we don't come to the totality of all the entities that can be talked about. What about the final totality? If that *is* another thing, it is *not* the final totality! For then, the totality is everything plus it. But if it is not another thing, it is not *the totality*, either, for we have no way of talking about it, of getting it into discourse. We cannot get this notion of totality simply by assembling discrete things—though we shall see, later, the point of all this in the chapter on "dialectical" logics. The kind of logic that Russell wanted when he and Whitehead wrote *Principia,* and the kind of logic that Quine wanted when he set out to tidy up the system depends upon ones being able to refer to discrete entities assembled, essentially, as classes. But the notion of discreteness involves the notion of a system in which such entities *are* discrete and, hence it involves a certain notion of totality.

We should remind ourselves that notions such as "class" involve many hidden properties and were these brought to light, the paradoxes might dissolve. The paradoxes may be influenced, for example, by the distinction between "internal" and "external" relations.[18] A is "internally" related to B if the relation makes a difference to A and B, and "externally" related if the relation makes no difference. For instance, we might think that a stone is the same stone whether it is in one pile of stones or another, but that John would be a different person if George and not Jim were his brother. It may even be that Susie would be a different person if she were married to George and not to Jim. Now classes are internally related to their members because the class of purple things would not be the class it is if it excluded any of the purple things that happen to exist or if it included any things that were not purple.[19] But the members of classes are not necessarily internally related to one another. If we have a class of purple things and a class of mauve things, none of them would be different if we drew the line differently so as to include some mauve things in what is now the class of purple things.

Now let us consider a famous example: suppose there is a barber who shaves everyone in the village except those who shave themselves. Does he shave himself? If he does, then he doesn't and if he doesn't then he does. One simple answer to this conundrum is just that there isn't any such barber—and so the problem doesn't arise. But that doesn't tell us why there should not be any such barber. If we think of the distinction between internal and external relations, we can see, in fact, that there could be such a barber and that no problem would actually arise.

The reason is that not all designated individuals sum to a class. This is so just because classes are internally related to their members and the members are not internally related to each other. For this to be so there must be some set of properties that don't sum in the required way. In the case of the barber, it is easy to see how this comes about.

The barber evidently shaves himself no matter what. Each person either shaves himself or is shaved by the barber. So imagine the case of Smith and imagine that we don't know if he is the barber or not. If he is the barber, he is shaved by the barber. If he isn't the barber, he is shaved by the barber. No problem here. The problem was in assuming that the class of persons not shaved by the barber sums to a coherent class when the class is defined by the property of being shaved by the barber. Clearly it does not.

There are various ways of solving these problems. But we set out to find a pattern of inference that would give us our freedom—mastery over our own discourse. And the outcome is not yet clear. To see what is at issue, we must first look at some other properties of such systems.

8. Some Conclusions

This was an admittedly rapid review of modern logic, formal systems and Gödel's results. We have barely scratched the surface. But we hope that we have given enough to illustrate a theme that has been emerging since the first chapter and to which we referred at the opening of this chapter. That is, that formalization in logic has been the attempt to lay down, in a rigorous manner, ideas that we first form more or less intuitively.

What we have also hoped to show is that work in modern logic, especially Gödel's, shows that imposing systems on our thinking seems to bring limits into play. Whether one is trying to tri-sect an angle using only a compass and a straightedge or formalizing the truths about the natural numbers, or trying to capture all the different types of sentences and inferences we use in ordinary language, limits do seem to arise.

So, perhaps we might say that imposing systems from above, that is, trying to lay out axioms or rules in advance, independent of those who might follow them and use them, will always lead to limitations. Indeed, this has been the underlying approach to the logic we have discussed, from Aristotle to Gödel, namely that logic *in the theoretical sense* is to be taken as independent of human minds. But there are other approaches to logic, approaches that are rarely, if ever, discussed in standard logic books. Such approaches try to take into account the simple fact that reasoning is done by reasoners. We now turn to such an approach.

QUICK QUIZ #6

1. What does it mean to say that "systems have limits"? What does "different branches of logic" mean?
2. What is the main difference between elementary and non-elementary logic? What does elementary logic talk about? What is meant by the "completeness of elementary logic?"
3. Why are some inferences valid in predicate logic but not sentential logic? What is the main difference between sentential and predicate logic? What are the two types of quantifiers? How are they related?
4. What is a "formal system?" Why are formal languages important? Are they important? What does it mean to say that a formal system is consistent? Complete? What does "provability within a system" mean?
5. What are Gödel's incompleteness theorems? What does it mean to "formalize arithmetic?" What is "essential incompleteness?" What is relative consistency? Is that good enough?
6. Did Gödel tell us anything about human consciousness? Are we just computers? Did Gödel tell us anything about the nature of logic? Of arithmetic? Are we just stuck with assuming the consistency of arithmetic?
7. Does "Russell's paradox" have philosophical significance or is it just a clever word game?

Notes

1. William Stanley Jevons (1835–1882). His major work was *Pure Logic,* London: 1864. For Boole see Chapter 2.
2. Some of the logical work of John Henry, Cardinal Newman (1801–1891) is found in his *Essay in Aid of a Grammar of Assent,* London: 1870, reprinted New York: Doubleday, 1955. His collected works also include essays on formal logic.
3. Though Frege is given credit, specifying where the break is between "traditional" and "modern logic" is not itself a simple matter. It was often said that Russell broke with Aristotle by insisting that we cannot infer legitimately from "All S is P" that "Some S is P." The propositions—or statements—involved do not usually now take these Aristotelian forms but rather forms like "("x)(Fx _ Gx) and ($x)(Fx and Gx). (These translate roughly as "For any x, if x if F, then x is G" and "there is an x such that x is F and x is G." The "$" signify the "existential" quantifier "there is a." The universal quantifier "any" or """ is given by the convention under which the bracketed x, if not modified in any way, is taken to mean "any x whatsoever." Gottlob Frege used the quantifier-variable notation, which made possible the various distinctions thought crucial.
4. Cambridge: The University Press, two vols., 1910, 1927.
5. A "substitution instance" is just a case where one can fill in the details of a formula expressing a principle without changing the logical nature of the proposition expressing the principle. For instance, we may say "Either A or not-A" is a logical principle. "Either Socrates is mortal or Socrates is not-mortal" is a substitution instance of it.
6. The closest branch of mathematics to logic is set theory. But there are reasons for thinking that set theory can make do with a more restricted notion of "set" or "class." "Set" has been defined in recent times to mean "non paradoxical class," and it is part of the business of logic to deal with the paradoxes so excluded. Quine (see *Philosophy of Logic*, Cambridge, MA: 1970, 1986, pp. 97–102), clearly opposes the total integration of logic with mathematics. He thinks that logic depends on notions that are basically obvious, that there is an important relation between logic and reality, and finally that logic is ubiquitous—it serves mathematics as well as all the other sciences and therefore cannot be literally a part of mathematics. Obviousness, as we have seen, is problematic. The question of logic, mathematics and reality has to do with the fact, as Quine notices, that mathematics favours certain special subject matters while "logic favours no distinctive portion of the lexicon"(p. 98).
7. There are a number of ways to do this. We describe only one.
8. There are a number of different ways to provide axioms. We provide only one.
9. Kurt Gödel (1906–1978) was perhaps the most celebrated logician of our time. He spent his mature years at the Institute for Advanced Study in Princeton, New Jersey.
10. However, this does not go completely unchallenged in the general case of systems. Some systems allow, but do not "encourage," contradictions; they are called "para-consistent systems." Fascinating, but unfortunately beyond the scope of this text. For more on para-consistent logic, *cf.* G. Priest, R. Routley and J. Norman, *Para-Consistent Logic*, Munich: *Philosophia Verlag*, 1989.
11. Slightly more technically, we say that the natural numbers provide a *model* for FA.
12. There are a lot of technical details we have omitted here; the reader is invited to consult more advanced texts.

13. Gödel developed a technique of representing statements about numbers by numbers themselves. This has become known as "Gödel numbering." It is not terribly difficult to understand but it does take some time to explain it. *Gödel's Proof*, by Ernest Nagel and James R. Newman. New York: New York University Press, 1958, contains a simple discussion of just how this numbering works.

14. Again, we have to skip over some technical details since what, exactly, G is about is a subtle question.

15. Peano (1858–1932)n was an Italian logician and mathematician whose work on number theory is still regarded as fundamental.

16. There is a question of terminology here. We are using Russell's notion of classes. Sometimes in modern set theory "class" is defined so as not to include the Russellian classes which produce paradoxes. Hence, for instance, in *The Vastness of Natural Languages,* Oxford: Basil Blackwell, 1984, the authors, D. Terence Langendoen and Paul M. Postal, use the expression "collections" to denote what Russell meant by classes.

17. This famous essay has been reprinted many times. It is most easily available in *From a Logical Point of View,* Cambridge, MA: Harvard University Press, 1953, and New York: Harper, 1963, pp. 80–101. The quotation is from pp. 91–92 of the Harper edition.

18. This notion is explored in Leslie Armour, *Being and Idea, Developments of Some Themes in Spinoza and Hegel,* Hildesheim: Georg Olms, 1992.

19. This is so in *one* sense at least. The idea of "making a difference" is not itself perfectly clear. But notice that we draw a sort of line between purple, say, and mauve and we give meaning to the words by including some things in one class and some in the other so that what constitutes the class tends to make it just the class that it is.

Chapter 4

JOHN DEWEY'S LOGIC

1. Introduction

We have seen that logic became increasingly abstract, cut itself off from experience, and eventually ran into problems. The problems of formalization remain lively topics of debate. But now we turn to John Dewey, who wanted to keep reasoning tied to experience.

Dewey did not condemn the study of formal systems. Rather, he regarded it as an example of the "spectator theory of knowledge," according to which the knower and the known are *completely* independent of each other. Dewey held that logic should study not only formal systems but also the full range of our experience. He also held that our logic is to reflect the "human world," not the "world in itself." Dewey's approach to logic is along the lines of the practical reasoning we spoke of in the first chapter. Since Dewey regards reasoning and inferring as kinds of thinking, we shall begin with his view of thinking.

2. Dewey's View of Thinking

Dewey held that thinking is a response to a problem. Problems are interruptions in the smooth flow of experience. Thought is successful when the blockage is resolved and experience flows smoothly again. Dewey held that experience could be coherent and satisfying: coherent when it provides meaningful information that we can use to control future experiences, satisfying when it meets the demands of reflective human beings.

Further, Dewey held that concepts like "truth" and "knowledge" had to be developed out of the interaction between theory and experience. But these concepts were *not* arbitrary.[1] He held that humans are governed by a kind of "intellectual honesty," and sometimes considered this "ideal of honesty" as virtually religious in character.[2]

So most humans are driven to a kind of experience that can be articulated in a structural, coherent and consistent manner. Most reject any reading of experience that fails these criteria. That is, they reject the idea of fragmentary or contradictory experiences. Thought develops out of this attempt to render experience coherent amidst all the daily frustrations of life.

Consider a simple example: you are walking down a path.[3] So long as it neither forks nor ends, and you pass nothing tempting, you will keep going. If you come to a fork, you have an option; this is a "rupture" in your otherwise smoothly flowing experience. You might take the right fork out of habit. So the fork is not seen as an option. However, the more it is seen as an option, the more likely it is to provoke thought.

To demand a rational order to experience is to demand a way to deal with the options to produce a satisfactory experience. The immediate "end" when facing a fork is a decision, but that decision becomes a means to some other end—like a quick route home. *That* end, in its turn, is a means to some other end. So Dewey said that there is a continuum of means and ends.

For Dewey, thinking was ultimately an *instrument* one used for a purpose. Nonetheless, thinking may become an end in itself because it can generate a desirable quality of experience. One desirable quality of experience is an open-texturedness, the kind of freedom constituted by live options, provided that one is able to deal with those options. Thinking, therefore, does become a dominant end in the lives of human beings but Dewey's ultimate insistence on the ends – means continuum appears to be derived from the fact that desirable experience is experience in which there is openness and possibility. Even the most desirable end, in consequence, leads to new possibilities and extends the ends – means continuum.

There are, therefore, two sides to the desirable build-up of human experience. On one side is a growing structure of effective thought, a growing rational order. On the other, are the new possibilities for experience offered by that structure.

3. Dewey's Five Steps

Dewey most commonly set out his analysis of the situation created by thinking in five steps.[4]

1. Recognize the situation that permits options.
2. Formulate the problem.
3. Create a hypothesis about the problem.
4. Deduce consequences from that hypothesis.
5. Apply the deduction (sometimes called "verification").[5]

These steps stress that reasoning is necessarily connected to the situation faced. The first step requires a mode of conceptualization and the second amounts to specifying the demands one is going to put on the situation.

Suppose that one faces assertions and wants to come to a judgement (Dewey's "settled opinion"). But assertions may or may not go together to form a judgement. There are options. One may either be given a proposal for judgement or one may formulate such a proposal. In sum, there is always the possibility of judgement.

Dewey likened logic to dancing and the law.[6] Both attempt to order a set of potentially discrete and confusing actions. So it is characteristic of the problems of logic that different orders will lead to different judgements. If the options consist of different *forms* of argument, that is one characterization of the problem. If the options consist of different ways of relating the concepts in the assertions, that is another characterization. And so on.

For Dewey, there was no *single* answer to these questions. Aristotle's logic and modern logic each have their place. Since Dewey connected inquiry and the inquirer, it is always a *particular* situation facing some inquirer, and the test will be the subsequent character of the inquirer's experience.

So a logical structure has meaning only insofar as it illuminates someone's experience. It could not contain or refer to *everything*. If it did, it would have a meaning independent of anyone's experience. There is always someone doing the reasoning, and *whoever* does it always transcends the constructed system. The construction always involves a last link that is the constructor's *act*. For Dewey, what the inquirer may infer depended not just upon the immediate case of inference, but upon the *situation* (Dewey's word) in which one finds oneself. Consequently, the system is constantly being extended and no two inferences ever have exactly the same status.

Standard logic, that is traditional and modern logic, envisions logic and inference as objective and divorced from all inquirers. But it gives rise to puzzles because it neglects the system that generates it and the situation of its user. It can never extend itself far enough to be meaningful in itself. Furthermore, it cannot, really, consist of indefinitely many discrete components that have constant meanings throughout the process. The meanings are always shifting with the situation of the user.

For Dewey, each inquiry began against the background of the inquirer. This background increases after each inquiry. Although successive inquiries will have common properties, no two inquiries will be identical. Consequently, there are no final, absolutely clear rules and so Dewey merely offered us the five steps.

Recall that logic dictates that one should translate ordinary language statements into the proper forms. Inference rules then enable one to validly move from statement to statement. Finally, recall that an argument's validity does not depend on any content, just on form. A standard logician would ask: where are the propositional forms and inference rules in Dewey's system? Perhaps Dewey simply bypassed logic and its issues in favour of *psychology*?

Dewey challenged this radical separation of logic and psychology. He insisted that formal logical concepts arise out of our everyday dealings. Logic and its rules have arisen out of our everyday dealings with each other and the world, just like the laws of society have arisen.[7] Also, these dealings always have a particular context: it is always a *particular* person in a *particular* situation. Standard logic has omitted all notions of acceptance or license on the part of the user and his or her situation.

Dewey attacked both the "two move" structure of the modern proposition and the notion entertained in the copula verb.[8] Consider the following propositions:

> Aristotle's Logic: All S is P, Some S is P
> Modern Logic: ("x)(If Fx then Gx), ($x)Fx

For each, one *starts* with something and *then* says something about it. For Aristotle's logic, one starts with S and says something, P, about it. For modern logic, one starts with some x and says something about it (that if it is F then it is G, or that it is F). Aristotelian and modern propositions presuppose that we get entities into our language by assigning predicates to them. We distinguish entities from one another by assigning certain predicates to some and different ones to others. This "two-move" structure presupposes that objects are first "there." One points at them and then names them.[9] For instance, one points at a given object and says "cat." It is then possible to move on to assemble things pointed at, properties of things pointed at, and so on.

Dewey doubted the presupposition of the "two-move" structure. He insisted that mere pointing is ambiguous. Suppose you point at an object and say "cat." I might think that you are pointing at its colour and calling it "cat." Another person might think that you are pointing at its texture (furry) and calling it "cat."

Dewey's complaint about the copula verb stemmed from several concerns. It is not true that a cat simply *is*. Of course *something* is there, what Dewey calls a "brute given." But when we go further and start saying things about this something, what we say depends on contexts of meaning and interest that are given by the observer.

QUICK QUIZ #1

1. Why is Dewey's account of "thinking" important to his logic? Was he right about thinking?
2. Can you imagine a kind of human experience that poses no "problems" in Dewey's sense of "problem"?
3. Discuss Dewey's "five steps" in problem solving.
4. Discuss Dewey's comparisons between logic, dancing, and law.
5. What is the "two-move structure" of the modern proposition? Why does Dewey attack it?
6. Discuss the difference between standard logic and Dewey's logic regarding the status of the thinker.

---

4. A Deweyite Proposition

Since inferences depend on the form of propositions, let us construct a proposition with a form of which Dewey would approve. The form must reflect the nature of everyday experience. Even though we will make several simplifications, the Deweyite proposition will quickly become quite involved.

Consider the assertion: (A): "Apples are edible." Translated into Aristotle's logic this would be: "All apples are things that are edible." Translated into modern logic this would be: ($\forall$x)(If x is an apple then x is edible). For Aristotle's and modern logic, (A) would be translated into the simplest type of proposition; it marks something out and says something about it. For Dewey, (A) will be a combination of assertions.

Dewey said that there must be an original assertion, (OA), which specifies how this situation is identified within someone's experience. Human appetites focus attention so as to divide experience into objects that could then satisfy those appetites. For instance, hunger divides your experience into two classes, edible and non-edible objects. Hunger then focuses your attention on the edible class.

But before dividing experience into *edible* and *non-edible* objects, experience has to be divided up in terms of objects *per se*. To experience an object as distinct from another, the objects have to be separated in terms of space and time. We can call these "focusing" variables because they produce the original experience frame. Let us call this focus (or experience frame) F. This frame is a Cartesian coordinate system for four-dimensional Euclidean space: three axes for space, one for time. The observer, or the subject, can be thought of as a "point-consciousness" located at the origin of the frame. We will first presuppose that at any space point there is only one object but many properties.[10] We will have an ordered 4-tuple: x^1, x^2, x^3, x^4, where x^1, x^2, and x^3 stand for spatial points and x^4 is temporal. To begin, we have:

$$(1) \quad F = F(x^1, x^2, x^3, x^4)$$

We can simplify this by writing the spatial coordinates in terms of a single variable: s^i.[11] We will rewrite the time coordinate in terms of t^i. Equation (1) becomes:

$$F = F(s^i, t^j)$$

So, in the experience frame, F, there is a position, s^i, at a particular time, t^j. To break out of this immediate spatio-temporal moment, we need some means to sum times and spaces. Here again, we can borrow from the riches of mathematics, the sigma operator, Σ. In general this operator says[12]

$$(2)\sum_{j=0}^{N} s^j = s^1 + s^2 + \ldots + s^{N-1} + s^N$$

Let us now begin our escape. We start by enlarging the temporal dimension of our experience frame. Since the frame fans out from a mortal point consciousness, it has a temporally bounded existence. Hence, t^j ranges over a finite set of values. Again, we have to make the assumption that time is discrete (an assumption Dewey may not have liked) in order to employ the sigma operator. So, we suppose that there are n moments in an experience. This can be represented as follows:

$$(3)F = \sum_{j=0}^{n} (s^i, t^j)$$

So this equation tells us that there is an experience frame involving a point at s^i over a time from $t = 0$ to $t = n$. At any given moment, that is, any given value of t within the limits 0 and n, experience is not limited to a single point of space. So we have to accommodate the fact that experience is infinitely spatially extended at a given moment. To do so, we again borrow from mathematics in that we nest our sigma operators.[13] At each moment t^j, the range of experience will be the totality of the s^i's.[14]

$$(4)F = \sum_{j=0}^{n} \sum_{i=0}^{\infty} (s^i, t^j)$$

Now, as many philosophers have remarked, essentially following Berkeley's criticism of Descartes, we do not experience "points" or extension in any way. Rather, we experience that which fills in extension. Various objects will be spatio-temporally characterized by unique subsets of 4-tuples. As an extremely simple example, a short experience of a dot would be represented by the set (s^i, t^j), in which s^i provides the information regarding the spatial points comprising the dot and t^j gives the totality of time involved in the experience.

But let us pull back and look simply at a single point at an instant. Suppose that it is a point on the surface of a MacIntosh apple. Again, idealizing somewhat, this point is characterized by several properties: redness, hardness, smoothness, sweetness and the like. This, too, must be accommodated into our experience frame. Not surprisingly, another nesting of the sigma operators will accommodate this aspect of experience. So we could represent the properties by p^h—and h ranges over a set of properties indexed by the natural numbers from 0 to z. Fixing the spatial–temporal coordinates we would have the following:

$$(5)F = \sum_{h=0}^{z}(s^i(p^h),t^j)$$

Now, putting the ideas of an extended spatio-temporal framework back in with the properties, we would end up with something like the following:

$$(6)F = \sum_{j=0}^{n}\sum_{i=0}^{\infty}\sum_{h=0}^{z}(s^i(p^h),t^j)$$

But note: the various p^i representing properties presuppose that we have some way of relating our language associated with the scheme to the actual spatial points within the experience frame. Of course, how language relates to the actual world is one of the thorniest philosophical questions. Dewey, unlike Russell, did not think that language simply mirrors the world. Rather, the relationship is shot through with conventions. Consequently, these conventions must be built into the Deweyan proposition.

Clearly the difficulty here is that the conventions under which we operate are numerous and often extremely complicated. Let us try to represent this by attaching a convention to each property, p^i. For instance, the property, "sweet," would be represented by p^{hc} (where h is the property's index and c is that property's associated convention). We now have the following:

$$(7)F = \sum_{j=0}^{n}\sum_{i=0}^{\infty}\sum_{h=0}^{z}(s^i(p^{hc}),t^j)$$

Now, we have to fill in this abstract structure by connecting it to the lifeline of an actual person. Experiences at any given time are influenced by prior experiences. As Bergson and Husserl stressed, it is an artificial schema of experience to represent it as a series of isolated and self-contained "drops" (to borrow a term from A. N. Whitehead). Consider the experience of music. If we only heard each note in isolation from all the others, we would never hear the melody. One must have some sense of the past (the previous notes) in order to hear the melody, which, of course, is not in the external world all at once. The melody is something that exists over time.

Again we borrow from mathematics. One could say that experience illustrates a recursive structure. Now, in a recursive structure, succeeding terms are defined by their predecessors. This, of course, is much stronger than we want here, and would leave no room for any novelty.

So we want a person's experience at a given time to be partially defined by that person's previous experiences. Moreover, we want to escape a purely idiosyncratic notion of the proposition. We do so by referring to other persons' experiences. We express the objectivity of the proposition by reference to *intersubjectivity*.

Let us call the information from previous experiences "reports." They will be of two types: first- and second-person, designated by R_{fp} and R_{sp} respectively.

$$(8) F = \sum_{j=0}^{n} \sum_{i=0}^{\infty} \sum_{h=0}^{z} (s^i (p^{hc}), R_{fp}, R_{sp}, t^j)$$

But even this does not meet Dewey's apparent needs. We now have to translate this proposition into an impetus for action.

5. Action

The goal is to move from (P): Apples are edible, to (P') Eat apples. There are two moves involved here: We need an *a priori* probability for P, and we need to determine when one should act on P.

The A Priori Assignment of Probabilities to P

The initial probability assignment is wide open. However, once you have acted on it (eaten an apple), you will have a new report and will use it to revise the original probability assignment. Sometimes we can estimate the *a priori* properties of things. For example, if a die has six sides, the probability that any given side will come up is 1 in 6. If a coin has a head and a tail, the chances of either one is 1 in 2. Even here there are some complications. One should always remember that the chance of getting a one or a six in throwing the die is always the same. If you have thrown one thousand ones in a row, the chances of getting a one are unchanged—still one in six. Of course, if you throw the die an infinite number of times, all the possibilities will turn up. It is reasonable to suppose that if you throw the die a thousand times you will get at least one six, for the chances are additive. You have one chance in each throw. If you throw the die a thousand times, a sixth of them or about 166 of them should be sixes. It would be very odd if the number were less than one, but it wouldn't prove that the die was loaded.

Notice, too, that the chances of getting two sixes if you throw two dice is 1/6 times 1/6, or 1/36. The chances of getting a six on either die is 1/6 plus 1/6 or 1/3.

Dewey was generally suspicious of *a priori* probabilities. It seems that he thought that we should estimate probabilities by counting the empirical reports. This is the best we can do with things like edible and inedible apples. If it is true that there are only two possible states, edible and inedible, one might think that the *a priori* probability was 1 in 2 for each case. But not half the things in the world are edible. Furthermore, it is difficult to divide the world into "edible" and "inedible." If "edible" means "well-suited for eating" one can do it. But there are things that *can* be eaten in some sense (wood chips, for instance) which are not very well suited to eating. Then, there *are* "opium-eaters," but some people don't think opium is suitable for eating at all.

Acting on P

A physicist will act first on the most likely hypothesis and last on the least likely. Moreover, many highly likely propositions will be ignored. In our ordinary lives, we do not act on propositions simply because they are likely. The propositions that we act upon are not *merely* the most likely, they have to have something more. We act upon the proposition that is the best choice at that particular time.

For Dewey, every proposition contained an evaluation of its candidacy for action *vis-a-vis* whatever other propositions present themselves. The problem is in how to determine when one *should* act on a proposition. So there is a value question involved.

Dewey held that we should replace the traditional notions of "truth" and "falsity" with "degrees of warranted assertability." But this conflates the probability question (the degree of warrant) and the value question (the degree of assertability). Let us try to sort this out.

Consider the probability question. Recall that the form of a Deweyite proposition specifies a reference frame, a range of objects associated with logical places and a property associated with some of those places. The association is represented by first- and second-person reports.

In our case we have apples located in certain places and times and reports saying that apples and edibility are associated in some cases. So objects (designated by "apple") and properties (designated by "edible") will be associated with some degree of likelihood.

The association of objects and properties must be the kind to which we can assign a likelihood associated with a number, but the "&" could designate not only class membership, implication, or identity, as it does in modern logic, but might also represent a *causal* relationship. For instance, "&" might represent the psychological propensity to associate, or the likelihood that these will be discriminated jointly in the experience frame. For particular cases, it will have to be spelled out.

Some properties are *intrinsically* associated with the experience frame, for instance the property of having a succession of places in space and time. We cannot *test* to see if this holds. This property, then, would be assigned Probability 1. Perhaps the most difficult problems in science are those that demand a revision of the experience frame's basic structures. (Einstein's revision of space and time is a good example.)

We also have to estimate the relation holding between the inspected region of the experience frame and the frame's properties. The apples we inspect may all be edible, but what is the likelihood that tomorrow's apples will not be edible? We would have to compare the number of apples found to be edible to those found to be inedible. This leads into the classic problem of induction.

6. Induction and Experience Frames

Recall that a valid argument could not have true premises and a false conclusion. Now consider the following argument:

> *Joe has three dogs.*
> Therefore, Joe has two sheep dogs.

This is invalid, although it has some inductive strength. But suppose we add the following premise.

> Joe has three dogs.
> *Joe has at least one sheep dog.*
> Therefore, Joe has two sheep dogs.

This is still invalid, although it is a stronger inductive argument. Now consider the following:

> Joe has three dogs.
> Joe has at least one sheep dog.
> *Joe's mother claims that he has two sheep dogs.*
> Therefore, Joe has two sheep dogs.

This is a still stronger inductive argument. However, it remains *possible* that the premises are true and the conclusion is false. Inductive arguments have *degrees of strength*. However, there are no degrees for validity; an argument is either valid or it is not. Consider the following argument:

> *All the apples eaten* so far *have been edible.*
> Therefore, the *next* apple encountered will be edible.

This is not valid. But most would accept the argument based on the idea that the future resembles the past.

Recall that Dewey began with a problem within experience and tried to solve it by introducing what we called an experience frame. The frame enables us to identify components of experience. These components may change, although the frame *itself* does not. Your experiences yesterday are different from today, although they are all located in space and time. So the future has to be similar enough to the past to even be the future.

If the future is identical to the past, nothing changes. We could not act on any proposition. In essence, there would be no sense in even saying that the future is different from the past. If the future is *radically* different from the past, then there is no way even to relate the future to the past. (We could not even relate them by saying that "the future comes after the past" since this presupposes that they are similar in that they are both in the same time order.)

In this case we could not say which course of action would be better since they would all be equally irrelevant. Again, the future has to be like the past but not identical to it.

So our choices *do* lie, as the propositional form proposed suggests, between 0 and 1 for any given association or cluster of associations. We then make an arbitrary choice between 0 and 1. After we act on a proposition we must then make two reasoned choices. First, should we change the initial probability? Second, if we do, *how* should we change it? One would think that each positive case of association increases the reasonableness of a *higher* probability and each negative case will increase the reasonableness of a *lower* probability. But, there is an important point here: this does not say that the probability will increase or decrease but only that the reasonableness of increasing and/or decreasing the *assignment* is influenced in this way.

Suppose that we discover that Delicious apples and crabapples are edible under different conditions of preparation. We may decide to leave the probability assignment and change the conventions defining what "counts" as the object we are seeking. Similarly, we may change the convention about "edibility" if we discover something about the way in which body chemistry is altered by eating one thing or another. We have already suggested that we may, sometimes, want to change the experience frame, and it should be evident that we might also want to change the way in which we conceptualize the association involved.

When conventions are well defined (as in the sciences), the experience frame becomes quite precise. In such a case we then can use mathematics to speak of the associations. For example: force, mass and acceleration are associated as follows: Force = mass x acceleration.

QUICK QUIZ #2

1. Translate the following, "All candy is sweet" into:
   (i) Aristotle's logic.
   (ii) Sentential logic.
   (iii) Predicate logic.
   (iv) Dewey's logic.
2. Why was Dewey suspicious of *a priori* probabilities?
3. Why don't we act on the most likely propositions?
4. Explain the difference between a deductive and an inductive argument.
5. Why does a traditional logic not permit a valid inference to future contingents?
6. Why does Dewey's logic permit a valid inference to future contingents?

---

7. What to Do in a Crunch

Although conventions in science become well defined, they do sometimes change. For instance, Einstein changed the way mass is related to force. So there are always choices to make. Should we alter the initial probability, refine the experience frame, sharpen our account of the association in question or change the conventions? The propositional form does not help us answer these questions. We have to look at the context in which propositions arise, that is, when we are faced with a problem.

Dewey likened a proposition to an invitation to do something. So acting on a proposition will bring about some desirable consequences. Desirable consequences come in many types, but they all bring about a state of experience more satisfactory than its predecessor.

Consider the following statement: "there is a single law that accounts for gravity and electro-magnetism." For Dewey, this was not a proposition, but a "propositional disguise." To find the proposition that this disguises, we have to find a suitable experience frame, a set of objects to which it relates and at *least* one pair of properties that are supposed to be associated in a certain special way (the way that exhibits the meaning of the phrase "a single general law"). But we would still think of the propositional disguise as a description of a state of affairs. For Dewey, this was not completely incorrect, although it is misleading.

Dewey insists that we are only interested in a proposition because it poses a problem for us. There are, of course, many different types of problems. As we have seen, the general idea of a problem is that it is a rupture in the smooth flow of experience. An intellectual problem is a special kind of a rupture. Our physics works until it cannot account for something that we see. We have run into an incoherence or unintelligibility or a block in experience.

The different sorts of ruptures inhibit action. They hinder our control of our own affairs; they are blocks between our desires and their attainment. The desire to understand is not merely an intellectual curiosity created by a society that gives certain people time to stand about in laboratories and think. The most remote of our objects of thought are really features of a general background picture of the world that colours all our actions.

For instance, you suppose that time will not run backwards, the laws of gravity and thermodynamics will hold and large objects will not simply appear when you cross the street. You live your life so that these very general questions do not intrude. In other words, you cheerfully assign probabilities of 1 (or close to it) to propositions that may in fact be rather doubtful. So the physicist or the philosopher who worries about such questions is not immersed in a non-problem but only in a problem that does not intrude on *your* affairs because you do not (or you lack the conceptual apparatus to) subject the appropriate regions of your experience frame to close analysis. In sum: eating because hunger pangs disrupt one's experience is on a continuum with Einstein's struggle to construct a unified physical theory since disunity in physics disrupted his experience.

If Dewey were right, the conventional distinction between facts and values would dissolve: propositions are believed to have warranted assertability because they have a value; we think for reasons (good or bad) that one who acts on sound propositions will increase the quality of his or her experience. It may seem that the outcome would be a wholly private matter: one thinks that "p" is a proposition that warrants assertion because one thinks that one's experience will improve in quality through the action of asserting it. But this is not correct.

As propositions are refined so as to approach a stable probability (a high probability, one hopes), they do so by assimilating appropriate reports about actions. In the experience frame, your reports count just as much as ours, provided that we each make a report with the same qualifications. If we look into a Wilson cloud chamber, our reports have (perhaps) little or no significance since we are not trained to do this. Indeed, anybody properly trained would quickly see our lack of training and promptly ignore our reports.

In general, the quality of one observer's experience is as important as the quality of another's. Observers are also equal when making value judgements, unless it happens that a particular observer is better placed to seek some sorts of improvement than to seek others. The physicist may achieve more (overall) improvement in human experience by sticking to physics than by trying to solve the problem of crime, and the criminologist may achieve little by turning his or her attention to physics. This concern applies not merely to differences in expertise. It is also true that one will have more influence on the experience of one's spouse, one's friends and one's colleagues than on the experience of people to whom one has no close attachment. The intrinsic equality is modified by the *facts* involved and it is not wrong or foolish to suppose that one's responsibility may be greater to some persons than to others. But this stems from what Dewey regarded as simply another fact: value judgements are about the quality of something; the only object of possible judgement is the state of some experience. The qualities of experience that are open to judgement are not inherently mysterious. Hence, what is at issue is the quality of those experiences that one anticipates will be changed by adoption of one proposition or another as a basis for action.

Now we have to build into our experience frame the fact that a particular proposition is but one proposition among many. Our experience frame has to show that propositions are options. For instance, suppose that our proposition is option "I" in a set I, II, III, IV…. If it is likely true that apples *are* edible, then our experience of eating them will not likely be ruptured by hunger pangs that block our other choices. In that case, we will place a fairly high value on the proposition. Suppose that II is "steak is available at X" and that we think eating steak will produce a longer set of stable experiences than eating an apple, we may then place a higher value on II than on I.

But suppose the apple is here and the only doubt is about whether apples are edible, while the probability of "steak at X" is only about 1/2. We shall have to balance the satisfaction against the likelihood and, to do this, we shall need other expressions that allow us to insert the experience of values for being sick if apples are inedible, being hungry if we search for the steak, and so on. Again, there is no fixed way of balancing the values. We will have to adopt some species of arithmetic and *then* have a rule for changing the numbers when the results are in. It is true that some values will outweigh all others—*if* God exists, then, by becoming "one with God" we may be able to achieve the highest order experience permanently or even eternally. But though that is so, the probability that God exists *might* be quite low. The chance of orderly action that would effectively make the proposition into a judgement (i.e., give it a probability that turns out to be stable after a series of planned actions) may be very low indeed. The possibility, even, of getting an intelligible association relation within a given experience frame may not be high. In that case, the likelihood of improving one's experience by eating steak might outweigh the desirability of solving one's problem for good by pursuing the God hypothesis. Dewey would simply have said that we ought to choose but should do so in such a way that our actions, gradually, will be modified as we conduct our exploration. Since the process will be a long one, we should stop long enough to eat from time to time. All of these questions are questions that we shall meet again when we discuss moral, theological and scientific reasoning. But it is important to notice here that Dewey did not think that the three are different in *principle*.

For now, let us add to our propositional form something that takes account of the additional subject matter. We will want to say that there is an experience frame or focus of experience (F) within which there occur propositional options. We can name them Op^I, Op^{II}, and so on—with an assigned value that asserts that there is an object (a), at a place and time (s^1, t^1) conventionally identified by the word "apple" (C^1). Further, there are reports, my own (R_{fp}) and others (R_{sp}), that this object is associated with a property (b) conventionally identified as edibility (C^2). This association has an assigned probability (x).

This will be complicated further if options (Op^I, Op^{II}, Op^{III}, Op^{IV}...) are spelled out. The first question to ask is whether or not we can break down such propositions into more convenient sub-units, each of which we could consider separately. The form looks like an amalgamation of many sentences including, "My experience has a spatio-temporal organization. There are objects in it. Some of the objects are what we call apples. It is reported by me (and others) that some objects of this sort are edible. I estimate the probability that apples are edible as high. Compared to other propositions that present themselves as options in my present state, "apples are edible" presents itself as having a high likelihood. If I am right, and I eat an apple, the quality of my experience will be improved by a discernible amount."

The classical approach would be to divide all these seeming assertions into suitable logical types and to investigate, independently, the structure of each of them. And, as we saw, we can spell out the different kinds of reports, experiences, and linguistic conventions in various sorts of propositional fragments.

Dewey's thesis, as we understand it, was that trouble starts when we come to value problems. We make value propositions a separate class, and then rightly complain that there is no way to validate them. If we separate value and factual propositions, then they do not bear on each other. We think of linguistic conventions apart from the role they play in enabling us to formulate the structure of our knowledge, and then we say "How arbitrary they are!" and proceed to develop a separate branch of our logic to deal with arbitrary linguistic generalizations. We fail to notice how first-person propositions go together with other propositions, and claim, therefore, that they are logically different. Before we know it, we may have inferred that since there is no route from first-person to third-person propositions, we are all somehow locked up inside our own heads.

Dewey's writings imply that separating facts and values leads to the strange world that many philosophers say is the real one: a world where values are arbitrary, experience is always private and inductive generalization is impossible. But if Dewey were right, this might all be misguided. Dewey did not expect us to analyze all our assertions into the complicated form we suggested since only the most important of them would be worth the time. Nonetheless, these worthwhile ones may be more complicated than the propositional form we adopted. To do this might be the work of days or even years.

Getting our assertions into a Deweyite form is more difficult in *some* respects than translating ordinary assertions into Aristotelian or modern propositions. However, there is a payoff. After getting a Deweyite form, we do not seem to encounter the difficulties which Aristotle's or Russell's logic create for us: there are no totality problems, for we do not need to introduce such notions except as features, perhaps, of an experience that will pose no more problems. But although this is an envisionable end, we have no reason to think that we shall ever get there. There are no problems of the completeness of proofs, for there are no complete proofs.

But Dewey's account, like traditional logic, restricts the things that we can say. For Dewey, we can only talk about experience. We only formulate propositions that lead to potential action and do so because we estimate both the likelihood of the proposition's results and the value of these results. The question of whether there is a world independent of experience does not and *cannot* arise in Dewey's system. However, it is not a subjective system since it provides clear procedures for assimilating first- and third-person propositions. For Dewey, the question of "a world independent of *me*" broke down into two different questions—the question of whether or not some things are simply presented in experience whether I like it or not, and the question of whether or not there is a public experience. Dewey claimed that there are some things in experience that are just given and not capable of being disposed of by any *conceptual* device, and that there *is* a public experience because there are public probabilities and public evaluations.

Dewey's system dissolves the traditional distinction between deduction and induction. Every inference extrapolates from the current evidence and changes the past assignments of likelihood. Induction simply consists of the ascription of likelihoods and a commitment to change those ascriptions on production of more evidence. There can, apparently, be no deductions proper—though Dewey sometimes suggested otherwise (especially when he talked about what amounts to fragments of real propositions.) Consider, on a traditional view:

> All horses are graminivorous.
> *This creature is a horse.*
> This creature is graminivorous.

According to our reading of Dewey, "All horses are graminivorous" means something like:

> There is a spatio-temporal reference frame in which there occur objects conventionally called "horses," and every instance so far identified turns out to be associated with the events commonly called "being graminivorous" in such a way that those whose experience has been found to be rendered more satisfactory by the presence of horses have found this satisfaction increased by adopting the feeding policy suitable for graminivorous creatures.

But it by no means follows from this that "This is a horse" entails "This is graminivorous." All that follows is something like:

> "If you think this is a horse, your best policy is probably to treat it as graminivorous." (This does not strictly follow, but follows as the best option available out of several which are bound to seem more foolish.)

Note that whatever follows in Aristotle's or Russell's logic, real life is on Dewey's side. For instance, Dr. Skinner may have conditioned the next horse you meet to eat nothing but peanuts.[15] One may *rightly* claim that Dewey abolished the universal quantifier "all." Indeed, his proposal is not a part-by-part translation of "all horses are graminivorous." He refused to make the leap, as modern logic does, to talking about mind-independent totalities in logic. Dewey might ask, "what justifies such a leap?"

Dewey did make exceptions. And, at least on our analysis, we may see why: to make the scheme work at all, we will be compelled to follow whatever *rules* we adopted when we set up the initial probabilities. It will follow necessarily that the next case of a graminivorous horse will increase the likelihood that horses should be treated as graminivorous so long as the original assignment policy is the one governing the transaction. Within the appropriate pieces of *arithmetic*, strict deduction holds. But we are not bound to that arithmetic. We can change the whole system when a more subtle mathematical device comes along. There are, therefore, as we might think, propositional fragments between which, under stipulated conditions, strict deductive procedures hold. It will also, therefore, be true that paradoxes can easily develop within those propositional fragments, but, in that case, the fact of a paradox will be one that entitles us to change to a new system. For we only buy the mathematics so long as it proves *useful* to us.

Does this answer all our questions? Not really. Some of the difficulties are obvious. We chose the original experience frame rather arbitrarily, and one thing the system doesn't tell us is how we would generate alternative frames. It also doesn't tell us when to abandon the one we have. If we assign the initial probabilities between properties in some ways, we shall soon see that a given frame creates difficulties. If we assign them another way, we may go on forever without ever discovering our error. We suggested that some associated features have probabilities of 1 because they are associated with the frame itself—for instance, properties of space and time. But we may not find out that a given association has that property because we may disguise its occurrence in the proposition by assigning probabilities such that the evidence goes to resolve some doubts and not others.

For instance, scientists used to think that the universe was completely filled with a substance called "ether," and thus space was not thought to be empty. Ether was used to explain how light managed to travel between the sun and the earth. Scientists attributed all sorts of properties to the ether and designed experiments to its other properties. Since the ether was taken to be a general feature of the frame under investigation, all experimental results were understood to change the likelihood that ether had certain properties rather than others. Ultimately, someone tired of this game or we might be still at it. That is, someone designed an experiment to determine whether the ether *itself* existed.[16] It took a reconceptualization to separate the component notions.

One flaw, therefore, in Dewey's system is that we can become locked into ways of looking systematically and ordering our propositions so as not to change that way of looking at things. To put it another way, Dewey's system works well for the self-correction of small and middle-sized concepts and less well for the correction of larger ones, which occupy a different place in his scheme. It also, as we have seen, does really restrict what we can say. Dewey thinks we have the best reasons possible for restricting ourselves. But was he right?

8. The Tensions in Dewey's Logic

Dewey's logic offers a way of coping with a set of tensions. If one sees it as the description of a set of static states, it will appear riddled with "contradictions." The difficulty with Dewey's scheme is that it is a way of coping with these tensions at a certain level of experience. It therefore tends to trap us in the immediacies of experience, giving us just enough control over them to be able to manage our affairs. In so taming the tensions, it tends also to obliterate their significance. Why is there this tension in experience and in logic and between experience and logic? The question remains largely unanswered in Dewey's theory.

The hope—however forlorn—of a dialectical logic is to explore these tensions in a way that will enable us to make them more intelligible. What we need is a way of reasoning that will enable us to know how and when to pass from a view that emphasizes one side of the tension to a view that emphasises the other.

We can see Dewey was trying to measure and assess the strengths of the various elements in experience. But this is, in itself, very difficult to do. Furthermore, one can always stay on one's own side of the dialectic by a little conceptual juggling. The capitalist may insist that the worst off might be still worse off if the costs of socialism were added to the social process, even though there might be more justice. And he can say this no matter how much injustice there might be. The socialist can argue that any kind of individual action can feed greed and create injustice. And he can say this however oppressive his own bureaucracy may have become. So we seem to need a more sophisticated way of dealing with these tensions. Let us now turn directly to that possibility.

QUICK QUIZ #3

1. The unknown plays an important part in Dewey's logic, but not in Russell's. Explain this difference. Is the effect of the unknown a weakness of Dewey's logic? Why or why not?
2. Dewey's logic is related to experience, but what seems to be really important is the notion of "focus" or "experience frame." Give a critical analysis of this notion.
3. Dewey's logic depends on the notion that human beings must make choices. It also forces each of us to make a number of choices each time we engage in inference. Explain some of these choices.

Notes

1. See Russell's amusing, but rather unfair, essay, "Dewey's New Logic" in *The Philosophy of John Dewey,* ed. Paul Arthur Schilpp, New York: Tudor, second edition, 1951, p. 135–56. For more on Dewey and "truth," see Leslie Armour, *The Concept of Truth,* Assen: Royal Vangorcum, and New York: Humanities Press,

1969, p. 141 and 202 ff.

2. See Dewey's *A Common Faith*, New Haven, CT: Yale University Press, 1934.

3. The example is Dewey's own.

4. The account differs a little between *How We Think,* Boston: D.C. Health, 1910/ 1933 and *Logic, the Theory of Inquiry,* New York: Henry Holt, 1938.

5. Sometimes in *Logic, the Theory of Inquiry*, Dewey does not talk about verification but about the various operations which we perform on our experience in order to generate facts and meanings.

6. See *Logic, the Theory of Inquiry.*

7. *Logic, the Theory of Inquiry,* New York: Henry Holt, 1938, p. 102; reprinted in Joseph Ratner, ed., *Intelligence in the Modern World, John Dewey's Philosophy,* New York: Random House, 1939, p. 886.

8. Here we are not so sure that we are on firm ground in knowing what Dewey is really doing, though it is very obvious from the text that the way in which Russell or Aristotle would characterize the situation is *not* Dewey's way.

9. Russell held this view in *The Analysis of Mind,* London, George Allen and Unwin, 1921, Ch. X.

10. This departs from Dewey's view since it presupposes that an observer passively "gazes upon" a field of independent objects in space.

11. This is done by changing from Cartesian to cylindrical coordinates. This also is intuitively satisfying since cylindrical coordinates reflect the fact that our experience exhibits, more or less, a kind of radial symmetry. The details are that s is a multi-valued function of R, 0 and P. R is the Euclidean distance from the origin to the object in question. 0 is the angle subtended by the line projected "straight in front" of the origin and the line projected from the origin to the object in question. Finally, P is the angle subtended by the R distance and the line projected vertically from the origin. The precise mathematical details of cylindrical coordinates can be found in any elementary calculus text.

12. Of course, to be more accurate here, we would have to rewrite the sigma operators in terms of integrals. That, however, would take us too far into mathematical details and distract us from the project at hand.

13. For those of a more logical than mathematical mind, this mimics the idea of nested quantifiers.

14. Once again we have made a simplifying assumption. Clearly one is not aware of the totality of spatial positions at a given moment. Experience, as Dewey and the other pragmatists—as well as Husserl and the phenomenologists—stressed, consists of a foreground and a background. What we are directly aware of is the foreground while that which we are indirectly aware of is the background.

15. B.F. Skinner, a Harvard psychologist, is perhaps the best-known expositor of behaviourist philosophy of the past thirty years. His skills include a considerable adeptness at animal training.

16. This is the famous "Michelson–Morely" experiment and its results form the cornerstone upon which Einstein built his theory of special relativity. A description of this experiment can be found in most introductory physics textbooks. Einstein's particular relationship to its results, however, is rather subtle.

Chapter 5

DIALECTICAL LOGIC

So far we have looked at two basic types of logic: standard logic (Aristotle's and modern elementary logic) and Dewey's logic. Standard logic abstracts from content and deals with the form of statements. This was fine provided logic dealt solely with logical truths. It ran into incompleteness problems when it dealt with arithmetic. Modern logic might be justified in that it gives formal structure to inferences that everyone would accept. Its problems, largely, have to do with its scope.

Dewey's logic does not abstract from content and remains connected to experience. Its difficulties involve choosing the experience frames. Different frames will give different structures to our experience and our inferences. How do we decide which first-person propositions—experience reports in their most basic form—to include in the structure? In our example regarding apples, it was fairly straightforward. We know from which propositions the judgement "apples are edible" is apt to follow. But suppose the judgement is "angels win football games for Notre Dame." Do we know what "experience frame" is appropriate, what conventions to employ, just what the first-person reports that link the proposition to actual occasions of experience might be like? The ingredients that justify inference in a Deweyite judgement are very complicated and rather numerous. The choices are numerous and apt to be what Dewey himself called "live options." Dewey's own recommendation, evidently, was that one must always wait to see whether one decided wisely. It will depend upon what kind of experience results. But sometimes we really need to know *before* we act.

So the problems can be seen like this. Modern logic illustrates Immanuel Kant's claim that reason, left to itself and isolated from experience, always leads to paradox. If there is no non-paradoxical way of separating form and content, does this not suggest that formal logic, in at least the obvious sense of that expression, is founded on a mistake?

Dewey's logic illustrates Kant's view as well. If reason without experience leads to paradox, surely experience without reason is unintelligible. In working with Dewey's logic one is constantly searching for rational frameworks. Of course, Dewey would say that the test of these frameworks is in experience itself. Can we live with the result? Are the natural developments of experience frustrated by them? But in answering such questions one is necessarily interpreting experience and this process of interpretation itself involves reason.

We ought to admit, then, that there are difficulties about these logics. Some of the problems may be solved by brighter logicians in the future. Others make it doubtful in principle that such logics will ever be rendered problem-free. The *ideal* solution would be a logic that combined the adaptability of Dewey's logic and the objectivity of standard logic.

But the ideal solution might be impossible. It would have to account for the fact that logic is a human activity. In Dewey's system, individual decisions are gradually "objectified" in a growing structure. But that process is evidently limited by the choice that is required to obtain the original experience frame. A more realistic solution might be a logic that provided a way of objectifying the choices that go into the construction of such frames.

Dialectical logics are an attempt to provide a principle for obtaining this result. In their modern form, such logics go back to Hegel. But there is much dispute about the correct characterization of Hegel's system, and the attempt he made in his two logics—*The Science of Logic*[1] and the first part of the *Encyclopaedia of the Philosophical Sciences*[2] —is not easy to understand.

We shall draw here on some earlier work—to be found, mostly, from *Logic and Reality.*[3] That book, however, was mainly an attempt to draw out some of the metaphysical consequences of a dialectical system, and to relate such systems to other logical structures and compare and contrast the result with rival metaphysical systems. The brief elaboration that follows will consequently differ somewhat in that our concern is with developing a logic that will satisfy the demands set forth in the first chapter.

.   So far, all the logics discussed started with statements and then translated them into the basic units (i.e., concepts) of the logic. The basic concept in Aristotle's logic is that of class. Modern logic's basic concept is the property. For Dewey it is the domain of experience. So, each of these logics has its own particular *type* of concept. What is common to these types of concepts is that they are all a way of marking out the world. So, in its most general form, a concept is a way of marking out the world.

This leads into many difficult philosophical issues, one of which is the problem of definitions. (We will discuss this further in a later chapter.) Consider the concept of "cat." "Cat" includes the creatures we normally think of as cats: domestic cats, lions, tigers and so on. "Cat" excludes things we normally think of as non-cats: horses, hats, automobiles and so on.

Now think about the concept of "person." This includes adult humans, but does it include a foetus? A newly fertilized egg? The definition of "person" is controversial and important. (Consider that not too long ago women were not included in this concept!) The definition of "person" is crucial to the contemporary debate over abortion. Consider the following argument:

> Killing a person is wrong.
> Abortion kills a foetus.
> *A foetus is a person.*
> Therefore, abortion is wrong.

Whether or not one accepts this inference will depend upon one's definition of "person." Dialectical logic uses the concept in its most general form. Dialectical logic is often called "the logic of the concept."

1. The Idea of Totality

Suppose we have to deal with the idea of totality. If we employ another concept much used by logicians, the concept of "class," we run into paradoxes. The same happens if we use the concept of "property." So the *concept* of "totality" is *not* the concept of a "class" and it is *not* the concept of a "property." Rather, the concept of totality is the concept of the system taken as a whole, without divisions.

Consider the following example, which comes from environmental ethics. Traditionally, we would think of a rabbit *and* its environment as separate. But this is misleading since the rabbit's environment is as much a part of the rabbit as its stomach. The rabbit depends on its grass, the grass depends on water and sunlight, water and sunlight depend on the earth's position in the solar system and so on. So the totality, rabbit-and-environment, is a single *functioning* unity, that is, a systematic unity. The totality is not merely the sum of the parts and it is not, of course, something added to that sum.

Now consider the eagle-and-environment totality. This is also a functioning unity. The rabbit focuses its environment in one way while the eagle focuses its environment in another. If we look at the world in *this* way, we have, instead of a world divided into bits and pieces, a world divided into perspectives. The world is the rabbit-and-environment from one perspective, the eagle-and- environment from another, the human being-and-environment from another and so on. The point is that each perspective embraces the whole. The "propositional unit" here is a series of assertions each of which describes the whole from a different point of focus.

So we do not have to understand objects in the world as "bearers of properties" or "sets of properties." We can understand objects as perspectives on the world. The object, "rabbit," is a particular way of organizing the world. However, the "rabbit organization" is not static. It is an ongoing process. It is *functioning*. (If it were not, the rabbit would be dead.) For instance, part of the rabbit perspective is digestion, respiration and so on. So a rabbit perspective could be conceptualized as a continuous process of organization. It is very misleading then, to point at a given rabbit and say "at that *particular* space and time is a rabbit."

2. Basic Relations Between Concepts

Since each concept is unique, any given concept excludes every other concept. But there may be different ways that concepts exclude each other. A given concept may have a unique way of excluding other concepts. For example, the concept of "totality" has a unique way of excluding other concepts. It does so by allowing only that subset of genuine concepts that is capable of focusing the *whole* of the particular region or universe of discourse being totalled. And there is a concept of all concepts that are not members of themselves if and only if it is not the case that this mode of conceptualizing excludes itself. Presumably, it *does* exclude itself. The point is that we are not in the fix we were with classes or with properties, each of which organized the data in a pre-determined way. Concepts may be shaped—must be shaped—to fit the case since they are a way of organizing the data appropriate to the case.

Again, each concept is unique. In consequence, each concept has a reference that we may call its general exclusion reference—it excludes all other concepts. This allows some kind of inference—if C^1, then not $C^2...C^n$. But this is not a useful logical property. First of all, it would give no clue as to how we might generate $C^2...C^n$ from C^1. But the whole set of concepts, $C^1....C^n$, is *not,* in principle, capable of total explication. For each concept is unique and each concept structures whatever it marks out in its own way. The sum of those ways is not another way of conceptualizing. There is a concept of totality; there is not a totality of concepts.

Concepts are related so that they do form a single system. Each marks something out and there are exactly as many concepts as ways of marking things out. A concept could not do any work unless it excluded some particular set of concepts. For instance, the concept of "redness" excludes the concepts of "yellowness," "blueness" and so on. The relation between "redness" and "yellowness" is a specific exclusion reference. Nothing can be red and yellow simultaneously. However, nothing can be red unless it is extended in space, like a surface. So the concept of "redness" is related to the concept of "being extended in space." The concept of "redness" functionally entails "being extended in space."

So, given a concept, we can generate other concepts. For example, the concept of "the right to freedom of speech" would specifically exclude "the right to suppress others." But it would functionally entail "the right to life" since it makes no sense to say that something dead has the right to freedom of speech.

In general, every concept may be said to have a specific exclusion reference and a functional entailment. These logical properties *are* useful and can be made the basis for a particular kind of logic. This logic is *dialectical* because a concept generates others as a condition of its meaning and function.

Consider the concept "red." For it to be *meaningful*, it has to mark something out. But if everything were red, then "red" wouldn't mark anything out. In other words, for "red" to be meaningful, not everything can be red.

Something would have to be blue or green, for instance. For "red" to be *functional*, that is, for it to be useful, we would have to generate *at least one* of its functional entailments, for example, "occupying a spatial surface." In other words, we would not know how to use red if we did not know that being red entailed being a feature of a spatial surface.

So if we are given (1) a concept, and (2) its function, we can infer at least one of its specific exclusion referents and at least one of its functional entailments. But this still does not get us very far. Moreover, what we generate will depend upon what we start with and that makes it all rather arbitrary.

So far we have general principles but they do not seem to do too much. Some people hold that this is about all such a logic can do since we are tied to what is given by languages, experience, and conceptual structure. How could we conceptualize what has not come to our attention in *some* organized form? And, if every concept is unique, will it not, obviously, be the case that each inference pattern will be different—even that each inference on this model is unique? We can only expect that every such scheme will help us to utilize the logical powers of a concept amongst its immediate neighbours. But these principles *seem* rather powerful. It is as if we had harnessed Niagara Falls and only succeeded in lighting a ten-watt bulb with it.

The explanation of this somewhat puzzling situation depends upon two facts: one is the fact that some concepts exercise an organizing function over others. The way that colour words operate, for instance, has to do with the way in which they are organized by such concepts as that of "space" and "surface." (We will encounter the second fact at the end of the next section.)

3. The Determinable-Determinate Relation[4]

The concepts of particular colours are most likely determinate forms of the determinable, the concept of "spatial surface." If this process is continued, it leads to the suggestion that there is a highest order determinable that governs, in some measure, the operation of every concept. Finding that highest order determinable may be very difficult, and the specification of its logical function may be even more difficult. Perhaps there is no highest order determinable. Then some concepts might not be determinates of any determinable. But that seems to interfere with a basic meaning condition for functioning concepts.

In general, we know what words like "red," "blue," "green" and "yellow" *mean* because we can see how the concepts connected with them are associated with some determinable or determinables to which they are related. If we could not do that, we would have to rely upon a form of ostensive definition, which would not work: we would have to define such words by pointing at instances of red, blue, yellow, and so on. But one who points at red or blue things must be able to make clear that she intends to call attention to a feature of spatial occupancy. Otherwise, she would face the problem Dewey calls attention to—she would simply be pointing at everything in her line of sight. Unless her pointing marked out only one uni-propertied thing, this difficulty would have to be taken seriously. Her pointing must have, at least, an orientation and an object, and cannot, therefore, have a simple object. The usual practice is to point at several things that appear to have only one property in common. But in the case of the coloured things, the result may be to call attention to that property or to the aggregate of the geometrical shapes involved. Logically, one would have to distinguish, somehow, the case in which "blue," ostensively defined, is a colour, and the case in which "blue," ostensively defined, is, for instance, a polygon. This is to say that the uniqueness demanded is unattainable: ultimately, a single uni-propertied thing would have to occupy the whole domain of obtainable discourse. But, then, it could as well be conceptualized as anything or as nothing. Hence, it seems to be a rule that every property is a determinate of some determinable. A highest order determinable *itself* appears to violate this view in that it is a determinate of the determinable "order of the totality." In fact, however, it reflects its own content and its own content reflects it—the limiting case, presumably, of a dialectical relation.

Hence, pending some examination of the potential difficulties of the notion "highest order determinable" we can conclude that every concept is related to some other concept which orders it. One of its functional entailments, that is, is a place in some order.

The other fact involved is that we can escape from the "trap" of the situation created by the way in which our language is capable of structuring our concepts simply because an analysis of the functional entailments of any concept set always extends beyond the scope of that concept set. For instance, in seeing how colour words work, we learn something about space.

4. Space and What We Know about It

Arguably, we do not know anything *directly* about space. We do not "see" space; rather, we see the objects within it. The verb "to see" is, after all, associated with the concept of successful identification. If there were no objects in a given space, we could have no knowledge of that space if knowledge of space depended upon seeing. But by understanding how colour words operate, we work out (some) of the functional entailments of the concepts involved. This generates the concept of space. We can then explore the functional entailments of the concept of space.

Mathematicians have explored the concept of "space" in great detail. This has led to an awareness of all different kinds of "spaces." Our everyday space is often called "Euclidean space;" another kind is "Riemmanian space." According to Einstein's theory of general relativity, this is the true space of our universe.

QUICK QUIZ #1

1. How do concepts, in general, mark out the world?

2. Explain why the definition of "person" is crucial to the abortion debate.
3. Explain how the concept of "greenness" functionally entails the concept of "being extended in space."
4. Is there a good reason for developing a logic of concepts as opposed to a logic of propositions?
5. Modern logic encountered a problem with totality. Does dialectical logic? Does Dewey's logic?
6. Discuss some basic relations that hold between all concepts. How do these help us to develop a logic?
7. How does the determinate-determinable relation help generate ideas needed for a dialectical logic?
8. The concept of "space" is the concept of a determinable. How does understanding this logical notion help us to understand our claims to knowledge about space?

5. Bona Fide Concepts

Because the beginning of such explorations is critical, one must start with a *bona fide* concept of sufficient generality. A *bona fide* concept marks out some feature that truly is a feature of reality.

A bad beginning would be the concept of "dragon" since we doubt that dragons exist. However, since we can form this concept it would seem that it has *some* relation to reality.[5] There are fires, snakes, breathing things, flying things and things hostile to humans. We incorrectly combine these into a *complex* concept that does not apply to reality. (If the concept did apply, the world would be quite different from what it actually is.) So it is better to begin with a *simple* concept since it could not fail as a result of an incorrect combination.

Another bad beginning would be a concept not sufficiently general, such as "freedom of speech." There are various ways that this concept could fit into a conceptual system. It might mark out a feature of a domain of rights that would exist whether or not humans did. So its functional entailments would mainly consist of other concepts that marked out other members of that domain of rights. But it might be that there are no such rights unless humans exist. In *that* case, its functional entailments would be rather different. But we cannot tell if we cannot locate both these elements in relation to a concept of sufficient generality to include them both.

So we need a concept that is both sufficiently general to have some logical relation to every other concept and has a place in any possible order of concepts such that this place will be the same for any conceivable ordering. Such a concept would be the ideal starting place for creating the appropriate generation rules for additional concepts. It ought to be the case that any conceptual ordering—any *specialized logic*—will turn out to have a demonstrable place in the *universal logic* that this most general concept generates.

6. The Most General of All Concepts—Pure Being?

"Pure being" is simply the concept of that which *is* in the most *general* sense of the word "is." For instance, a *specific* sense of "is" would be how a physical object "is." A physical object "is" in space and time. Another specific sense of "is" would be how a number "is." A number does not exist in space and time; however, that does not mean that numbers are nothing. Another specific sense of "is" would be potential existence, like your existence tomorrow.

"Pure being" is common to all of these specific senses of the word "is." If you can imagine any other sense of "is," then "pure being" would apply to it too. "Pure being" is the point of intersection of the contents of imaginable universes. Such a concept must figure in any possible ordering insofar as any such order represents a possible ordering of some part of some universe of discourse, reference or objective existence.

Although "pure being" is an extremely general concept, it is not, by itself, useful.[6] The *conception* "pure being" expresses the simplest and most minimal *concept*. In dialectical logic, concepts are logical entities; they are features of real or possible states of affairs. Conceptions are linguistic entities, that is, words.

Some conceptions might not express a concept. We may have a conception of a married bachelor or a square circle but it may be that those conceptions do not represent a possible way of ordering things. It is probable, for instance, that the concept of a "square circle" would have amongst its functional entailments the non-occurrence of the concept of "circle"—a concept that we have some reason to believe has a place in the system of concepts proper.

7. The Most General of All Concepts—Nothing?

Notice that if you try to say anything about the concept of "pure being," you end up changing it. If you say that "pure being" is material, then you have restricted its application to things in space and time and so it would no longer apply to numbers or even a piece of music.

The nineteenth century German philosopher Hegel claimed that the concept of "pure being" collapses into the concept of "nothing." If you say anything about the concept of "nothing," you end up changing it. If you say that "nothing" is just pure emptiness, then this "pure emptiness" is either nothing or some kind of thing. If pure emptiness is nothing, then you have only repeated yourself. If pure emptiness is *something*, then the concept "pure being" would apply to it. According to Hegel, "nothing" and "pure being" have a *dialectical identity*—each tends to collapse, on analysis, into the other. For nothing also simply "*is*," and "*is*" *without structure*, and, therefore it seems to generate the concept of "pure being." But this is rather confusing and seems to confuse the notion of nothing as the negation of whatever there is and the notion of nothing as the alternative to any organized state of affairs.

We think that the real dialectical relation is between "pure being" in the sense of the original conjunction of everything that is, in all the senses we mentioned, and a notion that Hegel does not explicitly employ, the notion of "pure disjunction." "Pure conjunction" is the notion of that which has the most perfect and simple order that unites other orders. "Pure disjunction" is the notion of that which has no order at all.

Now the concept of "pure being" has as its general exclusion reference all the concepts there are—including "nothing" in the sense of "pure disjunction." But its specific exclusion reference is, evidently, "pure disjunction." It is comprehensible by contrast with that notion. Between them, the notions divide the world on the broadest level of abstraction.

Another way to think of the pure being/nothing distinction is the distinction between "any kind of ordering" (pure being)/any kind of disordering (nothing). "Pure being" and "nothing" are the same in that both do not discriminate between one state of affairs and another. "Pure being" does not discriminate between different orderings, while "nothing" does not discriminate between different disorderings. We might say that "pure" being and "nothing" have the same property, the property of indeterminacy. So "pure being" and "nothing" *together* have a joint specific exclusion reference, the notion of "indeterminacy."

We can see, therefore, why they tend to collapse on analysis. One has to have them in any system but one can only have them on condition that one has something to contrast them with. A system in which they function, therefore, must have some further concept. But so far as we can tell, now, that further concept may be the only one needed, though we may guess that it, in its turn, will require others. This further concept is the functional entailment of both the original concepts. If they are going to work, in other words, they must have, between them, the property of entailing the concept that is determinate.

The situation is simply this: we know that every system needs "pure being" and "nothing." But no system will work without one further concept: "determinacy"—the concept of whatever it is that has the property of being particularizable. The concept of "determinacy" governs the logical structure of systems like Russell's. Under this concept one orders things according to their specificity: for every property, in such a system, a given entity will or will not have that property. Since the entities are particularized, it will be possible to deal with them one by one. (Entities that can be dealt with simply as particulars have the kind of individuality characteristic of Russell's logical atomism.) [7] The development of systems of determinacy is, simply enough, the classical development of the logics we have already seen. But determinacy, if it is not supplemented by others, yields paradoxes: since it determines the components of pure being, it represents a totality. But as we saw, one cannot represent totalities in just that way. We have to represent totalities, and we have to represent them in some other way.

What has happened here is interesting and not, in a dialectical system, very difficult to specify. Every concept, as we saw, structures the objects of the world in one way by excluding other ways of structuring that world. If it did not, it would do no work. This is true of even the simplest concepts at the beginning of the system. Since there is another way of conceptualizing the world (in principle) and since it denies expression to that other way within its own structure, it ends up creating paradoxes—just those that we saw in logical systems that emphasized determinateness.

A brief examination of the way even the simple system now under discussion has developed will reveal a rather general reason for the situation. We start with "pure being," which is what must be included in every possible system. We exclude "pure disjunction," which, of course, is what is excluded from every possible subsystem within the totality of systems. We then find that these concepts will not function (1) without each other and (2) without yet another concept. But this additional concept is developed from the way that "pure being" interacts functionally with "pure disjunction"—it is built, that is, upon the relevant functional entailment.

8. Systematic Unity

The way this functional entailment runs from unspecified unity through the unspecifiable diversity of "pure disjunction" to the notion of determinateness means that the original notion of determinateness will emphasize a certain sort of diversity—diversity as specifiable through a set of discrete parts, each of which is an independent object. Suppose that you have a collection of objects: a dog, a house, a hat and a pencil. This collection consists of independent or discrete objects and can be specified by the notion of "determinacy." This is the minimum conceptual force we need to prevent the collapse of our very elementary system into unintelligibility.

But consider another collection of objects: the bodily organs of a dog. These objects are interdependent; they function together, forming a system. The dog's body can be classified by the concept "systematic unity." In terms of dialectical logic, the specific exclusion reference of "determinateness" is "systematic unity"—the notion of a set of objects organized as a totality. This totality, of course, must be expressible, and to express anything, we must exclude something. The totality, then, will have to be represented as a set of ways of viewing the same range of data. That way, it can have a structure— one that will not lead to its collapse back into the simplicity of "pure being."

Just as the notion of "determinateness" governs a conceptual region within which the components must be conceptualized as a set of discrete objects, and this makes possible propositions which refer to one or more of those objects and to the relations to them, so the notion of "systematic unity" governs a conceptual region within which propositions must be expressed in a different way. To generate a new conceptual region is to demand another dimension to our logic, within which different propositional forms and infer- ence rules will run.

QUICK QUIZ #2

1. How can we distinguish *bona fide* concepts from merely apparent ones?
2. Is the concept of "pure being" the most general of all concepts?
3. Do we need a concept of "nothing" in our logical systems?
4. What logical problems does such a concept involve?
5. Does the idea of "systematic unity" provide a useful way of looking at the world?

9. Conceptual Structures

Once we recognize that there are alternative ways of expressing the same situation, and that, importantly, the truth about those situations requires that we express what is at stake in two or more different ways, we generate for ourselves additional problems. We must not only look at individual propositions but at the growing system of ways of conceptualizing things. What, after all, links those ways? The first answer, no doubt, is that the link consists of just what we saw—the unfolding of sets of concepts by a process that traces their specific exclusion references and their functional entailments. But the system of concepts is dynamic—it grows and, if we press its logic, it will grow more. Now, the notion of change presupposes some kind of fixed background. So the notion of a system in process, a system that changes, presupposes some background against which it changes. The background is, at least, the structure of our own thought. We make it grow. We stand in some relation to the system and we must make our expressions, somehow, bear witness to that fact.

We are in the position in which Dewey found himself. We can choose how to conceptualize—though we may now see our thought as governed by objective factors associated with the conceptual structures we are trying to generate. What Dewey called experience is, in fact, a set of conceptual structures, which, applied to the world, generates a certain context. There is not a neutral "experience"—a neutral experience would be one not influenced by our existing conceptual structures or by our conceptual choices.

If you look at an x-ray photograph, you will not see what a trained radiologist might see. Astronomical photographs are often similarly uninformative. In neither case is it enough to look harder. One needs the necessary conceptual structure as well as the skill that practice at applying the concepts produces. Skill in looking at x-rays, astronomical photographs, microscopic slides and the contents of Wilson cloud chambers is not, however, the kind of skill that fortune-tellers have developed for looking at tea leaves. In the scientific cases, many observers will generally agree about the results, and will agree, too, about appropriate conceptual structures. Tea-leaf readers, by contrast, rarely agree and the concepts involved are usually both disputed and vague.

But the sciences are not so different from some ordinary doings. You can regard your experience as a field within which you discriminate things in one way or another, or you can regard it as an assembly of discrete sensations. In either case, the focus you give it will determine, to an important extent, what you "see"—and that focus will depend upon what your interests are, what you are looking for, what you distinguish as foreground and background and so on.

Dewey's logic, you will recall, required an experience frame, a set of conventions that served as definitions, the identification of objects in that experience frame, and the identification of features associated with that frame— together with some first person statements that associated the various reports with someone's experience. Out of this one could generate judgements with various probabilities, which could be shown to depend upon the scope of the experience frame, the proportion of positive identifications, the effectiveness of the conventions and so on. (Indeed, the factors threatened to become very complex.)

Dewey's judgements tended to become objectively reliable (to acquire "warranted assertability") as the judgements came to express increasingly rich assemblies of intelligibly structured statements. But elements of subjectivity intruded rather strongly upon his logic—especially in the original choice of an experience frame and of the elements of convention that entered in. The objectivity was thus always relative (or so it seemed) to the experience frame and could be redefined by choosing either another experience frame or a different set of conventions.

10. Definitional Conventions

One thing that a dialectical logic might do is to provide the basis for choosing a variety of experience frames and how those different frames fit together. It might also show us how to overcome the difficulties inherent in the choice of conventional definitions. For those definitions will all involve concepts that have other specific exclusion references and functional entailments. In this way, we can see what a given convention might do for us or to us, and if we had reason to think that the choice of conventions might "load" the "judge-ment" that we were developing, we could determine in what ways this would be likely to happen.

We will try to set out the form that such judgement assemblies might have in due course. Before doing that, we must recognize that the role we play in the story is not entirely exhausted by the way in which we make our obvious choices about conceptual structures and definitional conventions.

Russell's logic holds that inference occurs among the symbols of the system. Dewey's logic holds that inference always occurs within experience— an experience that includes both the self-awareness of the inquirer and the object of the inquiry. But even in Russell's logic, the situation is not quite so simple. Suppose you wonder how to do a simple problem in propositional logic. We show you how it follows from the "truth table definitions." You say you still don't see, or perhaps, like Lewis Carroll, you demand some additional rules to link the propositions to each other.[8] We may go on to translate the problem into different forms, explain the theory of truth tables and so on. But at some time or another, you must develop the "insight" or give your assent. In the end, you either see or you don't. What this means is that every imaginable logic must have, to go with it, an appropriate structure of human awareness. As a rule we are content to say "well, some people see the point and some don't."

11. Logical Implication and Justified Inference

This is a good place to notice a point that W. E. Johnson thought central to the understanding of logic: there is a difference between simple logical implication, even when we take it to be valid, and genuine or fully justified inference.[9] In Johnston's view an "implication" is only a "potential inference." Implications generally have the form, as we saw, of statements like "If P, then Q"; but genuine inferences made in the real world have the form "P, therefore Q". There is, as you will recall, a classical argument form called *modus ponens* which goes like this:

> If P, then Q.
> *P.*
> Q.

You will notice that this argument form contains both Johnson's formulae "If P, then Q" and "P, therefore Q." But Johnson pointed out that one has to have a specific kind of knowledge to make the real inference. For instance, one might have an argument of the form:

> If anything is a quark, then it is too small to see.
> *X is a quark.*
> X is too small to see.

Now we know that this is a valid implication in Johnson's terms even if we don't know anything about quarks or about seeing. But to make the real inference, you have to know that x is a quark. Therefore you need to know the elements of the physics in question. You also need to know about seeing, and that some things are too small to be seen (by humans? by dogs? by God?).

In the end, human knowledge plays a part in what Johnson called inferences, by which he meant inferences both real and justified.

A dialectical structure makes it clear, however, that there is at least something more to be said about the complex relations between logical forms and human knowledge and awareness. For we can see that, as a dialectical system develops, our own awareness develops with it—but not, exactly, in a parallel way.

To understand the discussion about "pure being" or "pure disjunction," you had, already, to have a notion of what was to be contrasted with it. By contrasting those simplistic states with the ordinary notions of determinateness that we all carry around with us, you could make sense of the position. When we attempted to explain the dynamics of the system in relation to our own self-consciousness, again, you had to be aware of a stage in the dialectic that lies beyond what we have been calling systematic unity. (The natural next steps in the system seem to be "determinate process" and "pure process"—for what links "determinate being" and "systematic unity" seems to be that they are determinate, static states, and what they exclude is the notion of "process." If we put together their uniting property and their joint specific exclusion reference, we will get notions of process.)

An interesting rule about such systems seems to be this: any stage in a dialectic has to be understood from the perspective belonging to the stage beyond it. Thus, though one works with Russell's logic, say, at the level of determinate being, one can only gain the insights necessary to see the validity of arguments by framing the components as a unified field. When one understands that, "since P implies Q, and Q is not the case, then P is not the case as well," one does so by putting it together as a system. One realizes that were the components changed in any way, the outcome would also be changed. That the totality belongs on a different level is a lesson that in practice has proved difficult to learn. Similarly, it is only from the perspective of one involved in a process that one can understand a dialectic system, even though, if one looks at its components, it is merely a set of static states. To grasp its point, one must represent the system as involved in a kind of logical time. This rule about "understanding" is not very mysterious. We could state it otherwise by saying that the interpretation of any system of information must contain more than the system itself—it is a reflection of that system in a certain context. Merely repeating the properties of the system will not, in itself, interpret it.

At some final stage, the ideal system would surely turn back on itself. The "highest order determinable" of which we spoke earlier is probably the property of "being an actual or possible object of knowledge." For it is at once a property that everything in principle (though not in practice), has, insofar as it can be spoken of, and it is a way of ordering all the other properties. An idealized system would summarize everything as what it is *and* as an actual object of knowledge. The ultimate dualism of system and interpretation would disappear. But it is not the case, in all likelihood, that we *can* generate such a system. Even if we could, we could only represent it from a certain perspective. The final notion of what Hegel called "The Absolute" (literally, just that which is not relative to anything) is difficult and elusive. Short of it, we must reckon with the duality of assertion and understanding.

12. The Concept of the Absolute

The concept of the absolute is, however, worth some discussion here. The "absolute," we said, is *literally* what is not relative to anything else. But just what is it to be relative? In dialectical systems, concepts are shown to be more or less adequate or inadequate depending on their relations to one another. Thus the concept of being collapses into the concept of nothing because each, in a sense, is the idea of what is but is not anything in particular. "Pure being" is to be understood only *in relation to* (or relative to) the concept of "nothing." "Nothing," similarly, is to be understood only in relation to "pure being."

"Pure being" and "nothing" (as well as both of them together) are intelligible only in relation to that which is determinate, that is to the concept of "determinate being." This is to say that, *without* the concept of that which is determinate, "pure being" and "nothing" and the relation between them would be unintelligible. "Determinate being," in its turn, is relative to some way of being determinate, to quality and quantity. Can anything exist without having some quality or other (i.e., without being red, or large, or smelly, or sublime)? Can anything exist without having some quantity? But quantities and qualities can exist only in relation to something else, namely, that which has qualities and quantities, i.e., substances of one sort or another. (If Jane is clever and beautiful, it is not the beauty of Jane that is clever nor her cleverness that is beautiful but Jane who is both.)

Substances in their turn are either occurrences or continuants and so the concept of time and process must be invoked to make them intelligible. They are, that is, either things (like rocks and trees and people), or *abstracta* (like the number two or "justice" or the "class of all classes") or events (like an automobile crash or a flash of lightning). There is, notice, a tendency to lump things and abstracta together and to call them continuants (existents at more than one moment of time), and to contrast them with events so as to get a neat "dialectical opposition," but this is the sort of thing of which one should be suspicious. At any rate, if something were existent and were neither a thing nor an *abstractum* nor an event, we would not know how to talk about it.

Of course these categories themselves tend to break down. One can analyze things (and perhaps) events further. For what it is to be a continuant is to manifest a certain property at more than one time. Properties that occur more than once are called "universals" and so the concept of universal turns out to be essential, too, for the system. The manifestations are "particulars." But "events" are not just manifestations of particulars. They have to occur at places and times, and places and times imply a kind of grid that is itself a universal. Abstracta are more puzzling. Is the number 2 or "justice" just a universal—i.e. a property that can characterize something else? Or are there "really" numbers? And is justice "real"? Since Plato, philosophers have been arguing these questions.

Our concern here is not with such arguments but with the process by which concepts are understood as relative to one another. If this analysis were to go on forever, we would face a contradiction. Every concept would depend on some other concept to which it was relative. The situation would be like that of a group of mountain climbers all roped together, none of whom was anchored to the rock. But if all concepts are relative to one another, there is no way in which meanings can finally be attached to any of them. Hence the claim that one depends on the others would be empty. We would then be saying that each concept has a meaning, but that no concept has a determinable meaning. Yet to know that each concept has a meaning, one has to have determined at least one meaning. Such claims would surely be contradictory.

But if all the concepts are finally anchored to a rock, what is the rock? What is it that is or could be relative to nothing else? The idea of the Absolute is an attempt to answer this question. In a sense the Absolute is the "highest order determinable," of which everything else is a particular expression, but which, itself, is not a determinate form of anything else.

This gives us an idea of "being" but not of the abstract "pure being" that begins the dialectic and collapses into "nothing." Thus we said earlier in this chapter "at some final stage, the ideal system would surely turn back on itself."[10] The "highest order determinable" is probably the property of being an actual or possible object of knowledge. For it is at once a property which everything in principle (though not in practice) has, insofar as it can be spoken of, and it is a way of ordering all the other properties. An idealized system would summarize everything as what it is *and* as an actual object of knowledge. The ultimate dualism of system and interpretation would disappear.

Probably the best that we can do is to represent such an Absolute from a certain perspective. We cannot *say* everything that needs to be said about it, if only because we must always distinguish between our assertions and what they are about. If this is so, we must reckon always with a certain duality of assertion and understanding.

Still, we *can* think of ways in which the Absolute might present itself. Thus we spoke of the idea of a "systematic unity." We can think of the world not as a collection of bits and pieces of things but as a unity expressed in a number of different perspectives. We are hard-pressed to say where the rabbit ends and the world begins because the air the rabbit breathes and the grass it eats are as necessary for its survival as is the beating of its heart. But we can think of the world as rabbit-and-environment. Such a world focuses the totality from the perspective of the rabbit and each thing in the world that is really distinguishable must have its perspective in much the same way. Thus we get a totality that does not, like Russell's totality, break down into a set of discrete parts that cannot be assembled, for each part reflects the whole.

Again, in organic unities we can see totalities assembled in ways that may indicate the nature of the Absolute. The butterfly encapsulates its entire past. We can infer from it its history as caterpillar or chrysalis, but its past is not a series of discrete parts. Its present, too, is a whole within which a complex set of parts is arranged so that each is unintelligible without the others. There is a kind of holographic relation so that each is reflected in the nature and needs of the others. Existing biological entities are not perfect wholes, of course. Each has some extraneous parts and many parts for which substitutions can be made. But if we imagine this process of interdependence carried to its limit, we may get a glimpse of the totality.

Immanuel Kant speculated that human beings might be related ideally to each other in such a way as to form what he called the "Kingdom of Ends." A Kingdom of Ends is a system within which each person is necessary to the whole and within which each person contributes to the ultimate expression of what it is to be human. Thus the question of the Absolute is ever more pressing. In our understanding of the environment and of the biological and social sciences, we have had to envisage the notion of new totalities. In considering the possibilities of a peaceful order, we need, somehow, to extend this notion to political science.

The question about whether or not the Absolute is intelligible is the question of whether or not these models do finally make clear the notion of something which is not relative to anything else and which can function as an ultimate totality. Still we must be careful to ask questions about all such ideas:

- Are these models clear?
- How would we improve our understanding of them?
- What difficulties do they pose?
- Can we relate them to our actual and ongoing experiences?
- Could they be instantiated?

QUICK QUIZ #3

1. What are the basic conceptual structures required for dialectical reasoning?
2. How might a dialectical logic help us choose between different conventional definitions?
3. Do dialectical logics provide insights into logical implication and justified inference?
4. Can the concept of the Absolute be made intelligible? Is it a useful concept?

---

13. More Limited Ideas of the Dialectic

One may argue, of course, that one does not need to represent our understanding of judgements along with the judgements themselves. We do not normally represent the validity conditions for Aristotelian syllogisms *and* our understandings of them. We generate the validity rules and demand that the understanding be forthcoming. But failure to notice this duality leads to a peculiar kind of myopia. We think we have fixed univocally what we want to express, when, in fact, if we could see both the conceptual form of the expression and the conceptual form of our understanding, we would have to face the fact that there is no simple resolution of the questions about form and inference.

The dialectic, then, is capable of generating the frames of reference for both the explication of the situation and for its understanding. The problem, largely, is to determine where the issues arise, what conceptual frames are appropriate for them, what the conditions for understanding are and how we are to move to understanding.

At any given moment as Dewey pointed out, the problem of generating these formulations and of coming to a judgement depends upon the situation we face—the problems we have, the questions we want answered, and, of course, the character of our experience.

The Russellian system, as we saw it, provides a schematization for things that meet certain conditions of discreteness and independence. This scheme was based on a "logical atomism" and it went best, or so Russell thought, with a certain characterization of experience: one in which one's experience appeared as a set of what Russell called "sensa," what Hume had called "impressions" and what more usually are called "sense data."[11] The notion that there is a "basic" experience lying under all its conceptualizations has always seemed attractive—not least, obviously, to logical atomists. Dewey's account questions this notion and dialectical logic suggests that it is merely one of many ways of focusing one's experience.

We need to be clear about our limitations. If we must always try to distinguish what we say from the things we are trying to talk about, then it is true that there will always be something that appears simply as "given." The dialectic is capable of generating the basic concepts that suggest modes of organization for experience. It is also capable of generating accounts of the ways in which concepts in a given framework are related to one another—and of generating accounts of inference rules. It is equally capable of generating accounts of the conceptual situation that will lead us to look for different modes of experience. Once we know, for instance, that the structuring of *experience in terms of sense data* goes with the notions of determinate structures expressed in one kind of logic, we can begin to look for its dialectical twin, *experience in the mode of systematic unity.* We are aware—as Gestalt psychologists have properly insisted—that experience can be structured equally well as a field and that we can become aware of the unity of our own field of experience.

Yet there will always be, in any mode of conceptualization, something relative to that mode that is simply given. One cannot, for instance, generate the concepts of colours without some suitable experience. All the structures we have met in this discussion can be represented as a series of levels, each appearing intelligible by reference to the level above it. ("Being red" is a way of "being coloured," "being coloured" is a way of "occupying a surface in space," "occupying such a surface" is a way of "being discrete and particularized"—and so on.) The lowest of these levels in any system has no further specification. It simply is. But we get there by adopting some suitable conceptual structure—and we can always substitute one kind of experience for another if we need to express, in more detail, the relations between discriminated objects at the most basic level.

We can express the relations between colours through the relations between different wavelengths of light, for example. In so doing we substitute for the experience which we usually call "seeing red" another experience relevant to our mode of determining wave lengths. It is interesting to notice what is going on here. We associate colours with wavelengths of light because we discover that the relevant experience classes can be correlated. But the correlation is not just "given"—it is not, say, like the relation between the business cycle and the length of women's skirts. Colouredness is related to notions of spatial surface *and* to notions of "seeing." "Light" is a notion that explicates both these further notions. Our ordinary mode of experiencing shuts out certain kinds of data. If one could "see" photons, for instance, one could not "see" anything else. We thus seek other sorts of experiences that will illumine other aspects of the situation. The move is from "seeing colours" to features of the specific exclusion reference of notions of colouredness, and back again to other experience forms that are not similarly excluded. The ability to see colours demands that there be some other structure that renders the process intelligible. We trace this through its conceptual connections and then trace those to other modes of experience. Thus there is not a brute "given" associated with any of the "objects" of knowledge—though there is always some given relative to any structure we choose.

We can now choose between several procedures: one would be to generate the succession of basic concepts in the dialectic from "pure being" through to whatever conceptual structure might bring an end to the process of generation. At each level we could seek the appropriate experiences and so build up a picture of the world. This would give a set of general answers to questions about the available conceptual framework, the available levels of experience and so on. It was some procedure like this which Hegel undertook in his *Science of Logic* and in the *Phenomenology of Mind*,[12] a work that sought to reveal a dialectic of experience that would go with the dialectic of concepts in the *Logic*.[13]

But although Hegel may at times have looked forward to generating a complete system of knowledge (represented in part in his *Encyclopaedia of the Philosophical Sciences*), it must be obvious that beyond the generation of a structure that would cast light on general metaphysical issues, we cannot expect to generate such a complete system all at once. Many kinds of experiences would have to be sought, an untold range of concepts generated, and the relations between endless interlocking systems of concepts investigated. If we could not answer any serious questions about particular issues until we had a complete conceptual system and a complete system of knowledge, we would be in a bad way.

14. Dialectics and the Incompleteness of Knowledge: Dialectical Logics and Other Logics

Another procedure, then, the one we might use for more straightforward and mundane inquiries, would have to be constructed rather differently. It would have to start, generally, with questions raised because we face what William James and John Dewey liked to call "live options."[14] A question that involves a live option, in their terms, is posed by a fork in the structure of experience or in a logical structure with which we are presented. In a sense, we are always in this position because we outrun any system that we have constructed up to the moment. A judgement, as Dewey would have it, represents our decision to take one option rather than another. We ask if apples are edible, and we choose to eat them or not. We ask if it is the angels who win football games for Notre Dame and we bet our money or we don't. But at the same time, we want to know what goes into these judgements, and we need a way to make them more objective—to assure ourselves that we are moving generally in the direction of sound judgement with each inference move (and not continuously away from it), and we want, finally, to achieve that condition of freedom that set off our inquiry in the first chapter.

Such a structure, like Dewey's, must represent propositions and inferences as open-ended structures—structures focused on a judgement that is subject to change as new elements are entered. Such structures must then represent both forms of certainty and forms of uncertainty and be structured so as to have growth points. Ideally, all that we know at a given time should be representable in a single structure that can be revised in several dimensions. For even a simple query like "are apples edible?" has implications that extend over the realm of what is known. (Eating anything will make some change in one's body chemistry, which will alter in some way, however insignificant, our susceptibility to things like radiation from distant parts of the universe, or which may change our glandular secretions so as to make us more or less susceptible to emotions generated by certain kinds of literature and so on.) Once again, however, our practical situation tends to dictate that the available information be assembled according to degrees of relevance. Though we should express the logical situation in a way that will make it possible for all judgements to bear upon one another and, ultimately, for them to be amalgamated, the actual situation is bound to dictate that we have a rather large number of judgement structures operating to some extent independently of one another at any given time.

15. The Structure of Question, Answer and Presupposition[15]

What, then, do we need by way of structure? First, we need the question itself and an account of its logical structure in terms of presuppositions. One who asks "Is the moon roughly spherical?" supposes that there is a moon and that, since it has one or another shape, it is a determinate entity. This conceptual situation needs to be related to the alternatives that an analysis of the situation will generate. (The moon may also be a collection of sense data, a feature in a field of experience and so on.) We will relate the problem to the dialectic of concepts in the region to which it belongs. Then we can determine what will count as an answer—for questions, if meaningful, have answers. The alternative forms of the question will also have answers and, in seeing the range of what could count as an answer to different forms of the question (e.g., "What experience patterns lead one to talk about the moon?" "What sense data would count as giving relevant information?"), we gradually build up a picture of the form in which the answer is likely to relate to the issue that gave rise to the question. At this stage of the inquiry, we draw upon what we know of the conceptual frames into which the issues can be fitted. The next stage, obviously, is to generate accounts of the situations in which the answers would be intelligible. We need to generate the conceptual equipment required to understand the situation and to question it.

From one of these two pieces of information we can generate accounts of the kinds of experiences and the kinds of actions that will generate discriminating data. Discriminating data are the kinds of data that make us prefer one answer to another. We then begin to see how some answers are closed off and others are left open. From the open possibilities, we can estimate the effect of a given answer on other judgements that we might, anyhow, think acceptable. (We now think, for instance, that bodies in the solar system beyond a certain size tend to be roughly spherical and that they are all subject to the same physical forces and so on. If we found a large sharp-angled pentagon floating about in space, what would we conclude?) We try, that is, to render a given judgement coherent with its neighbours—where "coherence" means that there is both consistency and a natural path of inference from one to the other. The final judgement will be influenced by the fact that each of the neighbouring judgements will have some openness about it, too—that since we do not have a complete system, there is opportunity for error.

What we have, then, are not independent "propositions" but clusters of assertions that bear upon judgements. Some of them, those that relate to the original dialectic of basic concepts, have about them a good deal of objectivity if the rules for generating the dialectic are sound. So too do some of the original presuppositions of the question we asked, but those, though we can substantiate them logically as we explore the range of possible answers to the question, are subject to the influence of other questions we might ask— questions that might have other presuppositions and so turn out to conflict with them. (Some we reject because no data turns up. One might have asked "Is the moon alive?" but perhaps that would turn out to be a wrongly framed question.)[16] Then there are the intelligibility conditions—conditions that limit what we say, anyhow, about any region of the universe. Somehow, the world must be conceived so that it makes sense when described. Otherwise, we cannot get the issues into discourse at all.

Then one begins to assemble the appropriate bits of experience. As we saw in Dewey's system, these assemblies come in two forms—first person statements about what someone actually experienced (and these are statements we must just accept) and other statements about similar experiences in various analogous situations (and these, because they are logical assemblies, are subject to questioning).

Our picture, then, is something like this: given a question, Q, which has a basic conceptual frame, C (with alternatives C^1, C^2, C^3...), presuppositions (P^1, P^2, P^3...), and a potential answer set (A^1, A^2, A^3...), *then*, given intelligibility conditions (I^1, I^2, I^3...), a set of discriminating experiences (E^1, E^2, E^3...), a judgement, J, follows, with a likelihood, X.

16. The Uses of Likelihoods

We will call the result a likelihood, because the notion of "probative" has been taken over by the friends of arithmetic and used for simple calculations like the chance of getting heads ten times in thirteen coin tosses.

The difficulty in this scheme will be obvious. To generate a likelihood, we will have to give weight to the various elements and guess about such things as the likelihood that the original conceptual frame was well generated, that the potential answer set was completely discriminated, that enough attention and integrity went into the delineation of the reported experiences, that they are a good sample of the available experience—and so on. We will also be faced with problems about various ways of fitting the structure together. For example, when we have a conceptual frame that relies upon discriminating sets of determinate entities, we have to have translation rules in which those entities figure, not as individual things, but as patterns in a total system of systematic unity. This is an important break from the kinds of logics that regarded the world as collections of individuals—whether concrete or abstract. The "patterns" we are talking about here are not individuals in any sense.

But in fact, the initial weights we give and the initial structures we develop do not matter *in themselves*. If we were to regard the judgement that we have framed as isolated, as the sole basis for a single earth-shaking decision, of course then it would matter desperately what weights we gave to the initial structure. The fact, however, is that the judgement must figure as a member of a growing set of judgements and the moral lesson is not to predicate any world-shaking decision on a single occasion of judgement. (It is not wise, for instance, to change one's life on the basis of a single religious experience generated by hearing a televangelist. This is so just because the weights one can give to a single occasion of judgement are arbitrary.)

The point is that, whatever weight we give, the system will force us into constant revisions. The question itself generates alternatives to when we see what we can substitute within its logical form. The conceptual frame generates more basic concepts, each of which leads to a different way of assembling the data. As we saw, a single experience invariably has simple "givens" within it—and every one requires translation into a situation in which it is not a given. There is no limit to the assembly of experiences.

What we do, therefore, is to assign arbitrary weights that are susceptible to correction according to the various processes upon which that weighting depends. Even if one assigned the weights in a wildly wrong way, the principle by which the weights were assigned would generate corrections if the process were carried out. The judgement is never *simply* wrong—for the conceptual structure behind it guarantees that it has some connection to the possible orders of things. We may be wrong in estimating its likelihood, but that likelihood is simply proportional to the weights we have assigned to various factors.

Inference, now, is not the product of a simple relation between premise and conclusion. It is the product of the interplay of all the factors. It is not, anyhow, the conclusion we are concerned with but the practice it sets in train—the practice that will lead to its gradual objectification. This, however, leads us naturally into the questions of belief and persuasion that are next on our agenda.

QUICK QUIZ #4

1. Short of providing a full-blown account of the Absolute, are there other subsidiary and useful ways of developing dialectical logic?
2. Hegel's dialectic seemed to suggest that we need a complete system in order to understand the world. How do dialectical logics cope with the fact that we do not have such a system?
3. Does the "logic of question and answer" play a part in solving some of the problems of dialectical systems?
4. What role does the notion of likelihood play in the development of dialectical logics?

Notes

1. There are currently two translations of this work, first published in Nurnburg in 1812–1816. The oldest, by W.H. Johnston and L.G. Struthers, two pupils of the Cambridge philosopher J.M.E. McTaggart, was first published by Allen and Unwin in London in 1929. It is very good, but its technical terminology is meant to go with McTaggart's commentaries. The same publisher produced a newer translation, by A.V. Miller, in 1969. It is sometimes easier to read, but it interprets Hegel in ways with which not everyone would agree.
2. The standard English translation is still William Wallace's *The Logic of Hegel*, Oxford: Clarendon Press, 1874.
3. Assen: Royal Vangorcum; and New York: Humanities Press, 1972.
4. More on this can be found in W.E. Johnson's three-volume *Logic*, Cambridge University Press, 1921–24. A paper-back edition was published in New York by Dover in 1964.
5. For more on problems regarding existence see Charlie Dunbar Broad's *Philosophy,*

Religion and Psychical Research, London: Routledge and Kegan Paul, 1953.

6. Pure being is not the "highest order determinable" since it cannot reflect the diverse richness of actuality and possibility.

7. For a discussion of logical individuality in this sense see Chapter 13.

8. See "What the Tortoise Said to Achilles," in *The Complete Works of Lewis Carroll,* New York: Random House, n.d., p. 1225–30.

9. See Johnson's *Logic,* Vol. III, p. 1ff. There is a summary by Howard E. Smokler of Johnson's point in the *Encyclopedia of Philosophy,* New York: Collier Macmillan, 1967, Vol. IV, p. 292–93.

10. See page 95 of this text.

11. David Hume, 1711–1776, the Scottish philosopher and historian, is the most celebrated and strictest of the British empiricists. He discusses these notions in his *Treatise of Human Nature* (1739) and his *Enquiry into Human Understanding* (1748).

12. Hegel's *Phenomenology of Mind,* the earliest of his major works, was first published in 1807. The English translation by J.B. Baillie, London: George Allen and Unwin, 1910, revised 1931, is quite clear but, like most Hegel translations, it is often disputed.

13. In fact, Hegel, of course, wrote the *Science of Logic* and its shorter counterpart in *The Encyclopedia of the Philosophical Sciences* in the hope of casting light on some of what we would think of as general metaphysical questions. See the earlier notes to this chapter for references.

14. James (1842–1910) was closer to the commonly understood notion of "pragmatism" than Dewey. But Dewey's ideas owe much to him, especially his view that knowledge and action are tied together. The notion of "live options" is a crucial part of this view of knowledge.

15. The "logic of question and answer" owes most to the work of R.G. Collingwood (1889–1943) whose many works illustrate its use.

16. Only a few years ago, no one would have entertained such a question. But now there are people who think that one should regard the whole of the earth as forming a single living organism. If they are right, then the question "Is the moon alive?" becomes quite sensible even if the answer is "no!"

Chapter 6

BELIEF AND ITS JUSTIFICATION

Basically, logic tries to sustain and expand truth through various transformations. That is, we start with a true proposition and we infer other true propositions. We do not want to move from truth to falsity. We may not know whether or not what we believe is true, but we want at least to know that we are justified in our beliefs. In sum, we do not want to get into a worse position with respect to truth or justification.

We want to add to our beliefs and continue to have justification for them or to replace our present ones with better ones. This means that the functions of inference are closely related to the problems of belief. A belief is something like John Dewey's judgement, a "settled opinion." One makes inferences, therefore, to reorder one's beliefs, to test one's beliefs, to arrive at beliefs, to quell one's doubts.

1. Belief And Inference

One starts with a belief or a doubt—and a doubt may be the expression of another belief. One ends with another belief or doubt. In between are various "interim" beliefs—for example, the belief in the soundness and efficacy of the rules of inference one uses.

Belief has been a vexing topic for philosophers. We will look at the following questions: what does it mean to "believe something?" Do we have to know that what we believe is true to be justified in believing it? If all inferences have to *start* with propositions, some propositions have to be given. Must we simply believe these propositions without further recourse?

2. The Mental State Theory of Belief and Its Problems

Most of us claim to know what we believe. But how do you *know* what you believe? The common answer is provided by the "mental state theory of belief." Suppose Linda believes that she likes ice-cream. For Linda to know that she believes this, she simply looks into her own mind and inspects its contents. Linda would know what she doesn't believe by introspection as well.

The mental state theory has a long tradition in Western philosophy.[1] Believing is like a mental colouring of propositions. Doubting is like a mental colouring as well. We can "see" this colouring through introspection. But think about the consequences of this view of belief. For person X to know what he or she believes, then X must introspect. So only X can say just what X believes. However, can we not deceive ourselves? Put another way, do we not sometimes say to another person, "you do not know what you believe?"

Imagine the politician, Rubbertongue, who consistently claims to worry about racism. But whenever legislation is proposed that would protect people from racism, Rubbertongue announces that while he supports the principle, the act is "untimely." After numerous such occurrences, we might say that Rubbertongue himself does not even believe what he says. Or, we might say that he thinks that he believes what he is saying but he really does not. Inevitably, if he is at all given to reflection, there will come a time when he is not *sure* what it is that he believes.

Imagine a young woman, religiously raised, who continues to follow her faith into adulthood. Gradually, however, she builds up a series of beliefs that dramatically conflict with her religious beliefs. There must come a day when she asks herself just what she believes and finds herself not altogether sure how best to characterize it.

The point is that "looking into the mind" may be more like looking into a muddy lake than into a clear pond. But the uncertainty as to *what* one believes on this theory is not even the biggest difficulty. The theory holds that belief is a kind of mental colouring of a proposition. This is a little too metaphorical: what does it really mean? Our question then is "what are the criteria of belief?"

What is it that we look for when we introspect on whether or not we believe something? Do we ask if we assent to a given proposition? Surely the best sign of assent is *action* is it not? So when we claim to believe something, we are saying that we are willing to act on it. But acting on some proposition is a *public* criterion for claiming that you believe something.

We might just say that there is a *feeling* of belief. And this feeling of belief must be present before we act in any way. But sometimes propositions that "feel best" may not be the ones we actually believe. For instance, one may be on a jury and feel much sympathy for the accused but still believe that the accused is guilty.

Suppose that belief manifests itself as a feeling in the mind. Call it B. There would also be a similar feeling for doubt. Call it D. Suppose that you ask yourself whether you believe some proposition, P. Upon introspection you "feel" P along with B. So you say that you believe P. Suppose that you ask yourself whether you believe some other proposition, Q. Upon introspection you "see" Q coloured D. So you say that you doubt Q.

But are you sure that P was felt along with B? Maybe you made a mistake in your "observation." How could you decide that you "felt" B and not D? You would have to have some kind of criterion to distinguish B from D. But a criterion is a rule that can be applied to something.

Note that rules can always be publicly expressed. If belief is essentially private, you cannot state the rule. Or, again, any criterion that you could apply to yourself, you could communicate to others—and then they could tell you what they believed, *and* what you believed if you were able to convey to them whatever it is to which the criterion is supposed to apply.

Simply put, the things "rattling around in the mind" are very hard to pin down. One may think this thing is like yesterday's. But how does one know? Criteria for identification have about them the feature that one may lay things out, one beside the other, and tell which descriptions fit them and which don't. But what you can't do with B is lay it out for inspection by yourself or by anyone.

Indeed, one often learns about oneself by reflecting on what one does, and not, primarily, by looking into one's inward depths. One knows that one is a novelist by seeing that one can write novels, and decides that one is a philosopher when one see one's papers in the *Journal of Philosophy* and one's books on the shelves at the bookseller's.

Such concerns have led some to embrace what is called the behaviourist theory of belief.[2]

3. The Behaviourist Theory of Belief and Its Problems

According to the behaviourist theory of belief,[3] those who believe P will know that they believe P because they will find that they act in certain ways and not in others[4] whenever the circumstances for action are appropriate. The behaviourist looks to see whether those who claim to believe that flowers feel pain when they are cut will picket florist shops. The believer would do *something*. If not, is the profession of the belief serious?

The problem lies in the fact that a given action is always compatible with many beliefs. Although Smith picketed the flower shop, perhaps he did so because he just enjoys picketing and does not care about flowers.

4. Is There a Better Theory?

Neither of these theories alone seems to work. We think that there are a number of aspects to belief and that each theory captures some while missing others. But believing is indeed a complex activity. It certainly contains the following elements. One who believes that P is true must:

1. Have a propensity to act in certain ways and not in others.
2. Be able to assert "P" in a way that distinguishes "P" from "not-P."
3. Have a preference for "P" over some other propositions.
4. Be prepared to subscribe to no proposition that entails "not-P."
5. Intend on some occasions to utter "P."
6. Will on some occasions utter "P."

It happens that 1 and 2 are "behaviour"-entailing situations, 3 expresses a certain attitude, 4 is a logical condition, and 5 and 6 refer to states of mind that are, to one degree or another, ascertainable by behavioural checks—though not completely. Together, these conditions mean there will be some publicly inspectible ingredients, but also some ingredients that refer to mental states. Some of the latter are such that the believer is in a better position to know what the case is than anyone else—but not to the extent that no one else has any chance of knowing it. Together, also, the six conditions explain why we are sometimes in doubt about the beliefs of others and sometimes not (much).

But they involve a kind of oscillation. One has to do some things and then reflect on them—action and reflection go together in our attempts to determine what we believe. They also involve some value notions—there is an element of preference without which we would not say that we believed. The preference may be based on objective facts but it still involves the notion that the belief has, and must have, some value.

What is represented in the list is a kind of dialectical tension that always exists between the world and us. We act, reflect, evaluate and then act again. There is a process involved. Hence we can understand the politician, Rubbertongue, whose actions gradually divide him from his beliefs. But can we understand Jane, who holds that tritheism is true but doesn't do anything? Yes, surely, for she finds that she has a propensity to do some things that she must guard against. She finds that she has a conceptual preference that she would express if, say, someone deeply involved in a scholarly way with the problem of the Trinity should ask her advice. Of course, she does not know for sure what she believes until one of these elements is put to the test. She knows what she thinks is *likely* the case. And, indeed, after years of being quiet about it she might find, when the test does come, that she has changed her mind. This is part of the normal human condition. Thus armed, we can turn to the more difficult topic: the justification of belief.

QUICK QUIZ #1

1. It is said that belief outruns inference—i.e., that some beliefs do not result from inference. In what senses is this true or false?

2. Do you know what you believe? Is this knowledge a mental state? Why or why not? If it is a mental state, how would you identify it?

3. Must belief show in behaviour? Might you be wrong in thinking that you would believe some proposition, P? What kind of mistake would this be? Are there beliefs that could not be shown by any behaviour?

4. Are actions always or usually compatible with more than one belief? Do you believe that flowers feel? How do you know that you do or do not believe that flowers feel?

5. Are there alternatives to the behaviourist and mental state theories?

5. Justified Belief and Action

Let us begin by specifying some requirements of a justified belief. *The first requirement* is that a justified belief lead to some action that does not contradict one's own experience or that of others. One must bring in other sentient creatures because any act that contracts their horizons will lead to a possible failure in reports that might correct one's own reports, and because a belief is, *qua* belief, not something that stands in a privileged relation to any given believer. No one has any more right to a given belief than anyone else, for there is nothing about a belief that gives anyone privileged access to it.

It is interesting to notice that value judgements seem inevitably to arise in this context because beliefs are partial determinants of actions and because simple rationality seems to dictate that what is a desirable pattern of belief for one must be left as an option for others. This seems to be a perfectly objective piece of "moral knowledge." It is not the sort of proposition that has to be proven, for the reason that the onus of proof would be on the person who desired one state of affairs for himself and another for others.

It seems evident, too, that, since we have seen that any feasible logic will show inquiry to be open to development at any stage and phase, one cannot either (a) hold that a belief would be justified if it led to no action or (b) hold that a belief would be justified if it led to the closure of the horizon of development. The alternative is to hold that one ought to adopt beliefs taken as absolute or with no consequences that would lead toward self-correction.

Though there may be *components* of beliefs that are not open to question—i.e., propositions that assert that some concepts are genuine concepts in any system of thought, or second-order propositions that are about *what* to believe—there seem to be no clear cases of beliefs that could be adopted as final and open to no question. (The difficulties that this poses form the subject matter of the next chapter.)

6. Justified Belief and Consistency

The second requirement is that a justified belief (ultimately) be consistent with every other belief that has the same or a greater assigned probability. That is, one's belief system must be self-consistent and if beliefs conflict, one ought not to abandon the beliefs that one thinks most plausible. However, we often do not know whether or not our beliefs form a consistent system. For instance, is the proposition "God exists" consistent or inconsistent with the proposition "the world is evil"? It is difficult to say because the concepts involved belong to regions of discourse connected only by tenuous inferences. We would have to ask how each belief was likely to affect action. If one's concept of God were such that if God existed, one ought not to tamper with the world, which is the work of God, it would most likely follow that the two beliefs were inconsistent. One belief could lead to actions forbidden by the other. We most often discover that beliefs conflict when we see that they demand conflicting actions. We would then most likely have to choose by reference to requirement 1.

7. Justified Belief and Truth and Falsity

The third requirement for justified belief is criteria that will ultimately show it to be true or false. There must, in short, be an entailment to action of a rather specific kind—that which leads to inquiry. The reason, again, seems to be obvious. A belief that leads to no inquiry—an *impotent belief*—is dangerous. There is no way to show that an impotent belief is unsatisfactory, hence no way to eliminate it or assign it a degree of likelihood. Moreover, an impotent belief might well be inconsistent with other beliefs that are ultimately justi-fied. The point is not that beliefs *have to be actually shown* to be true or false. We cannot always do that. What we can do is to insist upon beliefs that *can be subjected* to tests.[5]

The tests may be many. Some are given by the first two criteria,[6] others concern the manner in which a given belief either intersects with experience or fits into a given piece of inference. But the point is the same: beliefs that fail to meet the requirements of criterion 3, like those which fail criteria 1 and 2, have the property of closing the belief system rather than opening it.

8. The Test of Assent

The fourth requirement for a justified belief is that it meets the test of assent. The belief must be such that after you have reviewed all its ramifications, you (*will-ingly*) assent to it. Cardinal Newman was surely right in his *Grammar of Assent* to insist that assent is a single act independent of all the other acts associated with inference and evidence.[7] One can always say "yes" or "no." Much (though not all) of Newman's study was concerned with matters of religion (some of which we shall have occasion to discuss later.) But the point is a rather general one. Whatever one is faced with, one can always revise the criteria for accepting it or rejecting it. The distinction between the freedom of mind (which seems to be essential in claims to knowledge), and constrained judgement, is that in *free* judgement one insists that, ultimately, one remains able to assent or dissent.

This point about "freedom of the mind" may seem strange, but consider it in the context of belief. Suppose one adopts a belief, X, but is unable to assent to X. If one acts on X, one surrenders one's autonomy. If one fails to act on X, then X becomes an impotent belief. In sum, beliefs failing criterion 4, like those failing criteria 1, 2 and 3, have the property of closing the belief system rather than opening it.

We are not suggesting that giving or withholding assent is a purely private matter against which public considerations have no weight. A reason for giving or withholding assent may be the effect of the appropriate actions on the lives of others, and one may not always believe that one's private criteria for assent are superior to the public ones.

9. Justified Belief and Intelligible Goals

The fifth and final requirement for a justified belief is that it must form part of a coherent policy that involves a commitment to some intelligible goal. There are not just matters of inner coherence, testability, assent and so on. For beliefs do not come singly but as parts of large sets of logical and psychological structures, which, together, necessarily establish a direction and pattern in experience. The direction will be there whether one realizes it or not. If it is not clearly specified, the danger is that considerations relevant to justified belief may fail to be accounted for.

Notice that one who subscribed either to the behaviourist theory of belief or to the mental state theory in their most basic forms might well want to deny this condition altogether. For if belief were simply a matter reflected in action, so that the evidence that someone held a given belief was a single appropriate action, one might suppose that beliefs could be held automatically. Similarly, if to believe is simply to be in a certain state of mind, states of mind and beliefs may well be co-ordinated in a one-to-one way, and it may well be the case, again, that they could be considered automatic.

But if belief relates to thought and action in the complex way suggested in the last chapter, it turns out that all of one's beliefs bear on one another so as to create an ongoing pattern in experience.

A person who thinks that he can have beliefs subject to no corrective process would deny this criterion. Such a person holds that there is no ongoing and developing pattern of belief, action and experience. But if one accepts that beliefs are invariably relevant to some future context, that future context must be a part of what one decides upon as a justified belief.

Of course we cannot directly deal with future contexts, but we can see that they are partly determined by the direction possessed by our pattern of experience. If that direction is crucial to the justification of belief, then the policy governing that pattern must be one of the crucial determinants of the situation.

But why should we orient ourselves toward a hypothetical future? Why not confine our considerations to the immediate present? Part of the answer is that if the theory of belief that we have been detailing here is correct, it is true that we do not live in the span of a single present. For belief is a central ingredient in our nature. What one *believes* determines to some extent what one *is*. But belief is not a momentary state of affairs if this theory is correct. Rather, belief is spread across a time span so that we can only locate ourselves in a span that runs from the past into the future.

An important point is that our existence is a dialectical process—one determined by the way we put ourselves into the world and then reflect upon ourselves. We are never confined to a given category because, by believing and acting, we tend to create ourselves, and our thought always presses beyond our immediate state. If no coherent policy defines us in this situation, we become, once again, the victims of that ongoing process.

This set of criteria seems to be rather different from what we might have expected. Our task at this point is to see why, so that we can decide whether or not to withdraw from the initial premise *that justified beliefs extend the horizons of relevance.*

10. Why the Criteria are Complicated

Simpler answers (than the ones suggested in this chapter) might have included these:

1. A belief is justified when one knows it to be true.
2. A belief is justified when the proposition central to it is such that its denial amounts to a formal contradiction.
3. A belief is justified when it follows as a piece of valid inference from another justified belief.
4. A belief is justified when it is useful.
5. A belief is justified when it forms part of a set of natural human beliefs.

Proposition 1 is, on the whole, the theory that belief should be confined to the domain of knowledge. If one knows P is the case, it follows that P is true. If P is true, surely one is justified in believing it.

The difficulty is just that we do not usually know for certain that any proposition is true in the absolute sense of "true," and belief seems necessarily to outrun knowledge anyway, because we need to have beliefs to get started upon our settled inquiries. But the suggested criteria for a justified belief seem to leave open the possibility that one might know that P is true and still decline to believe it. Would that not be a serious paradox?

One might know that P is true, but acting on P might restrict the horizon of relevance, fail to yield a successful general policy and so on. But suppose, you will say, I know it to be true, anyhow. Ought I not to believe it—and believe it absolutely?

The distinction, here, we think, is the one we suggested earlier. There may be components in belief situations that have about them an air of certainty. But there are not *whole* beliefs that fall into this category. For whole beliefs include relations to one's states of self-awareness and to one's conceptual frames for action and so on. These seem to be in a process of development and any whole belief will thus contain elements that run beyond what one "knows to be true." It is not a simple matter of propositions if my theory is correct. But certainly, if one rejects that theory of belief and returns to the simpler behaviourist or mental state theories, there would be a paradox in holding that one knew P to be true and did not believe it. For then beliefs would be expressible as simple, single and atomic propositions.

Proposition 2 is, in effect, a logical theory about belief or about some beliefs. It holds that what justifies belief is valid inference and it might be called, along with proposition 3, a central component in a purely rationalist theory of belief and knowledge. Again, it will depend upon what you mean by "belief." If you think of beliefs as simple, expressible in single propositions, and if there are propositions that both express beliefs and meet criteria 2 and 3, then one ought to accept those conditions as justifying. And if reason is always the paramount justifier, then it seems likely that 2 and 3 might even be necessary and sufficient conditions for justified beliefs.

The difficulty is that we have seen no cases that approximate the required conditions and degrees of certainty. Propositions 2 and 3 seem to justify a very widespread scepticism, which, one might think, would paralyze action. But they seem to be demands that stem from standards we have no particular reason to uphold.

Again, however, it might seem very odd that our proposed criteria do not exclude the possibility that the conditions specified in 2 and 3 might be met, and that we still would not be required to believe the propositions in question. For these are logical conditions under which denial is apparently impossible. If a denial introduces a contradiction or if it says that a valid inference is not believable, one would be in logical trouble. It *is* odd, to rule out these cases, if the belief is simple and about propositions. But beliefs usually involve many propositions in complex relations. And some do not involve propositions at all. "I believe in God" or "I believe in Jane" are examples. It may be contradictory to hold that some propositions are true and that God does not exist. But one might have lost one's faith "in God" all the same. On the other side, that which one takes to be evil will turn out not to be, or one may "believe in" Jane even if only Jane could have taken the money out of the till. It might seem contradictory, but one might think that some explanation would be forthcoming.

Proposition 4 is a crude approximation of a "pragmatist" theory of belief, though we doubt that any pragmatists or instrumentalists would have accepted it without qualification. Certainly James and Dewey would have wanted to add qualifications and they have tended in the direction of the criteria we have suggested here. The most obvious difficulty is that one must ask: "useful for what"? Unless one spells out various criteria, there seems to be no obvious answer.

One can certainly think of occasions of utility combined with obviously unjustified belief. Some theories work, as it were, by accident. Some beliefs violate the implied moral criteria that we suggested formed part of a necessary analysis of the situation. Some are useful now and harmful later. It is not denied that utility has a place in the scheme—only that it has an all-encompassing place.

Proposition 5 comes, in effect, from David Hume[8] and represents something quite different. Hume had noticed that, by his own criteria (essentially criteria associated with empirical verification), no propositions about the world are ever finally demonstrated to be true. He was a sceptic in the sense that he thought that there was no *demonstrable* knowledge. He concluded that there is *never* enough evidence to overturn our "natural beliefs"—essentially those very general beliefs about the world that are common to all of us and prior to sceptical analysis or philosophical reflection.

This is interesting, for Hume asks why we would jettison some beliefs that we already have, given that we have no proofs for counter propositions. The answer, we think, is that our natural beliefs have no natural superiority. We can test them as well as any others by the procedures we have suggested. It may be that they fail to meet the criteria we have suggested or those you may want to suggest for yourselves. It is not that we are overturning them in the name of more certain propositions. Rather, we may overturn them because of certain criteria we can develop for justified beliefs.

QUICK QUIZ #2

1. Could someone have a true but unjustified belief? Explain.
2. Could someone have a justified but false belief? Explain.
3. Explain the three criteria of a justified belief. Why is it difficult to provide the criteria for the justification of belief?
4. What would happen if we dropped the third justification condition for beliefs? (This is a tough question, so here is a hint: Suppose that only the first two conditions held and so our beliefs were justified *solely* by not conflicting with our previous beliefs. What do you think could then happen?)
5. What consequences does our third criterion have regarding fundamental beliefs? (Think about fundamental beliefs such as the existence of God or a person's right to life.)
6. Should all beliefs be justified? Why or why not?
7. Must all justified beliefs lead to action? Why or why not?
8. Must all your justified beliefs be consistent with one another?
9. Must all justified beliefs satisfy the criteria for propositions that are either true or false?
10. What is the significance of the "test of assent"?
11. How is the idea of justified belief related to the idea of intelligible goal?
12. Why are the criteria for justified belief so complicated?

Notes

1. Rene Descartes' *Meditations on First Philosophy*, 1641, is still, perhaps, the clearest source of the "mental state" view of belief.
2. Ludwig Wittgenstein was an influential philosopher who attacked the mental state theory. See his *Philosophical Investigations*, tr. G.E. Anscombe, New York: Macmillan, 1953.
3. Alexander Bain's *The Emotions and the Will*, London: J.W. Parker, 1859, p. 568–98, offers perhaps the first clear example of this theory. However, in the seventeenth century, Blaise Pascal subscribed to the view that belief involved a moral commitment which should issue in the appropriate actions.

4. Behaviourists do not doubt that people "think they believe" propositions on which they do not act, but they doubt that statements of such alleged beliefs have any real meaning.

5. This view is primarily associated with Sir Karl Popper. (See especially his *Objective Knowledge, An Evolutionary Approach,* Oxford: Clarendon Press, 1972.) Popper pushes this view to its limit: a proposition can never be *proven* true, but it can be clearly *falsified.* Now, if no test can falsify a particular proposition, then that proposition is deemed "meaningless." On this view we ought to believe only those propositions that we have already tried by effective means to falsify and have not succeeded. Such propositions are not true, but merely *corroborated.* We shall return to Popper's view in section 5 of Chapter Ten.

6. They have to do, that is, with the tendency of a belief to suggest some action and with the consistency of beliefs.

7. John Henry Cardinal Newman, *An Essay in Aid of a Grammar of Assent,* originally published in 1870, New York: Doubleday, 1955.

8. See especially his *Treatise of Human Nature,* 1739, Book I, Section 4, paragraph 2 (the best modern edition is that of L.A. Selby-Bigge, revised by Peter H. Nidditch, Oxford: Clarendon Press, 1978) and the *Enquiry Concerning Human Understanding,* 1748, Section 12, paragraph 7. (A readily available modern edition is that of Eugene Freeman, Chicago: Open Court, 1971, made from the second [posthumous] edition.)

Chapter 7

UNJUSTIFIABLE BELIEFS, JUSTIFICATION AND PERSUASION

An ancient and confusing question animates this chapter. Its answer, inevitably, depends upon one's theory of belief, one's theory of inference, and the account one is prepared to give of "justification."

1. The Justification of Belief and the Reasonableness of Reasons

We must be careful not to confuse our animating question with the following question, which Peter Geach has discussed: "is it always reasonable to ask for a reason?" Geach held that sometimes we ought to accept the reasons already given, and that it makes no sense to keep asking for reasons for giving reasons.[1] For example, if one has a perfectly good mathematical proof, one needs (at least in mathematics) no further reason for accepting it. If one has good enough motives for asking for reasons—such as that getting them will free one from potential manipulation—no other reasons are needed. In the first case, mathematics is a discipline with clear enough definitions, in some regions at least, of ideas like "proof." It is settled that $2 + 3 = 5$. One can sensibly ask "should one do mathematics?" but not "is $2 + 3 = 5$"? The reason is that nothing is more certain than "$2 + 3 = 5$." Hence, one cannot plausibly imagine any further improvement in our situation as a result of further answers to further questions. So it appears that the best reason for doing something is that doing it will free oneself from manipulation. After all, if one is being manipulated, one is not free to do anything. Nonetheless, such good reasons can be overruled in particular circumstances. For instance, you do not continue "freeing yourself" by studying logic while your little sister drowns in the bathtub. It is not that you have a better argument for rescuing your little sister than for doing logic, but that rescuing your little sister is obviously more important.

2. Must We Start with Assumptions?

Our animating question, "must we start with *assumptions*?" is different. It is not a question about limiting enquiries in some particular context, but about not questioning some proposition upon which our whole edifice of reasoning is founded. It is clearly important and it has some practical outcome, because we are frequently told that, "one must start with some assumptions" or that "one's system must have some primitive or undefined terms" or "every argument presupposes something."[2] These expressions are not equivalent and they suggest some of the things that go into the background confusions and help to make our original question difficult to answer in any simple way.

It is true, to be sure, that *if* we think of inference on the Aristotelian model (whereby inference is the drawing of conclusions from premises according to pre-determined inference rules), *then* it would seem that every chain of reasoning contains at least one unjustified premise. For if every premise is justified only by deriving it from another premise, some premise is always left unjustified. One would not, we suppose, accept such a premise unless one could, in some sense, believe it to be true, or useful, or harmless. It would also seem to be the case that the inference rules one deploys to get one's conclusion would suffer the same defect—if it is a defect. There must be, one would think, at least one premise not justified by any *inference*.

One often meets this argument in religious or theological discussions. "Of course you can't prove the existence of God, but then you can't prove everything, anyhow, and the existence of God is a good premise with which to start." In such an "argument"—if it is one—it remains unclear whether or not the proponent would describe herself as a "believer" in any of its usual senses. And, when she says "the existence of God is a good place to start," we expect her to produce some other argument. What she seems to be doing is distinguishing inference from justification. She thinks, that is, that she has a justified belief, but she doesn't think her belief follows as part of an inference scheme.

3. The Relation of Inference and Justification

There we have one of the possibilities we have already seen: it may be feasible to separate inference and justification. The last chapter's proposal about justification and belief does separate justification and inference in the sense that what we demand as justification for belief is something about the subsequent openness of experience and something about the likelihood that beliefs accepted as justified will, if wrong, be corrected by the inferences and experiences they set in motion.

The other immediate possibility is that we can arrive at a different account of inference. We have seen that this is also true in Dewey's logic, and in a different way in dialectical logic. Both are designed to provide occasions and practices that will tend to correct original "assumptions." Since the systems feed back into themselves, original "assumptions" are not unchanged by the inferences. In Dewey's logic, inference, experience and action are linked. Inference leads to action, action to experience. Each new experience is given a place in the original scheme and that place changes the logical force of the original "assumption." In a dialectical system, the generation of additional concepts through the delineation of their specific exclusion references and functional entailments puts the original concepts in a new context. In this context, more of their shape emerges and they do not, again, have the same logical force. The combination of these techniques—one that changes the rational structure surrounding a belief and the other of which brings new experiences to bear on the situation—seems not to leave any untouched original "assumption."

We should not exaggerate the power of either of these techniques. The changes brought about may be slow and painful. One who starts badly will not find the outcome very satisfactory except in the very long run. But perhaps, as in the dialectical systems we examined, there are, at least in theory, ways of starting well by getting an unimpeachable first concept.

Even then, however, one must start at a very abstract level, and such a procedure may be of limited help in a situation in which one needs an inference relevant to one's immediate concern. But those situations are mostly what Dewey called "live options"—occasions in our experience in which there is an immediate fork in the road and a decision is imperative. There, the original alternatives are limited, and there is at least a sporting chance of starting with the right initial presumption. Thus we can conclude that we must always be left with unjustified assumptions on the ground that every argument starts somewhere.

4. How Do Definitions Figure in the Justification of Beliefs?

But what of the possibly related matter—the "definition" argument? The Russellian tradition has it that there are two ways of defining words: by reference to other words or by reference to experience, i.e., by pointing at things.[3] Some words seem definable only in the first way, others only in the second. Consider "disestablishmentarianism"—the practice of opposing the relation between church and state which currently holds in England. This word seems definable only in terms of other words; we cannot just point at disestablishmentarians. It is unlikely that we could find a set of persons with only that feature in common. Even if we could find such a group, it is unlikely that anyone could understand what feature we intended. But consider words like "red," "stinky," "sour," and "soft," which seem definable only by immediate reference to experience. It would seem that anyone lacking the appropriate experience could not possibly know what the words mean. However, we could develop more of the structure of the concepts involved and then exhibit the words in special contexts that do not require direct reference to experience. In fact, scientists often do this. For example, scientists correlate "red" with either a particular region of the spectrum of light or a particular wavelength of light.

Nonetheless, these correlations must, in principle, move other expressions into the foreground as "direct experience-referring expressions." It is something one does that ensures that one has determined the wavelength of light represented as red. There will be experiences that determine these occasions and words for them that will refer directly to the experience. Then, in any case, there will have to be established correlations between the determinants of the secondary expressions and the original expressions themselves. (We must believe, that is, that generally speaking, one in the presence of certain wavelengths of light sees red.)

Thus we have two points: in every system it seems likely that there will be two sorts of undefined expressions: those that, if they could be defined, could only be defined by other words, which, in their turn, must be defined by still other words; and those that, insofar as they can be defined, can only be defined by reference to experience. The first class probably includes structural expressions—words that figure in logic and grammar, and words which figure, perhaps, in certain classifications. The second class seems likely to consist of words that mark out experiences that cannot be further analyzed.

There have been philosophers who thought that indefinables might be reduced to a single class. If a kind of "pure empiricism" could be made to hold, language could be derived from putting together expressions that refer to basic and atomic sorts of experience. If a kind of "pure rationalism" could be made to hold, language could be developed out of original concepts whose function was, in some sense, logical.

It's doubtful that either scheme would work. The explanations for this are perhaps too numerous and complex to figure as a topic in this book, but there is probably a basic set of facts that might make us think that we will not be left with a single class of "undefinables." For one thing, it is simply true that experience is just what it appears to be. One cannot "define" all its contents. Some "truths" about it are expressible as a certain class of first-person propositions. They seem unavoidable and should be (as we saw in Dewey's logic) given a place in any system. But they must be expressed in words that will capture something of the logic of the situation. It seems improbable that this logic could be captured if it were not for the fact that some of the truths simply refer to basic ingredients in an experience that one must share or repeat to understand. There are, however, also "logical truths," which do not seem analyzable into propositions or assertions whose components refer to experience. They are not like first-person propositions. While certain first-person propositions are, in a sense, "necessarily true" they might not have been. They are true, that is, if someone utters them honestly. But the experience might not have occurred. The logical truths are "true for any possible world"—e.g., you cannot construct a coherent description of a world for which "P and not-P" happens to hold. The logical "truths," in their turn, will turn out to have undefined expressions in them because, otherwise, one would have to go on forever defining one word by another.

This is a (fairly) orthodox story about the situation of definitions. We should, however, be a little wary about accepting it without further investigation. In a sense it is true, but it disguises a good deal from us.

5. Options In Definition

Let us look at an expression we used as an example of words that are defined by other words—"disestablishmentarianism." If we can get straight about that, we may stand a chance of seeing what is going on with respect to words that depend upon other words. If we can get straight about these, our chances of getting straight about words that deal in experience may be improved.

Now "disestablishmentarianism," as we saw, is the practice of opposing the relation that currently holds between church and state in England. Part of what is at stake is that some of these expressions are evidently not of the sort that gets cashed in experience. The relationship that now holds between church and state in that country is a rather complex one: the monarch is the titular head of the Church of England, some of its bishops sit in the House of Lords, its clergymen (unlike all other clergymen) may not sit in the House of Commons (being classed with convicted felons, lunatics and peers of the realm) and the prime minister (who is quite often not one of its members) participates in the appointment of its bishops. It does not, however, receive any public funds.

No one would claim to have experienced this church-state relation— though many people have had experiences, such as getting married, that are somehow influenced by it. Nor has anyone who is a disestablishmentarian ever experienced opposing this church-state relation—though many have had experiences that count as opposing it, such as the experience of writing letters to the prime minister denouncing it. One might *say* "I had a strong feeling that I was opposing the Established Church" but one would really mean that while one was doing something (writing "@#*! The Church" on a lavatory wall), one had an experience (fear of the police in the next booth), which one interpreted as opposing the church.

Indeed, The Established Church is not itself an object *of* experience or an object *in* experience. (It is not a sort of bigger St. Paul's.)[4] One may see parish churches, bishops, clergy and so forth, but there is not something *else*, The Church, which one might meet on the street. The Church, in that sense, is a certain grouping or ordering of all these other things. It is not reducible to them, for it does things that none of these other entities do. It owns shares of common stock, for instance, and they are not owned by the parishes, bishops, clergy, or members. They are owned by The Church.

We can now see what is going on here. Words like "church," "parish," "establishment" and so on engender the possibility of defining words like "disestablishmentarianism" and its relative (one of the longest in the language) "antidisestablishmentarianism." These two words are not reducible to words that depend upon experience, but it is also not really true that we must choose between an infinite regress of definitions and simple acceptance of them as "primitive" terms whose meanings are "arbitrary."

For what we can do is to draw upon the rules that govern their use. These rules specify occasions for use of the words in question and the rules are associated with certain practices in which we indulge and which, for the most part, we understand. A church is a place where people do certain things and refrain from doing others. An "established church" is one that stands in a certain relation to certain governmental practices.

Similarly, of course, the most basic terms in our logics—or rather in special sorts of them like those of Aristotle or Russell or Quine—are also associated with certain *practices*, which we, as a rule, understand. If the word "implies" joins two other words of certain sorts, we make a practice of inferring that *if* the relation is believed to hold, *then* it is believed to be the case that, *if* the state of affairs designated by the first expression holds, *then* the state of affairs designated by the second expression also holds. It is a question of whether or not the *practice* is one that we are prepared to accept, and, under various conditions, the answer will be "yes" or "no."

These meaning assignments are, then, associated with beliefs—beliefs that certain practices hold, are comprehensible, justify the use of certain expressions and so on. But the beliefs are not ultimately beyond the scope of "justification" unless we cannot, in fact, determine whether or not the various practices hold.

Thus one of the two classes of definable expressions—those generally thought to be definable only in terms of other words—does not necessarily lead to special difficulties about the justification of belief. If there are such difficulties, they will be difficulties of practice rather than of theory. It may, that is, be quite difficult to cope with expressions about "the Established Church" in England, and it may be quite difficult—as we have seen—to cope with certain logical practices. One reason for choosing these examples was to show just how this might be so. We can see that getting any clear picture about the whole set of practices associated with ecclesiastical language about the Church of England (or about logic!) is probably very difficult.

Ecclesiastical vocabulary is more slippery than a bag full of eels. Books are being written all the time in a rather vain effort to explain it. But that is just because the practices are numerous and hard to identify. Similarly, just what practice is normally associated with words like "implies" is a matter over which, as you know, people puzzle all the time. We may not always, then, be able to justify our beliefs about certain things when the words and expressions about them are of a certain kind. But we can usually find some way to do it. However, we are inclined to think that there are limits to this defence and we would like to call your attention to a puzzle that we find quite difficult but which may lead us to some conclusion about basic and "unjustifiable" beliefs.

6. The Problem of Defining Words Dealing with Time

Consider time and the words associated with its definition—"past," "present," "future," "earlier," "later," "is," "was," "will be" and so on.[5] One cannot "point" at time. One can at most point at a non-typical segment of it, the present. (The past is gone; the future has not yet come.) Nor can one, easily, define temporal expressions by reference to other words. It seems a matter of principle that one cannot define temporal expressions by non-temporal ones. (We are, admittedly, inclined to think of time as spread out in a kind of "space" but the image is, very likely, unfortunate.) Thus, there is a tendency to say that the future *is* what will be, just as the past *is* what was. (The "is" is italicized because it has puzzling features about it. It seems to refer to the "present.") Unhappily, these new definitions seem to imply additional temporal series or sequences.

There is an "earlier/later" series in which everything remains fixed. If Julius Caesar was murdered before Charles I was beheaded, then it is now, always was and always will be the case that the place in the series occupied by those two events remains unchanged. But the "past/present/future" series does not remain unchanged. What *was* future *is* present and *will be* past. But what do "was/is/will be" mean? We make it sound as if there is a realm marked out by "earlier/later," which is explicated by a *process* described as "past/present/future" and *that* the process is intelligible in terms of another process described by "was/is/will be." This may or may not be nonsense, but it seems certain that it is not a helpful notion for one who wants to define "time."

One solution might be as follows.[6] It is true that we cannot point at time, i.e., we cannot have a "simple first-order ostensive definition of time." But it is also true that the present consists of all that can be pointed at. We can get a meaning for "ostensive" because we can define some terms (given a context as we have seen before) ostensively. From *that*, we can derive a "definition" of "present." We can then define "past" as the set of closed possibilities (the past *has* happened), and "future" as the set of open possibilities.

Rather than noticing the difficulties in this series of definitions, let us expand on it a little. We can *associate* the terms so defined with others: the past is what, in principle, could be remembered; the future is what, in principle, could be anticipated. If we work with our experiences of memory and anticipation, we can build up a notion of time through associating experiences and practices with temporal expressions.

Nor is this all: we can get some notions *about* time because of certain facts about experience. There are several levels of consciousness: there is immediate sensation, which is, if you like, the wholly present. There is reflection—a state whose time span is longer than immediate sensation. There is mental construction—a state whose specious present may be quite "long," therefore some events are past while others, which were contemporaneous with them, are still present. Some states of mind, like anticipation, create a kind of future of their own. Given the original "definition" of the present—whatever can be predicted—we can build on it.

But notice what is at stake. The notion of time is obviously a complex *kind* of construction. That is, it seems that we construct time (in a sense of "construct" that is not quite standard but distinguishes it from mere passive reception).

Suppose, then, we have beliefs about time. "Time is real" is one of them—one that enters into all of our calculations. We cannot "defend" this belief or "justify" it by reference to affairs that do not enter in some measure our creative processes. Once we have decided that we can approve, or accept, the notion of time that we "construct," we can proceed to fill it. We decide that the data fit best on a temporal axis, and we generate theories in physics, chemistry, biology, geology, history and so on that exhibit the data as distributed along a temporal axis. All our "beliefs" in this area are tied, in a sense, to our "belief" about time. But "time" could only be defined by construction and association—by what we *do*. Is our belief that "time is real," true or false? Justified or unjustified? It may be *false* if we believe that time is independent of any other state of affairs. For the notion of "time," then, is a very special kind of construct." But the belief is true if what we mean is that we really do make this construct, we really do live out our lives in time. The belief may be unjustified if "unjustification" always means collecting objective evidence about it. Finally, the belief in the reality of time is justified provided "justified" means "providing a framework which makes experience intelligible."

We suspect that there are a number of structural concepts that influence experience and that may be like this. (As we previously discussed, "space" appeared to be an indirect construction from experience.) One way to uncover the nature of these beliefs is to examine the problems about definition.

So far we have not discovered any cases in which problems of definition, *per se,* render any seemingly sensible beliefs in principle entirely unjustifiable. But what are we to say about words like "red" and "stinky," which are defined by direct reference to experience? If, having offered such a definition, one believes that something is red, does one not have on one's hands an unjustified belief? After all, though the suggested technique guarantees that most of us will use the word "red" on the same occasion, who knows whether we are actually aware of the same colour as one another?

Is it not the case, then, that one cannot go any further? Well, not *quite*. For, again, it is true that, as we saw, one can move the context of the discussion of "redness" in a way that will add something else to the discussion. There is no certainty that if two people are subjected to light rays of the same wavelength they will have the same or similar experiences. But we can carry this association further: we can compare our optical apparatus, our brains and so forth. If we find no differences, the case builds toward the likelihood that we have the same experiences. True, it never quite gets there, but what is interesting is that we could list the factors that might lead to different results and eliminate them one by one:

- Outer eye characteristics
- Inner eye structures
- Optic nerves
- Nerve paths
- Cerebral cortices
- Conceptual structures
- Linguistic habits
- Feelings
- Mental tones

One would think that something would have to be different for a differ-ence to occur—though there is not a simple rule to that effect. But a justified belief is not, for sure, a belief known to be the truth. We saw, earlier, that we cannot reach *that* kind of certainty, at least in every case. All we expect is that, by running through the factors, we can expand the horizons of relevance—bring out more data with the likelihood that findable mistakes will be found. However, there remains the problem about residual unjustified beliefs.

We have dealt with "assumptions"—initial premises in arguments that may be associated with beliefs to produce residual unjustified beliefs. And we have dealt with the "primitive" or "undefined" terms—features of unexplicated matter that may well drag along with them unjustified beliefs, or even, if one can call such things "beliefs," semi-conscious or wholly disguised beliefs. These cases turn out to produce unjustified "beliefs" only on certain assump-tions about inference, about definition and its relation to meaning, and about what "justification" might amount to. But we have found nothing, so far, that remains beyond the realm of justification.

QUICK QUIZ #1

1. Distinguish between the assertion that not all beliefs can be justified and the assertion that one should sometimes refrain from asking for further reasons.
2. Does every argument presuppose something?
3. Do all justifications involve inferences?
4. What part do definitions play in the justification of beliefs?
5. Are there only ostensive definitions and definition in terms of words?
6. What do our attempts to define "time words" tell us about definitions?

---

7. The Analytic/Synthetic Distinction

We might explore other proposals about what qualifies as a belief not open to justification. For instance, Quine has argued that one can always choose to make some propositions analytic[7] and to regard those as independent of evidence. For example, we could regard "All men are mortal" as *analytic* in that we decide not to call anything a "man" if it lacks mortality. So no evidence would change our minds regarding its truth status. But we could regard "All men are mortal" as *synthetic*, as an empirical generalization. So evidence would change our minds regarding its truth status. One might argue that we must accept some propositions as *analytic* since we need some "guiding propositions" that determine what counts as evidence and how to collect evidence. If we regard the "guiding propositions" as synthetic, we would need some evidence for them. But, how could we recognize the evidence for the "guiding propositions?" We would need "special and different guiding propositions" for recognizing and collecting the evidence for the original "guiding propositions." We might, in that way, produce an infinite regress. Now analytic propositions seem to be simply taken as "given" and, if we have any beliefs about them, it would seem that they might be "unjustified." However, we do not need to take this view because, like Quine, we can ask questions about how well this way of ordering the evidence works for the purpose we have in mind. We can give our analytic propositions grammatical justifications. *Alternatively, we could say that we do not have beliefs about them but only beliefs about the outcome of using them to marshal the evidence.*

Again, we could deal with the situation as Wittgenstein seems to have in his *Investigations*, and later, perhaps, in his notes, *On Certainty*.[8] At least part of Wittgenstein's thesis was that we are stuck with certain features of our ordinary language. If we turn our language on itself, we change its meaning and foul our investigation. Suppose one doubts that one knows what "doubts" means? More subtly, Wittgenstein thought the concept of certainty is associated with certain standard paradigms. How do we usually use expressions like "certain" and "doubtful?" For instance, a woman in good mental and physical health, at home drinking tea with her husband and petting her dog, is certain that she knows where she is. If asked if she is certain, what standard does she have? Usually, if she wonders whether or not something strange has happened to her, she uses a standard that involves ordinary experiences and images. If everything feels right and comfortable—as it does when she is at home with her husband and dog—she feels no special doubts. So what standard is she to use if someone questions her certainty when she *is* at home with her husband and dog? (Of course, every science fiction reader knows that she will soon find that she is not at home when she thinks she is, but that she has really been captured by Gorms and is on the other side of the Milky Way.)

8. Are We Just Stuck with Certain Notions?

One can argue that the rules for using expressions like "motor car" function as criteria so that we all know whether or not to say that a particular thing is or is not a motor car. If a philosopher were to come along and say "perhaps there *really* are no motor cars, perhaps there are only ideas in the mind of God," we might not be sure what he was saying. Is he saying that everybody, always, wrongly applies the words "motor car?" Or "there really are motor cars but they are not, in their turn, just what you think they are?" The first assertion would, of course, land you in problems. For you would be admitting that the criteria were applied quite correctly in the ordinary sense but that they were not the *right* criteria. But the ordinary criteria, in fact, give the meaning for "motor car." In this case, however, we are made to think that no one can ask questions about the world if the questions are like those of Bishop Berkeley—who did, after all, want to say that everything real is an idea in one's mind or the mind of God, or is some other feature of a spiritual substance.[9] There is, as it seems, a sensible question—Berkeley's question—that we cannot answer, and we are made to look as if we are simply "stuck" with a belief that we cannot challenge.

However, the second question shows that this is not quite so. We can accept the ordinary criteria and then go on to ask different sorts of questions about the result. These further questions are about how such concepts as "reality," "existence," or "being" are related to one another and to such other notions as "motor car." In one version of his thesis, Wittgenstein seems to have associated these ordinary "certainties" with behaviour—one acts in such a way as to exploit the knowledge or belief in question. To doubt it would be to suggest that one's actions sometimes do or at least *might* fail. But we cannot conceive of acting, perhaps, in a way that would succeed on Berkeley's view and not on the ordinary view. (Here we are exploring on our own what we suppose to be the consequence of Wittgenstein's thesis on "certainty," given one of its interpretations.) Does this leave us with a basic kind of "common sense" belief that we cannot imagine how to test or overcome?

Not really. For we might choose Berkeley"s thesis and then act, as a matter of fact, rather differently than we ordinarily do. That is, we might more cheerfully take certain risks if we thought that we were immortal spiritual substances and the world were within the mind of God.

We cannot easily imagine that there are no cars. (It seems certain that there are.). But we can imagine that cars are not merely (not that they are not *exactly)* what they seem to be. If we can find reasons for choosing between these hypotheses, then we might well hold that we are not, in this way, faced with necessarily unjustifiable beliefs.

There is, however, what seems to be a more drastic argument. The things we have been dealing with, analytic propositions about how the evidence is to be marshalled, basic common sense "truths" that seem difficult to challenge, and other conceptions like them, seem very much the sorts of things one might call "presuppositions." They are not, like assumptions, premises that are set out in the clear light of day for us to inspect. They are not, like the beliefs that may cluster along with unexplicated terms (those we may choose not to define or which resist definition in some way) part of the surface fabric. Rather, they may be things that pass unnoticed. Since we accept certain views about marshalling the evidence, we may not know just what we have presupposed. Since common-sense beliefs tend to permeate our ordinary language, we may find that they have not been subjected to any sort of test and so have not shown themselves in the mainstream of the argument.

9. Collingwood's Questions and Answers and the Choice between Presuppositions

There is, however, as R. G. Collingwood pointed out, a still more easily hidden set of presuppositions.[10] Collingwood noticed that all propositions that we are inclined to include as facets of belief function as answers to questions. One never knows, he says, what they mean unless one knows what question they are likely to answer. For instance, "horses are graminivorous" has one meaning if the question is "do horses mostly eat grass?" and another if the question is "do horses ever eat minerals?" In the first case what it seems to say is true, in the second case false. (One who utters it in the second case seems to be answering "no" to the question about horses and minerals.) It is usually—always, according to Collingwood—the case that a given proposition will turn out to be true for some questions and false for others. One who says, "London is larger than Manchester" is right if the question is about population, but he would be wrong if the question were about area, and if it referred to the city and not the urban area of London. One might think that such assertions were accidentally favourable to Collingwood's thesis. Surely, one may say, London *might* have been unambiguously larger than Manchester in every possible sense. But this is a mistake. It could not be larger in the sense of having more assignable predicates than Manchester (in the crudest sense of the expression) or larger in the sense of accommodating more possibilities for human experience.

At any rate, it is *often* the case that the same proposition may be true if it is the answer to one question and false if it is the answer to another, and one would think in principle that one could always contrive a question that has the desired result.

The point of this is that questions have presuppositions: "Do horses eat grass?" assumes that there *are* horses and that they eat something. "Has London more people than Manchester?" assumes that there *are* people in at least one of those places. "Is the moon roughly spherical?" assumes that the moon is an object that occupies a region of space.

Usually these presuppositions are, themselves, answers to further questions. But one of two things is obviously true: Either there are infinitely many such relationships or there is, somewhere, a presupposition that is NOT the answer to any question. If the former, there must somewhere be a belief, or at least a belief-component, which we cannot justify. We cannot justify infinitely many beliefs. If the latter, we obviously cannot justify what Collingwood called "an absolute presupposition."

Are we then, at last, at the unjustifiable belief? Not if the latter hypothesis is true. For what is assumed is that the presupposition that we ultimately settle on is not to be justified by a direct examination, and that this is the only thing that we would call "justification." Collingwood sometimes made this mistake. At other times, he seems to have suggested that between the various absolute presuppositions there stands a dialectical relation—that we can see, from the concepts involved, how we might move from one to another in the way discussed in Chapter 7.

But that is not the only possibility. Another, of course, is that presuppositions *do* give rise to questions. The questions *do* delineate a range of appropriate answers. Sometimes we cannot choose between the possible answers. But that seems to mean that the questions are wrongly put—they are like fishnets that catch no fish. In that case, we try other questions with other presuppositions.

Sometimes, too, the presuppositions are inconsistent with one another and it turns out that the question – answer sets for one are a good deal better than those for another. (Perhaps we hold the principle of sufficient reason on the grounds that it makes sense of the world given the questions we choose to ask, while its alternatives and denials do not.) In short, we might be stuck with some "absolute presuppositions" and then, again, we might not. We might choose to abandon as many such presuppositions as we can because we believe that the best beliefs *do* marshal the evidence and *are* consistent with one another.[11]

The conclusion, then, is that there *are* some serious problems. We do not know, for sure, that we can cope with all of them. But certainly, neither do we know for sure that we *must* be stuck with unexplicated beliefs. The *philosophical* problem of persuasion and its justification seems, primarily, a moral one:[12] Suppose we could persuade you to believe any proposition whatsoever? Under what conditions would we be justified in doing so?

10. The Justification of Persuasion: A Moral Concern

The answer seems to be perfectly simple: We would be justified in doing so if and only if the proposition were itself an expression of a justified belief or an expression of a component of such a belief. Yet there are obvious complications. One is that persuasion and justification may not be entirely separable. Suppose that we are on a sinking ship. It is imperative that we all act together or we shall all drown. The "justified" belief in the ordinary sense (forgetting persuasion for a moment), however, may be one that the captain can persuade only a small minority of the passengers to accept. The truth may be that the ship is sinking quite slowly, that the best thing for everyone is to gather all the necessary supplies in a systematic way and to wait until the ship settles before attempting to launch the boats. But the passengers may think it is going down quite fast and be unwilling to show such patience. The captain, then, may be wiser to use every means to persuade them to act rationally and survive together rather than to permit them to act impulsively and perish together. The choice is often between persuasion and force, and if the optimal belief is not one which can be inculcated by persuasion, it may be necessary to choose a less desirable belief. Like the captain of the ship, one may have to inculcate the best beliefs one can, given that the overriding aim is for everyone to survive. So one can argue that it is possible for a belief to become justified because it is the best of a set of several beliefs that a certain group of persons can be persuaded to accept.

This may not be so horrifying as it sounds. We have discovered, in any case, that belief is very complex and that few beliefs are likely to contain all and only elements whose justifications consist in the fact that they are known to be true. Yet the suggestion seems to be that some justified beliefs may contain elements known to be false—i.e., the captain may have to act on what she does not believe, the proposition that the ship will go down rather quickly, and she may be justified in getting the passengers to act in a way that sustains that belief provided that she can save their lives by getting them to act together. We should notice, however, that in this case, such a captain is not persuading them to accept the false element in the belief: they already believe that.

Consider, in this light, the case of the politician who does not believe that the capitalist system will work. If others cannot be made to accept his belief, it may be justifiable for the politician to recommend to them, say, stronger anti-trust laws. Passing those laws seems to express a belief that the politician does not have—that the capitalist system can be made to work. Actually, however, the politician's act only expresses the belief that the system will be improved by the new law. And no one is being persuaded to believe that the capitalist system can be made to work. The constituents, presumably, believe that for themselves. The problem, that is, is that the best justified belief in the situation *may* be one which contains elements that are reasonably believed to be false. If one is trying to advance a legitimate goal, one may be justified in accepting some of the elements in the beliefs of the audience even if they are known to be shaky. One would not, however, at least not on those grounds, be justified in persuading others to accept false beliefs, or to include false elements in their beliefs, if the falsehoods were not *already* contained in their beliefs.

11. The Myth of the Good Political Lie

Plato thought that the state might actually be justified in spreading lies (useful myths, stories), but this would seem to raise insoluble moral problems. It might be true that a ship's captain could be forced to choose between lies and disaster—between, say, telling the passengers that they will all hang if they disobey and letting them drown as a result of their self-induced chaos. But that suggests a desperate situation.

If we must choose between lies and disaster, it is by no means clear that we must choose lies. It all depends on the lies, the disaster and the people involved. We suppose that mothers in the London Blitz sometimes told their children not to be afraid, that "it would be all right" even though they knew that it wouldn't. The children were not in a position to understand what was going on and nothing would have been helped by having them in a state of nervous collapse. Children are not the only people from whom it may some-times be justified to "withhold the truth." Society, and even the law, generally discourage people from shouting "fire!" in crowded theatres, even if (perhaps especially if) there really is a fire since the ensuing panic will cause death. In this case, no one is in a good position to guarantee the good behaviour of the crowd.

By contrast, one might argue (perhaps against Plato) that the citizens of a country with a deeply corrupt government ought to be told just how corrupt their leaders are even if they are apt to get very angry and start a riot. This will be true if one believes in democracy in the sense that the people are able to choose for themselves better than anyone could choose for them. One who supports democratic government but hides corruption would seem to be in a contradictory position. One should notice, though, that it is important to know which principles one is defending. In one American presidential election, at least one of the candidates was driven from the race by newspaper exposures of his affair with a young woman who was not his wife. Here, again, we are telling the people the facts and letting them choose. But it was suggested, not unreasonably, that there might be another principle at work: even in a democracy citizens are entitled to a certain amount of privacy, especially with respect to matters which do not involve their capacity to exercise their public offices.

This brings to light another dimension of the problem of persuasion. Consider that the candidates in an election are trying to persuade the public to trust them with power. The question of what makes a person trustworthy is not easy to answer. Does it bear on the question if a candidate does not prove trustworthy to his or her spouse?

Sometimes the issue is even more convoluted. Winston Churchill persuaded the British public that Britain could be defended against the Germans. Many people believe he knew that the defence would be unsuccessful in the event of an actual German invasion. But Churchill, of course, was also trying to persuade the Germans that the invasion would be foolhardy. There are many beliefs which, if held firmly enough, affect the outcome. This is one example. Others may occur in the practice of medicine, since a patient's will to survive and belief in his or her own powers may actually determine the outcome.

Here there are various subtleties short of outright lies: we are faced with the possibility of withholding some of the truth, allowing the audience to keep its own beliefs, or inculcating beliefs that tend to become true if accepted. None of this permits us to call actual lies elements in "justified persuasion," even though we might not regard all liars as being in the same moral situation. It is one thing to accept, for the moment, a falsehood that someone in any case believes, and quite another thing to add a falsehood.

A falsehood must alter all the logical relations in one's existing belief structure—and so taint the entire system of beliefs. (Remember that coherence amongst beliefs is a condition of the justification of beliefs.) The point is, no doubt, that it is always wrong to inculcate falsehood, but not all those who inculcate falsehoods are in exactly the same position. There are other wrong acts as well. (Letting people drown is itself, no doubt, wrong and worse than telling them calming untruths.)

12. Some Wrong Acts are Better than Others

It may well be that there are relations between wrong acts such that some of them are preferable to others. But the choice would have to be one in which a wrong act of very great significance was the only alternative before one would say that inculcating falsehoods was justified, and *even then* one would not say that the false belief so inculcated was, itself, justified.

The second major difficulty is this: the justification of persuasion depends not only upon what is to be justified by way of belief but also on questions about the manner of the persuasion. That is, one may be right in believing that a new anti-trust act would improve the economic system. It does not follow that they would be right in persuading others of this proposition by, say, arousing in them a strong fear that they would face unemployment if the act were not passed. Whether or not one should be afraid of unemployment depends upon whether or not one is likely to be unemployed.[13] But the fear can be engendered independently of the facts. In the next chapter, we shall look at the classical accounts of "fallacies." Sometimes there are lists called *the* fallacies of persuasive argument. (We italicize *the* because some textbooks writers make it seem that these are all the fallacies or at least the really important ones.) Here the point is to notice that there are many modes of persuasion, and to determine what principles, if any, determine which modes are justified. We have seen that, beneath the minimal rational structure of belief lies feeling. Persuasion, in practice, more often seeks to work at the level of feeling than of rational belief.

13. Persuasion and Emotion

David Hume said "reason is and ought to be the slave of the passions,"[14] and a recent writer, Robert Solomon, has argued that justice in reality depends on a strong feeling which derives from our sense of "being with others," which militates strongly against both excessive individualism and excessive communitarianism.[15]

Hume believed that reason could not motivate us to action, and that it was, in any case, purely formal in the sense that it led us from one idea to another but could not generate any facts of its own. Solomon pointed out that there is a real feeling of justice in us and that it is this and not abstract ideas that motivates the great reformers. One must be very careful with such notions, however. It is easy to confuse the doctrine that persuasion itself ought to be rational and based on propositions one has good reason to believe to be true with the quite different doctrine that all justified beliefs are ultimately based on reason.

It is this second proposition that Hume is concerned to deny. Indeed, the expressions "rational belief" and "belief based on reason" are by no means identical. For instance, one might accept what Solomon said about the feeling for justice without thinking that one's beliefs about justice are themselves in any way irrational. One may accept outrage as providing a reason. It may be quite rational to accept that because nearly everyone who has thought carefully about the problem and been exposed to a reasonable understanding of the nature of human potentiality is outraged by certain kinds of discrimination and oppression, discrimination and oppression should be opposed. It is, at any rate, a reason for thinking that the thirst for justice caused by these feelings of outrage is justified.[16] Jefferson Davis, the President of the Confederate States of America, who led his people in a civil war that many people thought was fought in defence of slavery, in fact said "Slavery is repugnant to the conscience of all mankind," and one may think this is an admission that the feeling is nearly universal amongst thoughtful people.

It is not the feeling as such that justifies the belief. If outrage at racial discrimination is justified it is likely to be, as Adam Smith suggested, that we have a natural sympathy for one another. And our natural sympathies are evidence that we do feel real concern for people of other races. After all, discrimination is based on the belief that others are different from us in a way that makes them inferior. Our natural sympathy reflects the fact that we find it difficult to believe such nonsense once we have come to grasp the origins of our cultural biases. The sympathy is natural to just the extent that justification for racial discrimination invariably turns out to be contrived.

14. Justified Beliefs that Fall Short of Proof

The demonstrations available for opposition to slavery or discrimination based on race may even fall short of what one would be willing to call "formal proof" according to many notions of "proof." Without descriptions of each of the (perhaps infinite) set of human characteristics, one could not *prove* that *no* race is ever inferior to another with respect to *any* of them. Yet using, say, a logic like John Dewey's, it would be perfectly rational to suggest that one has sufficient evidence for the proposition that the quality of human experience in general will be better for so many people if one acts against discrimination that one *should* accept the need to act against discrimination. And, using Sir Karl Popper's notions of falsification, one is entitled to say that the claim that some groups are inferior has been tested so often and has so uniformly been found wanting (even if a few doubtful applications of intelligence tests suggest the contrary), that we are quite entitled to regard our belief that all races are equal as justified. All arguments of this kind surely belong to the domain of "rational persuasion" in that (a) good reasons can be given for the propositions offered and (b) a rational way is open for those with different views to assemble their counter-evidence. Indeed, once one has a reasonably wide notion of "rationality," attempts to justify non-rational persuasion become more suspicious. They may well have to do with a tendency to evade the results of genuinely free action.

Persuasion that attempts to work at the level of rationality expressed by the complex notion of rational belief has unpredictable results. The methods of rational persuasion make this fairly clear. One way of changing a rational belief is to present true propositions that conflict with the rational belief. So the holder of the belief has to resolve this conflict. But, the holder of the belief has several options. He might simply reject the presented propositions. He might reject his original proposition. But, he might reject some other previously held proposition that blocked him from integrating his previously held proposition and the ones just presented. In sum, attempting to change rational beliefs in this way sets in motion a rational appraisal whose result cannot readily be predicted.

Another way of changing rational belief is to create new tests for existing beliefs—to suggest modes of experience that will raise questions about the existing belief. If it is a justified belief in terms of the criteria suggested in Chapter 6, it will be subject to test and confirmation. Furthermore, one who regards it as important will seek as many tests as possible—if he or she is rational. But to seek genuine tests is to raise the possibility of another kind of large-scale reorganization. One who seeks to persuade in this way has, again, little reason to suppose that the outcome will always be the desired one.

Rational persuasion may again take the form of attempts to reformulate the criteria for inference and the canons of relevance that hold for the investigations and subject matters under review. But one who uses this method is likely to hope that those to be persuaded will adopt the favoured view of inference and the favoured canons of relevance. To achieve this end rationally—in the context of justified belief—one must again face the strong possibility that the review will lead the audience to make reforms quite unlike the ones proposed. For all one can do is suggest criteria for the review. The suggestion of one set of criteria that is rationally intelligible, however, makes sense only by contrast to another. One will, therefore, almost inevitably (if one does one's job well) suggest for them live options which one does not want them to act upon.

15. Rational Persuasion as a Tactic for Free Agents

In short, rational persuasion is a tactic for free men and women. It is irrational even to undertake it if the outcome desired is specified in advance of the investigations one sets in motion. For it can only be done at the risk that one will, and others also, come to quite new conclusions.

The irony of this situation can be illustrated in the history of thought. The fathers of the church, for instance, had difficulty with their missionary activities at least in part because their scriptures seemed to contain a great many ambiguities and even inconsistent doctrines. They set about finding a solution to this problem by attempting to generate coherent creeds and bodies of doctrine—propositions that could be components of rational beliefs. In doing so they were compelled to reason and so to develop criteria of inference and interpretation. They were also compelled to generate, as best they could, unambiguous accounts of the validating religious experiences and so on.

Inevitably, the result was the generation of a whole range of entirely new "heresies"—for each time they specified the desired result, they called attention to a variety of options. The options were "persuasive"" in the obvious sense that they were equally rational alternatives to the original beliefs. At the same time, however, the reformers thought that a particular belief must be obligatory, and that the obligatory belief tended to be the one that ultimately commanded the assent of a majority of influential bishops. But it was surely inevitable that there would be minorities who did not see the outcome as the majority did. Hence, heresy. We might well notice the logic of the situation.

16. Reason and the Generation of Alternatives

One cannot reason without generating alternatives. One cannot reach a solution without generating alternatives nor can one reach a solution without an act of assent. Therefore, one must expect that amongst those given to reason, there will be a plurality of beliefs about almost anything. Indeed, that plurality of beliefs is probably one of the crucial guarantees of the likelihood that, overall, we shall move toward the truth. For plurality of belief encourages the testing of belief. Without such testing, belief will tend to degenerate toward ossified feeling.

Nonetheless, those who set out to persuade usually have something in mind—the conversion of the doubtful. Whether they are selling religion, washing machines or political programs, persuaders normally want some specified outcome. They may or may not be aware of the theoretical reasons for thinking that rational persuasion can as easily generate dissent as assent, but the temptation, nonetheless, is to move below the level of belief and to approach the problem at the level of feeling.

It is true that we are not sure just what may happen if we change our own or other people's feelings. But it remains that most emotions are directed to specific objects—hungry people seek food, angry people pursue their enemies, fearful people hide, or seek power and so on. It also happens that, since we have language, and since the symbols, rightly manipulated, can simulate the effects of the objects they symbolize (at least in our minds and emotions), a great deal of persuasion is directed to symbolic construction of states of affairs that will engender appropriate emotions. (Oddly enough, one of the feelings involved is the feeling of being reasonable—but that can be engendered, as every television audience knows, by what *look* like arguments and are not.)

The interesting thing about this situation is that, in this way, persuasion tends to become a kind of force. As a rule, in civilized societies, persuasion is preferred to force. It is thought wrong to get one's way with a gun, or by blowing up a neighbour's house with dynamite, or by hiring a gang of thugs to terrorize the neighbourhood. It is thought wrong for at least the obvious reason that force gives its wielder an unfair advantage—an advantage to which he or she has no moral entitlement—and because it is not conducive to effective and coherent social action. (It is sometimes thought to be justified if used by the community as such and applied to those who "cannot be reasoned with." The slipperiness of this argument we have already seen.)

17. Rational Persuasion versus Force

But the distinction that now makes sense is that between rational persuasion and force. How good is the distinction between the kind of persuasion that works on feelings, and force? It seems that having one's feelings worked on is not, in effect, much different from having a gun at one's head. True, it is less dangerous, at least in the short run. (In the long run, such techniques may play a large part in filling the mental hospitals.)

It is not very different from force for the obvious reason that the only control one has on one's feelings is through one's reason. If, therefore, persuasion that changes feelings works at all, it does so by acting in areas in which one lacks sufficient rational apparatus to have control of one's affairs. It works, in short, where one is defenceless. Indeed, it may be even more undesirable than applying guns to people's heads. At least one can think about one's decision while having a gun applied to one's head (or one should be able to if one's rationality is deep enough). But having one's feelings manipulated works, by definition, in a way that prevents us from thinking clearly about it.

R.G. Collingwood once remarked that one cannot *make* a man do *anything* by force.[17] A human being always has a choice between resisting or being shot—not *much* of a choice but a choice, for all that. But one who can work on someone's feelings can *make* the subject do things. For then, by definition, one is without recourse to one's rational capacities.

It is true that people act, as Hume thought, on their passions. But reason helps to free them to act on the passion of their choice, and they surely cannot be held responsible unless they have acted in some plausible awareness of the alternatives.

In a society that values free and informed action as a basis for public policy, rational persuasion may not be everything, but persuasion seems justified only insofar as it includes the rational. Going beyond reason is always a kind of wrong act. But as we have noted, some wrong acts are worse than others. If one can show that the only feasible alternative to one wrong act is another wrong act, and that the second wrong act is worse than the first, one has a case for promoting the first act. If it involves irrational persuasion, so be it. But one must always be able to show that one went as far with rationality as the avoidance of disaster permitted.

We have to admit, of course, that we cannot distinguish clearly enough between kinds of persuasion for most kinds to be regulated by law. The most we can do is to hope to regulate persuasion itself by rational persuasion—a fact that may help to explain why many of our problems seem rather intractable.

QUICK QUIZ #2

1. How important is the "analytic/synthetic" distinction?
2. Are there some concepts that we are just "stuck with"?
3. Does Collingwood's "logic of question-and-answer" provide a way out of the dilemmas posed in this chapter?
4. Is it ever right to persuade someone to hold a belief that one is not justified in believing to be true?
5. Plato thought that the state might sometimes be justified in inculcating falsehoods. Are state lies ever justified?
6. If some wrong acts are better than others, are there some wrong things that one ought to do?
7. Discuss David Hume's claim that "reason ought to be the slave of the passions." Are emotions necessarily irrational?
8. Are all justified beliefs provable? Discuss the possibility of standards that fall short of proof.
9. Should free agents ever assent to irrational persuasion?
10. Does it matter that the outcome of rational persuasion cannot in principle be protected?
11. Discuss the importance of generating alternatives as a phase in the reasoning process.
12. Can anyone really be forced to do anything?

Notes

1. Peter T.Geach, *Reason and Argument,* Berkeley and Los Angeles: University of California Press, 1976. Geach is a noted logical theorist, though this is a simple introductory book.
2. Because questions of definition—and therefore of meaning—necessarily enter into this discussion, it will prove useful in several places to use the occasion to work the problem of meaning into the discussion.
3. The theoretical basis for the notion is well laid out by Bertrand Russell in a classical essay, "Knowledge by Acquaintance and Knowledge by Description" in *Mysticism and Logic,* originally published in 1908, reprinted Harmondsworth, Middlesex: Penguin Books, 1953.
4. Some collective nouns do name potentially visible things. If there were only two Mormons or two members of the United Church of Canada left, you could see "the Mormons" or "the United Churchmen." But you could not see "the Church of Jesus Christ of Latter Day Saints" or "the United Church of Canada." These expressions name institutions like "the state" or "the monarchy." You can see the Queen but not the monarchy and some policemen but not the state.
5. One of the most celebrated accounts of these problems is in St.Augustine's *Confessions,* Bk. XI, Chapter XV (Cambridge, MA: Harvard University Press, Loeb Classical Library, Vol. II, p. 239–44). A much-discussed modern account is in J.M.E. McTaggart, *The Nature of Existence,* Cambridge: The University Press, 1921–1927, Vol. II, p. 9–31.

6. See Leslie Armour, *The Rational and The Real*, Martinus Nijhoff, The Hague, 1962, Ch. VI, pt. 2.

7. "Analytic," here, means "true by definition."

8. *Philosophical Investigations,* New York: Macmillan, 1953; *On Certainty,* Oxford: Basil Blackwell, 1969.

9. Berkeley (1685–1753), a British philosopher, is widely thought to be the founder of modern idealism. According to him, everything real is an idea in our minds or in the mind of God, but by "idea," he meant, in his early work, much what we mean by "sensation." See his *Principles of Human Knowledge,* 1710, and *Three Dialogues Between Hylas and Philonous,* 1713. (There are many modern editions).

10. R.G. Collingwood (1889–1943), a British philosopher who was often thought of as the successor to the British Idealists of the turn of the twentieth century and who was associated with one branch of the Hegelian tradition. The issues discussed here can be found in his *Autobiography,* Oxford: Clarendon Press, 1939, and his *Essay on Metaphysics,* Oxford: Clarendon Press, 1940.

11. For further exploration of this question see Leslie Armour, *The Concept of Truth,* Assen: Royal Vangorcum; and New York: The Humanities Press, 1969.

12. There are lots of legitimate and interesting non-philosophical issues. Some are psychological; for example, just how do people succeed in persuading one another? One hopes that *rational* persuasion is a possibility. But it is surely not the only one, and not, one fears, the most likely one either. Other issues are sociological; what kinds of institutions and other social structures are associated with persuasion? Still others are legal. It is not in fact the case that our legal system permits every sort of persuasion. For instance, "undue influence," the power that male employers have often had over their female employees—has always been a legal issue. Recent concerns about sexual harassment have accentuated it. Still other issues are political and their investigation belongs to political science. What kinds of persuasion can a democratic political system in fact allow without destroying itself? (In many places, including the United States and in some Canadian jurisdictions, corporate contributions to some political campaigns are limited or prohibited.) Again, communications theorists study the ways in which communications systems function to achieve persuasion. All these factual inquiries also tend to influence our views about which moral issues are important.

13. And even on what will happen to one then! Perhaps one needs a holiday and has plenty of savings.

14. *A Treatise of Human Nature,* 1739, ed. L.A. Selby-Bigge, revised Peter H. Nidditch, Oxford: Clarendon Press, 1978, Book II, Section III, p. 415.

15. *A Passion for Justice,* New York: Addison-Wesley, 1990. The quotation is from p. 104 but the issue is discussed throughout the book.

16. One must be very careful, however. It is the outrage of those who have thought carefully and studied the matter reflectively that is evidence that something important is at issue. Thoughtless outrage, ignorant outrage, outrage by people with no experience of confronting the views of others and so on are surely different matters.

17. *The New Leviathan,* Oxford: Clarendon Press, 1942, Part I, Ch. 13.

Chapter 8

THE TRADITIONAL FALLACIES

1. Common Sense and Traditional Fallacies

Logic books traditionally offered a list of fallacies and many modern ones continue this practice. This is problematic since there are probably infinitely many kinds of bad arguments but no one can provide an infinite list. It was thought that there were common fallacies and that to identify an argument with a fallacy should halt all debate. But there is something odd about the traditional list. The "fallacies" are there because they normally fool people; however, they fool people because there is a grain of sense to them. That is, there is usually some context in which a given "fallacy" is not fallacious after all.[1]

Many traditional fallacies substitute something else—authority, emotion, social acceptability, self-interest—for reason. But the list usually includes at least one sort of fallacy that is strictly logical, that is, "begging the question" (it is often referred to by its Latin name, *petitio principii*).

2. How Does One Beg A Question?

It is not clear how to beg a question. One classic form emerges out of the problem of questions and presuppositions that we saw in Chapter 5. A standard example of a loaded question is "have you stopped beating your wife?" No real lawyer would ask this. But a real lawyer might ask, "Did you leave your gun at home on the night of the murder?" Whatever the answer, it would establish that the respondent owned a gun. But if R.G. Collingwood is right, *all* questions are loaded. (They have to be: a question has to bring to light the relevance of a set of answers. If it doesn't, it has no answer nor is it a legitimate question.) The problem is to beg the *right* question. The gun question is better than the wife question. But the gun question assumes that the respondent could have owned a gun and in the context of a murder trial would suggest that there is a reason for asking the respondent this question.

"Begging the question" is usually defined as assuming that which is to be proved. This can be done in two ways. Suppose someone says "God exists" and then offers the following argument:

The bible says that God exists.

The bible is trustworthy since it is the word of God.
Therefore God exists.

Clearly the truth of the second premise depends on the existence of God. This is the *dependency* form of begging the question. But suppose someone argued that "the state ought to allow freedom of speech" and then offers the following argument:

A good state allows everyone to express his or her views freely.
Therefore, the state should allow freedom of speech.

The premise and conclusion represent different ways of saying the same thing. This is the *equivalency* form of begging the question. Consider the following:

Public ownership is dangerous because it is a socialist practice.

This gives a particular socialist practice a name, "public ownership," and assumes what is to be proved, namely that socialist practices are dangerous. However, it may be important to classify things under their right headings. Suppose we say:

Advertising "$10 off!" without saying that it is $10 off an imaginary price is fraudulent.

This simply associates two ideas and is not wrong if you know that fraud is bad but had not thought about how to classify the objectionable act. Such a claim may well be the legitimate prelude to some further investigation—though it may be a trick if the further investigation is not forthcoming.

Assuming what has to be proved is a way of framing a hypothesis, and if hypotheses are to be tested in action, anyhow, a Deweyite might want to justify it. One should be on the lookout for such tricks; one should also investigate, anyhow, the association of the ideas that have been proclaimed.

3. Are There Good Arguments from Authority? (*Argumentum Ad Verecundiam*)

An argument from authority is basically as follows:

Person A says X.
Person A is an authority.
Therefore, X is true (or you should believe X).

Normally this is thought to be a poor argument, but it might in fact be a good one. If you do not understand physics, it is probably better to take your physics from a physicist than from a garbage collector. (It *might* not be. Some garbage collectors are surely learned. But the odds are against it.) There are, however, more interesting cases.

Suppose you buy a car and sign an agreement with the dealer that specifies that the Society of Arbitrators will settle any disputes. This obliges you to accept the arbitrator as an authority. But in signing the agreement you have established the arbitrator as *the* authority for any disputes you may have. There is nothing wrong with this if you have decided that the Society of Arbitrators provides as basis for good decisions.

Or you may join a religious organization that has someone who determines matters of faith. Again, this decision-maker has authority because you gave it to him or her. Thus, the question is: how should we establish authorities? Since religious dogma is complex, it may be reasonable to establish an orderly way of settling disputes. In the automobile case, having an authority may save everyone enormous legal costs—and do the job just as well as the courts (another authority!) would.

It is not reasonable to have *ultimate* authorities in physics or philosophy because they have established methodologies. True, the method in both physics and philosophy is always, itself, under investigation. But there is a difference between designing an experiment and peering into the entrails of a chicken, or between constructing a logic and checking inferences with it and looking into one's crystal ball. We know roughly what to do about these disputes, and it is not essential, as it may be in the used car business, or the church, for all the parties to come to a final agreement.

Appeals to authority, in the wrong realm, are like appeals to force or appeals designed to whip up popular emotion: they are ways of evading the issue. But in some realms, obviously, the problem is to find the right authority. Sometimes the authority is the right one just because the parties to a dispute *can* agree on him or her.

Since nobody can be an expert on everything, a good authority figure is limited to speaking about a particular domain and is also recognized as an expert by others in that domain. A good authority will have unusual skill at marshalling evidence, weighing arguments, constructing inferences—and will be free from conflicts of interest.

4. Not All Self-Interest is Bad

Appeals to self-interest are, in principle, an evasion of reason, although they are sometimes justified since one may have legitimate self-interests. But like establishing authorities, we have to offer reasons for these self-interests and allow others to argue for their own. Suppose you wish to stroll about downtown without clothing. If you are allergic to all known fabrics and will suffer from wearing clothes, that's one thing. If you won't suffer and you have no other legitimate claim, there seems no reason to believe that others have an obligation to put up with the sight of you. You might do it just "in the name of freedom," but you would have to know *what* freedom. Is it like your right to make unpopular speeches in the public square? Is it like your right to paint pictures that others find odious?

5. On Not Burning Down One's House

The great philosopher René Descartes advised caution when applying reason. Even if one lives in a bad house, he said, it is not always wise to burn it down. Reason may dictate vast social reforms, but overhauling society in a day would be catastrophic. So, while properly arguing your case, it is probably best to obey most existing laws.

Protestors rarely think that the police should abandon all the rules and shoot them. People who take up social disobedience, for instance by setting up road-blocks, firmly believe that most laws will be obeyed. They do not expect truck drivers to run them down, and rightly so, for the rules they break are usually far less important than the rules they expect to be maintained. But drawing such lines is not always easy.

6. The Appeal to Ignorance (*Argumentum ad Ignorantium*)

The appeal to ignorance says "it's so because you can't prove it false." Appeals of this sort are a kind of inverse appeal to authority. You make your utterance its own authority and put it up for challenge. But, again, this appeal is not always bad. Scientists, for instance, use it. Indeed, one reason why physicists accept the law of gravitation is that no one has yet proven it false. However, neither has it been *proven* true.[2] There are many material bodies in the universe of which we have seen but a fraction. The law of gravitation makes sense of what we see and it hasn't been proved false. Indeed, most scientific laws are accepted because they make sense of the available data *and* they have not been falsified. It is an interesting question—one that we saw, in part, in Chapter 6—as to whether, indeed, there must be very general "organizing hypotheses," root assumptions that approach such a point of generality that the best we can say about them is that they have not been falsified. The problem of the "appeal to ignorance" is that it depends *solely* on the claim "you can't prove it false."

7. Appeals to Emotion

Next we must turn to a list of appeals to emotion:

> appeals to pity
> appeals to pleasure
> appeals to force, awe and
> appeals to dread.[3]

This list could probably be indefinitely extended. All the items appear to be arguments but actually appeal to feelings and seek to change beliefs illicitly. But once again, we must be careful.

It is one thing to urge that one should help another because that other person deserves pity. It is another thing to arouse someone's pity merely for the sake of making a point. It all depends on whether pity is in order. An alcoholic about to freeze to death on the street surely deserves pity, and because he deserves pity we have a good reason to help him. A philosopher burdened with too many logic students may deserve our sympathy, but hardly our pity.

Appeals to pleasure are more complex. We may try to persuade you by making you feel good about believing what we want you to believe—and that is a trick. We may try to persuade you by urging that the result will increase your pleasure. Whether or not that is a good thing to do depends upon whether or not the pleasure is deserved. (It is acceptable to encourage people to believe that they will receive well-deserved pleasure from doing a certain thing or even from adopting a certain belief.) Finally, we may encourage you to believe that pleasure is *itself* good and that, therefore, you ought to believe *and* act in a way that will optimize pleasure. In that case, we would have to decide whether or not the view that "pleasure is good" is justified.[4]

No doubt frightening people into belief is a very bad practice. But if you were standing under a mountain with an avalanche coming down and thought that the radio warnings were nonsense, we might think it wise to scare you into moving. If you move and live, we may be able to restore your rationality. But if you die in the avalanche, it would give us slight comfort to know that we avoided a logical mistake.

Awe is another matter. Suppose some things are really awesome (and not merely awful). Perhaps one should stand in awe. What we ought not to do, again, is to arouse that emotion in you just for the purpose of persuading you to believe something.

8. *Argumentum ad Hominem*

To be true to tradition, our list must contain something quite different—the *argumentum ad hominem*, the argument directed "at the man." Suppose Smith announces a new theory and we ask, "should we believe a man who smells so bad and is a quirky vegetarian to boot?" The logical point is that the *nature* of the presenter of the argument is quite irrelevant to the *soundness* of the argument presented.

At least, this logical point holds if what we are doing is assessing the *reasoning involved*. It is another matter if, in a court, we need to assess credibility. A jury will do well to ignore the state's witness who has nine previous convictions for perjury. The odds seem to be against such a person telling the truth.

The difference is important: *Reasons* are just as good or as bad whether they come from philosophers or the Pope, the Mayor of Toronto, or the most muddled wino in town. A reason is a reason. It is to be assessed on its logic.

Credibility, however, has to do with truth telling; with the likelihood that the witness was in the right place, with the right skills or the lack of them; with how the observations were made, and so on. So witnesses do differ in credibility. Reasons differ only in logic.

QUICK QUIZ #1

1. The idea of a commonly recognized fallacy seems to involve the belief that common sense can identify bad arguments. Can there be good arguments that bad arguments are bad? Illustrate your answer by reference to some of the fallacies discussed in this chapter.
2. How do you beg a question?
3. Are all arguments from authority bad?
4. If morality is the transcendence of self-interest, must all self-interest be bad?
5. Why did Descartes argue that one should not burn down one's own house in an effort to be rational?
6. How are appeals to ignorance like and unlike appeals to authority?
7. Should one ever appeal to emotion? Does it matter *which* emotion one appeals to? How would you decide the answer to this question?
8. Why do people object to arguments "*ad hominem*"? Are such arguments ever justified?

Explain the following fallacies:
1. Professor Zip told us that democracy is the best form of government. I believe him.
2. When did you stop cheating on your taxes?
3. I criticize the environmentalists as well as the animal rights activists since every zany movement deserves equal amounts of my time.
4. Einstein told us that democracy is the best form of government. He should be taken seriously.
5. No one has ever succeeded in proving that God *does not* exist. It would be foolhardy to deny God's existence.
6. No one has ever succeeded in proving that God *does* exist. It would be foolhardy to assert God's existence.
7. Bring in euthanasia and you will systematically undermine the public's respect for life and the result will be the erosion of our social safety net.
8. You must travel by either car or train. Going by car is slow and difficult. Take the train!
9. The stove worked when you moved in and now it doesn't. What did you do to it?
10. Don't ever drink during the day. Do so and you will end up as a drunk.
11. Yes, you might not do that now. But that's what everyone did in my day.

12. Why trust her view of the basic principles of engineering? Look at her bad taste in clothes.
13. There was no way that I was going to hire Sam as my fashion consultant. I mean, look at him; he is so badly dressed.

9. The Search for a Theory of Fallacy

So far the discussion has proceeded at the common sense level. Since most common fallacies concern questions of relevance, let us give our discussion rational shape by trying to give a theory of relevance.

Consider the sentence "Bishop George opposes birth control."[5] This cannot stand by itself as a reason for you to oppose birth control. It would need to be connected to other premises in an argument. For instance, the following argument is valid:

> Bishop George opposes birth control.
> *You ought to oppose whatever Bishop George opposes.*
> You ought to oppose birth control.

However, this is not a usual kind of argument. In fact, Roman Catholics do not believe that they ought to oppose everything the Pope opposes. The Pope's authority is only in a narrowly defined area of "faith and morals" *and* when he speaks "*ex cathedra*," i.e., with the full official weight of his office. In practice there are complex procedures for making such pronouncements. Even then, they are binding only on the faithful who have carefully examined their own consciences. Catholic authorities would treat even the following argument with caution.

> X is official church doctrine.
> *Y is a Roman Catholic.*
> Therefore Y ought to believe X.

10. The Question of Relevance

Douglas Walton raises the question of relevance.[6] He has shown that it is quite difficult to clarify exactly what "relevance" means. He has also indicated some important factors regarding the cause of *irrelevance*. We will discuss three, and then go on to some others.[7]

The first is when there is too little overlap between the subject matters of the pairs of propositions that form the basis of an argument. The second is when redundant premises are used (or misused). The third is when there is an absence of appropriate premises.

11. The Overlap of Subject Matters

Consider the Bishop George argument. For it to work, its concepts must mark out some appropriate ground in such a way that, in combination, they acquire a firmer grip on it than either would separately. If it is important to know what God intends for unborn souls, then if Bishop George knows what God intends, what the Bishop says is important.[8] The concepts of "what God intends" and "human actions can bring God's wants about or frustrate them" are what counts.

What the arguer must show is how the various premises are related to this subject matter. The tactic therefore is to map out the crucial concepts and see what ground they cover and how they cover it. Now one might raise questions of relevance of a somewhat different kind and try to firm up the theoretical structure. It is possible to provide a kind of theory, but it is not clear that we know enough to apply this theory except in very small, well-marked domains.

Recall our discussion of determinables and determinates.[9] Every meaningful term that marks out a feature of the world can in principle be arranged in a determinate–determinable hierarchy. For instance, "red" is a meaningful term. It is one way of being coloured. "Red" is a determinate of the determinable "colour." "Green, "blue," "yellow" and so on would be other determinates of "colour." However, "colour" itself is one way of occupying space. "Colour" is a determinate of the determinable "space." "Measurable extension" and "dimensionality" are other determinates of "space." A determinate form on one level is generally the determinable that forms the next level below it. Thus "yellowness" is a determinate form of "colour" but it is the determinable of such colours as "canary yellow" and "lemon yellow."

Now, suppose someone wants to make an assertion about redness. The things that are relevant to redness will be other terms that belong to the same region, such as other things in space, and that can influence or be related to colours. Not everything, though, *can* be red. Consider the following valid argument:

> P is red.
> *P is an angel.*
> Therefore, P is a red angel.

This may be unsound since the premises violate the rule about determinates and determinables. As we have seen, "red" is a determinate of "colour," which in turn is a determinate of "space." But, many people think that angels are non-spatial beings. So "angel" could not be a determinate of "space." Therefore, angels and red things are most likely NOT members of the same region of the determinate–determinable hierarchy. That is, they are irrelevant to each other. In sum, there cannot be red angels.

Again, arguments like "Jones is a conservative and Jones has children, therefore Jones is a conservative father" are examples of equivocal terms. But they are also examples of meanings belonging to different sectors of the determinate–determinable hierarchy and are therefore irrelevant to one another. It is not clear that we *have* the kind of knowledge that would be needed to apply this theory, but it is often useful to ask oneself where in the determinate–determinable hierarchy to put the relevant terms.

12. The Redundant Premise

This kind of irrelevance consists of adding unnecessary premises. Sometimes it is harmless except for the spurious new weight given to the argument. For example, suppose that we have a *valid* argument such as:

> God wants to maximize the world's goodness.
> *Maximizing the world's goodness requires maximizing the number of free moral agents.*
> Therefore, anything that reduces the number of free moral agents opposes what God wants.

It does not help the argument to add the premise "Bishop George also opposes birth control," though the addition adds a certain spurious weight.

Recall that adding a premise to a theoretically valid argument cannot change the validity of that argument whereas the validity of *practical* arguments can always be changed by adding a new premise. This is because theoretical arguments only relate a succession of propositions to each other. The concepts concerned succeed or fail in marking out the appropriate territory. If they do so successfully, other propositions are genuinely irrelevant to them. But *practical* arguments recommend some course of action and are relevant to every belief that the agent holds.

Think of it this way. An agent must commit the whole of himself or herself with each action. It is not your foot that is guilty if you kick an old person out of the way as you scramble on to the bus. It is you. It is not your brain that deserves the prize if you discover a cure for AIDS. It is you.

Since the whole of the agent is involved, whether or not one should catch the 9 o'clock ferry from Halifax to Dartmouth depends on all of one's commitments and obligations as well as on all of one's hopes and fears. Any new information therefore may change the validity of the argument. New premises are redundant in practical arguments only if they do not bear on any of the elements that might influence choices. But to know what these irrelevancies are one has to know everything about the agent.

13. The Missing Premise in a Valid Argument

Examples of practical reasoning also give us a notion of what it is to be missing an appropriate premise even though we may have what seems to be a valid argument. Suppose we have the following practical argument:

Smith needs feed for his pigs.
There is no feed in the Kitchener shops.
There are no trucks and no trains.
Jones will lend Smith his pickup.
There is pig feed in Mount Forest.
Smith ought to drive to Mount Forest to pick up feed.

But a premise seems to be missing. Smith is an Old Order Mennonite who believes that driving cars is immoral. The conclusion, without the premise about his religious beliefs, commits him to some kind of wrong act, namely driving motor vehicles. Before we know whether he should do so or not, we need to know more still. Will his pigs die if he turns down Jones' offer? Does his religion permit exceptions for emergencies?

14. The Argument Situation

Walton also notices three other problems of relevance. The first deals with the way arguments go between participants and with the exchange of commitments. Basically, arguments tend to have more than one person and take place in a context. The context determines, in part, what is relevant and what is irrelevant. The second deals with the different kinds of refutation. There is a difference between showing that an argument fails outright and showing that a reasonable person would reject it. The third deals with the problem of symmetry in the exchange of arguments. In some contexts it is indeed reasonable to make use of one's opponent's premises.

15. The Exchange of Commitments

The first problem suggests a different way of looking at some *ad hominem* arguments—not exactly the kind that we discussed, but still arguments that attack the arguer. Indeed, arguments have a context. One may argue with another philosopher, or a political opponent in parliament, or be engaged in a formal debate. During the argument, one's rival makes various concessions. Some arguments simply involve persuading one's opponent or a third party. Once a majority of the members of the decision-making body have agreed on what law, that is what the law *is*. So it is crucial to assemble a majority. Without a majority, a legal vacuum may result.

This almost happened in Canada over the abortion question. It was difficult to assemble a majority on any position regarding abortion. But legal vacuums are not *necessarily* bad. Some argued that it was wise not to have any laws regarding abortion. Nonetheless, few would argue that it would be wise to have a legal vacuum regarding murder or even gun control.

Majority decisions are assembled by a give-and-take process. So it is fair to protest when someone makes a concession in a debate and then simply withdraws it. A perfectly *fair* position for someone to take at the beginning of the debate, or for a subsequent newcomer to take, would be *unfair* if taken by someone who had already made the relevant concession.

Behind this, perhaps, is a deeper issue. To argue, people must first agree on many things. Philosophers often fail to persuade other philosophers because there is no common ground. A Heideggerian who follows all her master's apparent attacks on logic, for instance, will struggle to find common ground with a logical positivist whose position centres on the acceptability of a certain kind of logic. An orthodox theologian and John Dewey might end up arguing at cross-purposes since they attach different meanings to "God." Arguments are therefore always directed to someone who holds some propositions true, some definitions sound and so on. It is pointless to carry on a discussion outside the range of these agreements.

16. You Can't Prove That!

The second kind of contextual difficulty involves disputes about what is to be proved or refuted. "You can't prove that God doesn't exist" is probably true but usually irrelevant in a theological dispute. It is virtually impossible to prove that there are no black lions or pink swans in the world. Even if you had everything under observation all the time, you might miss them or have defective colour vision. It may be that all an opponent has to show about God or pink swans is that there is no plausible reason to entertain any hypotheses about them.

Recall from our Dewey discussions that one must assign some initial probability to a proposition. One who thinks that rabbits are really cats in rabbit suits, has a difficult task since nobody else thinks this. In such a case the onus is on the arguer. But what about God? Dewey's God is probably met everyday by everyone. But is that true of the Christian God? One must specify what one has in mind.

What Walton calls "weak refutation" will do if the case is one in which what it is reasonable to show is that there is or is not some plausible ground for introducing the hypothesis at all. Something more is needed where the initial probability would, for reasons that have weight, be taken to be high.

17. The Symmetry Problem

The "symmetry" problem relates to both of the other two considerations. Assuming one's opponent's premises is like assuming his or her concessions. Denying one's opponent's premises involves the problem of refutation and its two forms: weak and strong.

Walton maintains that there are different kinds of argumentative dialogues.[10] Suppose you and we agree on some premises and debate what can be inferred from them. We differ, then, over which inference procedures should be adopted. You may refute us by showing that our inference procedure leads to conclusions that are less certain than our shared premises.

But suppose that we hold various kinds of conflicting premises. If you want to disallow some of ours, it might be enough to show that there is simply no positive reason for holding them. This is the weak form of refutation. For example, we may say "God exists" and you say, "there are no grounds for asserting that God exists." Your premises conflict with ours, but they do not contradict one another. You do not really attack our view itself, just the certainty behind it.

Sometimes strong refutation is in order. Suppose that we say "God exists" and this time you take the stronger position and say "God does not exist." Now your premises contradict ours and one side must lose the argument if the other wins.

18. Fallacy and Freedom

Our enquiry has been centred upon the notion that a grasp of the problems of inference and persuasion is central to the generation of genuinely free agents. The problems of relevance suggest ways in which people become muddled and, in effect, have their decisions made for them through the illogical manipulation of confused concepts. The issues about the structure of debate raise questions about freedom in another dimension. Freedom depends, very often, on being able to solve common problems of the sort that dominate political—and other kinds of social—life. If we cannot act together, we become the victims of a decaying environment or an economic system running out of control. Hence, to a great extent freedom depends on our capacity to develop devices that enable us to make collective decisions.

But like many of the arguments, freedom also depends on being able to think clearly about all sorts of subject matters. In the post-9/11 world where many conflicts are essentially doctrinal disputes over which participants seem unable to rationally debate, learning to reason about delicate subjects such as religion is vital.

This is a good point at which to begin to look at logic in some specific circumstances, beginning with religion.

QUICK QUIZ #2

1. Do we need a theory about why fallacies are fallacious?
2. Must the premises of an argument be relevant to one another?
3. Must the subject matters in an argument be connected in any particular way?
4. Are redundant premises bad?
5. Why is it particularly important to look for "missing premises" in practical arguments? Why is this a logical problem that does not arise in the same way in theoretical arguments?
6. How is the "argument situation" relevant to settling disputes?
7. Must there be mutual commitments between participants if debates are

to proceed rationally?

8. What do you do when someone says "you can't prove it's not so?"
9. What is meant by "the symmetry problem"?
10. How is the identification of fallacies related to one's freedom as a rational agent?

Notes

1. For more details see Douglas N. Walton, *Topical Relevance in Argumentation,* Amsterdam: John Benjamins, 1982. See also his *Informal Fallacies,* Amsterdam: John Benjamins, 1987, and *Handbook for Critical Argumentation,* Cambridge: The University Press, 1989.
2. For a discussion of questions like this, see Karl Popper, *Objective Knowledge,* Oxford: Clarendon Press, 1972, 1981. Also, see chapter ten of this book.
3. Evans, Gamertsfelder and Nelson, *Elements of Logic*, Dubuque, Iowa: William C. Brown, 1957.
4. That, of course, depends on many issues, some of which, though only some, will turn up when we come to talk explicitly about moral reasoning.
5. Bishop George is simply a fictional character.
6. *Topical Relevance,* see footnote 1 of this chapter.
7. The following owes much to Walton's work, although we have departed from some of his views and so he should not be blamed for the developments.
8. This is not meant to be a ludicrous example. The Roman Catholic Church believes that the Holy Spirit guides its work. But determining how that guidance does, or is likely to, manifest itself is admitted to be a complex matter.
9. W.E. Johnson, *Logic*, Three Volumes, Cambridge: The University Press, 1921–1924. (Also see our Chapter 5 on dialectical logics.)
10. Walton is drawing on Jaakko Hintikka and Esa Saarinen, "Information-Seeking Dialogues: Some of their Logical Properties," *Studia Logica,* Vol. 38, 1979, p. 355–63.

Part IV: Logic and Knowledge

Chapter 9

LOGIC AND RELIGION

This chapter involves two distinct issues. The first is how one reasons when faced with apparently irresolvable conflicts that depend on rival basic beliefs. The second is how introducing the concept of God affects one's logical system.

1. How Can We Argue about Rival Basic Beliefs?

The last chapter's discussion about how the structure of debates bears on arguments is relevant here. Insofar as religion influences conduct and society's organization, it is obvious in our modern pluralistic communities that some way must be found which will enable members of rival religions to live together.

When people have fundamental beliefs that collide head-on, should they simply kill each other? The question seems absurd, but there are currently about thirty wars in the world that have their origins in such disputes. Suppose that each group believes that it has *the* truth and that it would be better if the others had the truth as well. It may be that if the others are all killed, God will ensure that they have the truth. However, in *this* world, one has neither truth nor falsehood after death. So the issue seems not to be the truth we will all have after death but the truth some of us have and some of us don't have in this world. The first step in this case is to keep everybody alive.

2. Can One Person Make Another Do Something?

R.G. Collingwood once observed that no one can actually make anyone do or believe anything.[1] For instance, we could kill people, but that won't make them believe the truth. So one has to keep others alive and reason with them, not force them. Moreover, people must be well enough fed to think clearly and act on the truth when they find it. So we *can* argue about how we should *treat* others who believe differently.

The great philosopher Blaise Pascal said that if God exists, he has not told us who is saved and who is damned.[2] But he expects us to treat the saved as if they were saved. How we treat the damned probably doesn't matter, but since we don't know who is damned, the only way to be sure that God approves of what we do is to treat everyone as saved.

But can we also *argue* about our rival beliefs? Many hold that religion deals only with fundamental beliefs that cannot be countered by still more basic beliefs. Many hold that religion stands upon direct revelation, which one either has or has not.

3. Religious Concepts Have Logical Properties

But "direct revelation" is questionable. That is, religious beliefs use concepts and we have seen that concepts have logical properties and relations to other concepts. So there is a "logic" of these concepts. Moreover, we can explore this logic, investigate whether there is a special "logic" of religious concepts or a general logic for all concepts.

4. Are There Principles of Inference Valid for all Subject Matters?

However, one must be cautious. It used to be fashionable to talk about the "logic" of almost everything. For instance, the noted historian of logic, William Kneale, once remarked:

> if we think that the logic of tradition has been concerned primarily with principles of inference valid for all possible subject matters, we must reject as unprofitable an extension of usage which allows such phrases as "the logic of 'God.'"[3]

Kneale rejected the view that the workings of *particular* concepts form the subject matter of something properly called logic. He suggested that we might rename arithmetic "the logic of 'numeral',", mechanics "the logic of 'force',", and analytical economics "the logic of 'price'."

One may respond that many justifiable inferences derive their validity from the ways in which the concepts they employ fit together, and that they cannot easily be justified by reference to the concepts that logicians have most often chosen to examine.[4] And one might well say that official logic relies too heavily on "the logic of 'and,' 'or,' and 'if..., then'."

But suppose that logic involves "principles of inference valid for all subject matters." Now suppose that a given logic cannot handle a particular subject matter. Do we keep the logic and reject the subject matter as irrational or unintelligible? Or, do we keep the subject matter and modify our logic?

5. The Special Problems of the Concept of God

Such questions arise when the subject matter is the concept "God," the concept of an omnipotent, omniscient and perfect being. We can deal with this subject area by modifying our logic. So this might be an occasion for talking about the particular "logic of 'God'."

Recall that Aristotle and Lukasiewicz modified logic when faced with the problem of future contingencies. It is certainly not controversial to speak about the future in terms of everyday language. The concept of the future had a legitimate place in everyday discourse and this motivated logicians to modify logic to accommodate it.

But the concept of God is different than the concept of the future. It may be that there are logical reasons for saying that the concept of God has *no* legitimate place in our discourse and so why even bother trying to modify logic in order to accommodate it?

If it should turn out, therefore, that, to accommodate it, we had to make adjustments in our logic, we should expect independent reasons for this adjustment to be forthcoming before the possibility would be of great interest. Part of what we shall try to do, therefore, is to show that there might be such reasons, though our aim is to open up a line of enquiry rather than to complete its exploration.

The first difficulty is in getting the concept of God into our discourse at all. Recall that Aristotelian syllogisms can only be constructed out of components which have forms such as "All S is P," "Some S is P," "No S is P" and "Some S is not P." In general, a logic must have formation rules to have inference rules.

The formation rules depend partly upon the kinds of inferences proposed and partly upon the requirement that it be possible to use these rules to say something intelligible. If we want inference rules for all possible subject matters, we should be able to use our formation rules to say everything intelligible.

6. Logic and the Assignment of Predicates

The traditional formation rules enable us to arrange predicates into patterns. For example: The logical form "All S is P" marks out a subject "S" and says a number of things about it. First, all cases of S have something in common: they are all P. If S and P are filled in, it turns out that what we substitute for S (or P) will be a predicate that designates a property. Since there are rules for exchanging the positions of S and P, they are not intended to be of logically different kinds.

We have seen that in modern elementary logic:

"All S is P" would be expressed as $(\forall x)(\text{If } Fx \text{ then } Gx)$
"Some S is P" would be expressed as $(\exists x)(Fx \text{ and } Gx)$

The point of these examples is to illustrate that we identify "x's" by assigning predicates to them.

Predicates convey information about their subjects. For example, suppose we say:

Sally is smart.

The predicate "is smart" conveys information about Sally. Suppose we say:

> Joe is not smart.

The predicate is now being denied of Joe. So the Sally case involves a positive predication while the Joe case is a denial. However, in both cases we are given some information about the subjects.

In general it would seem that to get a subject matter into our discourse, we have to mark it off from other things by assigning it some predicates and denying it others. Once it has been marked off, *then* we can use our inference rules to reason about it. However, if we cannot mark the subject area off, it would seem that we cannot reason about it at all. But we shall see that funny things happen when we try to mark off the concept of God.

7. Does the Concept of God Swallow all the Predicates?

Recall that "God" is omnipotent, that is, all-powerful. In other words, omnipotence is the property of having all possible powers. But think about positive predicates: suppose that X is red. This X has two powers. First, X has the power to appear red. Now suppose that you have some Y that is green. Someone who is colour-blind might (mistakenly) see Y as red. So in one sense, Y has the power, like X, to appear red.

But there is a crucial difference between X and Y. Someone who is not colour-blind would see Y as green. Now suppose that you have a being that could not possibly be wrong about the colour it sees. Regardless of any tricks or lighting conditions, X would appear red to the being and Y would appear green. This is X's second power: the power to appear red to someone who cannot be deceived about colours. Y certainly does not have X's second power. Only other "truly" red things would have X's second power. Y's second power would be the power to appear green to someone who cannot be deceived about colours. The point is this. *Every positive predicate seems to denote a particular power.*

Because God is all-powerful, to mark off God we must assign him all the positive predicates. But here lies the problem. Suppose we want to talk about some Z. We mark out Z by assigning it a particular combination of predicates. However, this combination will also mark out some aspect of God. By introducing God we have introduced a fundamental ambiguity into our discourse.

QUICK QUIZ #1

1. Is it possible to argue about our most basic beliefs?
2. Can changes in human behaviour and/or belief really be brought about by force?
3. Must religious concepts have some of the same logical properties as nonreligious concepts?

4. Are there principles of inference valid for all subject matters?
5. Do we succeed in talking about things chiefly by assigning them some predicates and withholding others?
6. How does defining God as perfect lead to the ambiguity problem?
7. How does defining God as omniscient lead to the ambiguity problem?
8. Is the ambiguity problem really a problem?

---

8. How is God Separate from the World?

Something else appears to have all the predicates, although in a strange way. We might call this something else "the sum total of all possibilities." To mark this off we would use all the positive predicates. However, it would seem that this collection is not God. Let us consider two attempts to distinguish this collection from God. Both attempts engender problems.

Attempt 1

God is defined as the actualization of this collection of possibilities. But this would identify God and the world. It would seem to defeat our purpose, namely, to talk about the concept of God, not the concept of the world. It also commits us to an impossible account of the world. For in a world in which the actual and the possible coincide, nothing can happen or even seem to happen. That is, the position is that there is something, God, to which all possible predicates, except the negative ones, apply, and that they apply actually and not merely potentially. Thus everything conceivable has an instance and every instance is some aspect of God. If anything new happened, it would have to instantiate some impossibility to be distinguishable from that which, in this case, actually existed.

If something already existing ceased to exist, it would then be the case that something possible had no instance, and that, therefore, some possible power was possessed by nothing—i.e., that God, conceived of as omnipotent in the sense suggested, did not actually exist or that no perfect being existed. But it is a condition of the problem that things do seem to happen—that it happens, for example, that there is one moment at which we do not seem to understand the problem with which we are dealing and another at which we do. A static world is one in which, amongst other things, one cannot do philosophy.

Attempt 2

God is defined as a special combination of the collection of all possibilities. So God is not merely a heterogeneous collection but a very special kind of unity. But is this "special kind of unity" another property? If you say no, then God does not differ from being a mere collection of all possibilities. But there is a problem if you say yes. To see whether some being is omnipotent, you simply list all the possible powers. Logically, if X has all those powers, then X is God. But the collection also has all those powers in the list. So our logic forces us to say that the collection is God. But what property does God have that the collection does not? The problem is that we have already admitted that the collection has *all* the predicates. There are no predicates left over to distinguish God from the collection. In sum, attempt 1 forces us into a static world and attempt 2 leaves us unable to say exactly what God's special unity is.

Theologians have tried to avoid these problems by the doctrine of "analogical predication." This says that God does not have all (or perhaps any) of the typical properties. For instance, God has the power of knowing things but He knows things in a different way than humans know things. So God's power of knowing is the analogue of a human's power of knowing. Theologians have also claimed that human language cannot articulate God's properties as they truly are.

However, if God has the analogues of typical properties, then another problem looms. The powers and perfections that accrue from the ordinary properties will not actually accrue to God, but only some powers and perfections that are like them. And these are not enough to establish omnipotence and perfection since they are not *all* the possible powers and perfections—the ordinary ones are amongst the possible ones, too.

9. Predicates which Designate Ways of Having Properties

Some familiar predicates form an important sub-class in that they seem to mark out not properties but ways of having properties. These predicates are properties of properties. Suppose that, "Joe is educated." But had things been different, Joe might never have gone to school and learned anything. Although "educated" is a property of Joe, it is a contingent or possible property of Joe.

Predicates such as "possible," "impossible," "necessary" and so on seem to designate ways of having predicates. So perhaps God has all the typical properties but he is unique in that He has them necessarily. For instance, God is necessarily omnipotent. Other things have their properties contingently. But they apply necessarily not merely to God but also to the sum total of all possibilities. It is necessarily true of them that, collectively, these predicates have all the possibilities, and this would seem to begin to lead us back to the difficulties which we have just noticed.

This way of putting it opens up a serious question. We have been discussing three things: properties, ways of having properties and objects that have properties. How are we going to mark out the objects except by assigning predicates to them? If we cannot do it this way, then the implication is that there are things to which predicates are assignable but we cannot mark them out by assigning predicates to them. In the context of the schemes for getting subject matters into discourse that we have been talking about, this implies that the things with the properties cannot, themselves, be talked about. They become very like Locke's mysterious substances (of which Locke said they are "an uncertain supposition of we know not what.").[5] Indeed, they are, perhaps, worse off. For they are cases of "something I *could* not know what." They will, indeed, figure nowhere in discourse. This does seem to be a leap from a lukewarm frying pan into a very hot fire.

Faced with such difficulties, perhaps we should simply abandon talk of God. This concept may just make demands that our logical resources cannot meet. Furthermore, some of the difficulties may be *linguistic.* Perhaps the language we have been using has undesirable features and is even rather sloppy. Are some of these problems of our own making?

10. Should We Retreat from the Traditional Concept of God?

It is doubtful that any retreat is possible *with respect to the features of the concept of God that we have discussed in this chapter.* For the concept of God cannot just be the concept of a rather powerful and interesting being. The God of religion is supposed to be worshipped, to be given unconditional allegiance. Those philosophers interested in God are concerned with a being that is unique in a profound sense, or else God would not pose a special philosophical problem. A being that was very powerful but not omnipotent, or very good but not perfect, could not command our unconditional allegiance since he might always change and go wrong in some significant respect.

The traditional natural theology of the West embraces a God who has every possible perfection, who must have the powers and properties that he has, (and who, therefore, is immune to change and error). God cannot, logically, be surpassed in power or perfection by any other being. Any other notion seems to be religiously useless.

The *One* of the Neoplatonists and the *Brahman* of the Hindu tradition are in this respect even more all-embracing, for they include not just all being, but all non-being, too. The One and Brahman transcend *all possible* distinctions, even that between being and non-being. But that only emphasizes the difficulties that we have discussed and raises other difficulties as well.[6] Given all this historical background, we suggest that it would also be sensible to see whether further modifications will enable us to talk sensibly about God or whether the concept should simply be abandoned.

11. More About How Things are Identified

The difficulty regarding the concept of God amounted to this: by assigning predicates to things, we identify them and so get them into our discourse. But it seems that we could not get an unambiguous account of God and so we could not get God into our discourse. If we cannot talk about God, nothing counts as reasoning about the concept of God, let alone establishing that God exists.

Let us look more closely at identifying things. Suppose that you want to talk about pigs. To be sure that you have said something about pigs and not about something else, you must assign enough predicates to your description of pigs to exclude all non-pigs. If you say "pigs are alive," you have separated pigs from sticks and stones. If you say, "pigs suckle their young," you have separated them from everything except other mammals. To finish the job, you have to mark pigs out from other mammals by saying that pigs have bristly skin and a long snout. No doubt even this might not be enough. Suppose that you want to talk about a particular pig. You will have to refer to some point in space and time.

The pig example suggests that behind the procedure for assigning predicates, there have to be organized schemes. When we say, "X has property Y," we are doing two things. We are assigning X predicates and covertly referring to a universe of discourse within which the assignment will function.

But it seems that we only refer to as much of the universe of discourse as necessary. It does not help to make remarks about pigs unless you know something about what you are distinguishing pigs from. Suppose someone commands, "look for the bristly, snouty thing at position P." This command may *seem* helpful even if you don't know what you want to distinguish pigs from. We imagine that you would just go to "P" and look. But to even find P we must know that P differs from other positions and how P relates to those positions. Moreover, one may see indefinitely many things "at P." So we must know just how the expression "bristly snouty thing" is supposed to function.

For practical purposes, we need only a limited scheme for finding pigs. For theoretical purposes, we want assurance that we have not confused the pigs with something else. That is, we need an account of a universe of discourse complicated enough to prevent confusing pigs with anything else whatever. Otherwise we shall never know whether we have really succeeded in introducing an adequate notion of "pig" into our discourse, or whether we have confused it with something else from which it could have been distinguished. Of course we may never be able to achieve this ideal but we should want to know that it was, in principle, possible. Meanwhile, our discourse retains certain merely provisional aspects.

12. Talking About Everything

To mark an X out from other things one must refer, in some way, to all the other things from which X is marked out. To get an adequate description of "pig," you have, ideally, to be able to supply an adequate description of everything. Propositions that genuinely mark out, genuinely refer to everything that can be talked about in an intelligible way.

Thus there is established a complex set of inter-relations that is all embracing. In a sense, then, if we were searching for an ideal mode of discourse, we would have to drag the whole universe along with all the distinctions we wished to make. Everything has to be seen, for such a purpose, as related to and, indeed, intertwined with everything else—for the process of individualization is, itself, only finally possible when the complete context is supplied.

Normally, when we identify a particular class of objects (pigs) or a particular object (Porky), only a fraction of the system is involved. But the whole system might be needed in some cases, for instance, identifying the concept of God. However, even the entire system proves insufficient since it depends upon our using some of our predicates to exclude others. Naturally, we cannot quite get the concept into the system though we may think we can almost grasp it.

We have seen that if we want to be certain that we're talking about a particular pig, we need to mark that pig off from everything else. In other words, our particular pig is related to everything else. If anything else were different, the position marked out for our pig would be different, and the description required for the pig would also be different. If we were to construe the pig's relational properties as essential to some wider sense of the pig's description, we could then say that the pig's complete description entailed the complete description of everything. On this view, the universe would best be regarded as a single entity, and the particular components of it would be best considered as aspects of it to which we call attention by the manner and order in which we focus our descriptions.

We could not directly distinguish a thing by assigning properties to it, since all properties would turn up in every description. Moreover, we could not distinguish a thing by the way we ordered its properties for assigning and ordering would involve some measure of falsification. To assign some properties to X and exclude other properties, we have to assume the independence of X from other things. But this assumption is false since everything is dependent for the appropriateness of its description on everything else.

Now let us consider another procedure for distinguishing things. We admit that, to distinguish an X from the other things, X has to be related to all these other things. We want to organize the ways of distinguishing things into a hierarchy. First, every concept can be understood as a concept of the whole. Second, each concept is unique in the way it uses the whole to focus on a particular feature (or features) of it. That is, each concept will distinguish an X by excluding some aspects of the whole and including others.

So the concepts at the bottom of the hierarchy use the description of the whole to single out a particular feature, which we interpret as a thing or a property. As we move up the hierarchy, the concepts use the description of the whole to single out a feature. But they do so by excluding less and less.

The concept at the top of the hierarchy will exclude nothing to identify its feature of the universe. Presumably, this feature will be what we have called "perfection," the property of lacking nothing. This top concept cannot be thought of as the concept of a separate designatable thing—for there is nothing in this case with which to contrast it.

But we can distinguish the concept of "perfection" from the concept of the "sum total of all possibilities" or from their actualization. The concept of the "sum total" is the concept of something divisible into particular instantiations, and their actualization is their instantiation. The concept of "perfection" is to be regarded as a very close unity. left over when the residual error that accrued from implied atomization is removed. Think of it like this: The concept of perfection does not identify a thing; rather, it is that which makes the ultimate notion of an individual thing itself possible.

13. The Unity of Things

This is a rather conventional argument pattern that leads to one of the possibilities we discussed in the chapter on dialectical logics. But our interest is primarily to find (if possible) a way to talk about a perennial philosophical topic, the question of whether or not God exists.

In these terms, all properties will be reflected in such a concept but in a different way than the one previously envisaged. Whether this notion serves to make sense of the other features normally associated with the concept of God is, of course, another matter. For some of the problems posed by this are, themselves, difficult and peculiar. It is usually thought that the concept of God requires not only the features already talked about but many others as well. For example, we may ask whether the top concept is also the concept of a "person." The top concept seems to be the concept of that which unites and makes intelligible all distinctions. This is also what the concept of "person" involves. So in some sense, the top concept may also be the concept of a person.

In the course of looking at the pressures brought to bear on our logical schemes by the concept of God, we have seen that there is another way of looking at and classifying things. This other approach arises out of our normal ways of relating to the world.

All we have done is exploit the consequences of taking seriously a way of marking things out from one another so that the concepts we want to employ can be effectively introduced into our discourse. But now we should look at the consequences of introducing peculiar subject matters into our discourse.

There will be a different kind of inference pattern within the hierarchy of concepts. In such a scheme, we are dealing with concepts, not propositions. The range of concepts required depends upon the particular structures of the concepts with which we are concerned. Each concept attempts to conceptualize the whole of whatever is conceptualizable, since each purports to reflect the whole from a certain vantage point. To get the complete system of concepts, one will have recourse to the particular focusing aspects of each concept, and one must show how the workings of each of them requires the workings of the others to get the complete scheme.

For example, Hegel's logic is a scheme of this kind as one works from concept to concept by showing how they are dialectically related, that is, how the nature of each concept affects the next. But we shall meet more of these relations when we pass from religion to science—the subject of our next chapter.

QUICK QUIZ #2

1. If God is omnipotent must the concept of God swallow all the predicates? If so, can one talk about anything *other* than God?
2. How can one tell when one is talking about God and when one is talking about the world?
3. Discuss the problem of talking about the ways of having properties or predicates.
4. Is the traditional concept of God that was developed in Western philosophy outmoded?
5. How does one talk about one thing and not another without also talking about everything? Can one really do this?
6. Why is the notion that things always form a unity worth discussing?

Notes

1. *The New Leviathan,* Oxford: Clarendon Press, 1942, Part I, Ch XIII.
2. First published in 1670. See the modern edition of Louis Lafuma, Paris: Delmas, 2 vol., 1948, revised 1952, 1960, Pensée #11 in this edition, and in the English translation by John Warrington, London: Dent, 1960 (Everyman Vol. 874). Lafuma's #11 is Pensée #194 in the much-used Brunschvicg numbering (Paris: Hachette, 1950).
3. William and Martha Kneale, *The Development of Logic*, Oxford: Clarendon Press, 1962, p. 741. (William Kneale wrote this particular passage.)
4. See Gilbert Ryle, *Dilemmas,* Cambridge: The University Press, 1954, chapter VIII.
5. John Locke, *An Essay Concerning Human Understanding,* Bk I. Ch. IV, Section 18, Peter Nidditch, (editor), Oxford: Clarendon Press, 1975.
6. There are special difficulties about the One and Brahman, with respect to knowledge (how can we grasp them?), and with respect to their relations to the world (how can that which is said to admit no distinctions whatsoever be said to be related or not related?).

Chapter 10

LOGIC AND SCIENTIFIC INQUIRY

From the logic problems involving religion, we now turn to those involving science. Religion and science are related in many ways, although they may not seem to be. In general, both involve the truth and falsity of broad assertions about the world. The existence of God or the next world seem to be alleged matters of fact and seem to be so at least as obviously as the existence of quarks or the reality of n-dimensional spaces.

1. How Science is Like and Unlike Religion

Obviously there are differences between science and religion. Faith may play a role in each, but many say that it is a different role. People think religion bears more directly on morality than science does. For instance, consider the following. Suppose that God disapproves of casual sex. This alone might seem— *does seem to believers*—to be a good reason for restraining one's conduct. But suppose that science could make casual sex perfectly safe. This alone, according to many, certainly to the same believers, would *not* be a good reason for indulging in it.

But now consider the following: suppose that God disapproves of kindness to sick children. We doubt that many, on the basis of this alone, would stop being kind to sick children. Suppose that science were to establish that making holes in the ozone layer will lead to the destruction of humanity. This alone would be a good reason for changing our conduct. So the issues are not simple and can be disentangled slowly as we begin to explore at least some features of scientific reasoning, and then (in the next chapter) to look more closely at questions about morality.

The logic of scientific discourse depends on serious puzzles that arise when one asks two basic questions. The first is: "What is science about?" The second is: "What are we looking for when we look for scientific evidence?" These questions have much in common; however, they are not identical.

2. Science and Empirical Generalization

We begin by considering the traditional, "Baconian view" of the logic of science.[1] The Baconian view holds that science proceeds by empirical generalization. One gathers many facts and then searches for patterns among the facts. As instances that match the patterns are accumulated, "laws" are developed. For instance, the "law of gravitation" summarizes our observations of the movements of physical bodies under various conditions. The theory of evolution summarizes the evidence gathered from geology, palaeontology, embryology and genetics.

But the Baconian view has problems. It supposes that we *find* the patterns in things—as if we first randomly collect data and then determine that it has patterns. But nobody goes about randomly gathering data. People gather facts to test particular hypotheses they already have. So people search where they think that they will find the appropriate facts to support (or disconfirm) their view.

Doesn't this search for *appropriate* facts make us into the prosecutor who insists that the butler is guilty and then gathers evidence against the butler while ignoring evidence against anyone else? Might she not discover altogether too many suspicious facts about the butler while failing to find the real culprit? But on the other hand, could we even gather facts randomly? Finally, it is not easy to say what a fact is as opposed to a theory.

If we could get over these problems, we would then face problems not about the "logic of discovery" but about the "logic of assembly." For however many bodies we inspect, it does not follow that *all* bodies obey the "law of gravitation." This raises the classical problem of induction. There seems to be something illicit in passing from statements about *some* instances of x, to statements about *all* instances of x.

We could meet this by claiming to derive our beliefs only from those observed instances of x to the *next* instance of x. This greatly reduces our chance of large errors. But does it justify the claim? Apparently. Failing that, we could stop talking about "the next x" and talk about the "probability" of the next x being a "y" (where "y" is the property about which we are trying to generalize.) But is this any better? Does it not imply that we know something about the distribution of x's in the universe such that we can tell something about the likelihood of its being a y or a not-y? If the x's are all coins, and the choice is between believing that they are heads-up or tails-up, we may be able to say something about the distribution. Other things being equal, we might claim, we shall expect to find them half heads and half tails, and the likelihood that the next x we find will be a y is precisely one half.

We do not, however, know what chance there is that dinosaurs occupy one place in the evolutionary scale or another, what chance there is that a given universe will have a three-dimensional space (what is the largest possible number of dimensions?), or what the odds are that gravitational attraction holds for a given physical system.

3. The Philosophy of Inductive Generalization

Philosophers have laboured to find a basis for inductive generalization and have proposed many fascinating solutions. But they have not been very successful at convincing one another. They have greater success at persuading one another that the situation is paradoxical than they have had at eliminating the paradoxes. Consider the following:

(1) All crows are black.

By contraposition we have:

(2) All non-black things are non-crows.

Now, (1) is logically equivalent to (2). Therefore, whatever evidence supports (1) also supports (2) and vice versa. But now consider:

(3) A red fire engine is a non-black thing and is a non-crow.

Clearly (3) supports (2) and so (3) would support (1) as well. But searching the world collecting non-black, non-crow things to support (1) would be a bad way of doing science. Suppose that someone actually does this. Should we judge him or her mad?

Consider how our Baconian view answers our two basic questions about science. The Baconian view assumes that:

(i)   Science is about the world.
(ii) One should examine the world in as neutral a way as possible.
(iii) The possibility of science is related to the possibility that there are patterns in nature that lead to scientific laws.

QUICK QUIZ #1

1. Explain the difference between faith in religion and faith in science.
2. Explain how someone could argue that finding a green shoe in a closet is evidence for "All zebras are striped." Should someone argue in this way? Defend your answer.
3. Why is it often said that science is based on empirical generalization? What difficulties does such a view pose?

---

4. John Dewey's Critique of the Baconian View

In a scheme like Dewey's these assumptions quickly dissolve. First, one does not search for general laws in the Baconian way; rather, one seeks to solve specified problems. Second, one bases one's choices on one's initial view of the likelihood (*however* one determines these choices) and then modifies one's theories as one's experience confirms or disconfirms the expectations one has developed. On Dewey's view, science is not literally "about the world" but about the basis for predictions about our experience of the world. In Dewey's view, we translate statements about the world into statements about what people experience, and statements about scientific inference into statements about how experience develops or becomes stunted. We abandon "induction" for techniques that strengthen or weaken our existing pattern of beliefs. We could still ask: how do we know we won't fall up instead of down when we jump out the window? But on Dewey's view, the issue is about what it is reasonable to claim as justified belief.

We suppose that one would claim "the future" means "the experiences that come after the ones I am having now." As we have seen, "the future" must be sufficiently like the past for it to count as a set of experiences. One would then investigate what one could justifiably believe about the continuing structure of experience. Dewey is less clear about the line between "experience" and "the world" than we suggest, but he would insist that this distinction would require its justification in claims about the instrumental value of its component propositions as devices for understanding experience.

5. Sir Karl Popper and Falsification

Sir Karl Popper offered a simpler solution than Dewey. Popper claimed that it is a mistake to try to confirm a scientific hypothesis.[2] For instance, to confirm that "all crows are black," one must check all the crows in the entire universe. So Popper says we should not try to *confirm* hypotheses but try to *falsify* them.

We can falsify the hypothesis "all crows are black" with a single observation, that of a non-black crow. A hypothesis that could be falsified, but has not yet been, has a certain claim to reasonableness. Its claim depends upon the fact that, so long as we hold this hypothesis, if we go on with our observation, we stand a chance of finding out in the event that it *is* false.

Popper's view retains the possibility that science is "about the world" and provides a fairly clear notion about what counts as evidence in science. Nonetheless, we do not have any way of estimating the likelihood that a currently accepted hypothesis will someday be falsified. For all we know, every one of our present hypotheses is false, but none of them will ever be shown to be false.

6. The Problem of the Black Crows

Consider the crow problem. Some properties of crows seem to be rather loosely associated with the others while at least some would appear to be crucial. If a white bird, otherwise like a crow, turned up, we would probably call it a crow. If something turned up that belonged to a whole inter-breeding group none of whose members could fly at all but all of whose members were otherwise like crows, we might be more doubtful. In a sense, these are only definitional problems, but if one looks at them more closely, they become more complicated.

The species lepidoptera consists of creatures that pass through several stages in their lives—egg, pupa, caterpillar and moth. We *can* regard them as a single creature just as we regard the tadpole and the frog as the same creature in different stages of its life. The fact that we so regard them causes certain problems in biology. There is a direction or path in the lives of such creatures and it needs to be explained. If we regarded each stage as a different creature, we would have quite a different problem.

So the result of falsifying a hypothesis is not entirely clear. Have we just lost an arbitrary definition? Have we wrongly dealt with a class of things? Or have we wrongly assumed that several different things form a single unit? Can't we always regroup our forces and go on—as scientists did when they found they had to keep formulating more and more complicated hypotheses about "the ether"?

One way to get a tighter logical organization is to adopt what has come to be called the *hypothetico-deductive* method. On this plan, one uses one's original idea simply to suggest general laws. Then one makes formal deductions from them: "*If* anything is a physical body, it attracts other physical bodies directly as its mass and indirectly as the square of the distance between them. This *is* a physical body, therefore, it does attract other bodies..." *Then* one constructs an experiment designed to test precisely the property that has been deduced. All that is *necessary* in the scheme is a certain logical relation between the original hypothesis and the conclusion. It can indeed be given a probabilistic interpretation. "If anything is an x, then in nine cases out of 10, it will also be a y." (Here one must have a sample of sufficient minimal size to allow the probability to be checked.) Thus one avoids the classical problem of "induction" and also specifies the requirements so as to make it clear what it is that is open for falsification.

It is, nevertheless, *still* true that all our hypotheses might be false and never be known to be false. For the sample checked may not be representative, the range of falsifiable claims in the original hypothesis is certain not to have been completely explored (how many entailments does a single proposition have?) and so on. Here, the method only suggests that one behave reasonably in the face of one's hypothesis; it does not guarantee that the hypothesis is any good.

QUICK QUIZ #2

1. Discuss John Dewey's critique of the "Baconian" view of science.
2. Why did Sir Karl Popper think that falsification is more important than confirmation?
3. If Popper's view were closely followed would it lead to unnecessarily

frequent abandonment of hypotheses? Why or why not?
4. Explain why Popper's view, if closely followed, would not instil confidence in someone deciding whether or not to cross a bridge.

---

7. Kuhn, Hesse, Harré and the Nature of Scientific Models

As a result of all these and other issues, some philosophers in recent years—including Thomas Kuhn in the United States, Mary Hesse, R. M. Harré and others in England—have suggested a quite different account of the logic of scientific discourse.[3] They propose that when we are enquiring into a state of affairs, we actually employ models that we understand to cast light upon that which we don't understand. For example, traditional mechanics is based on the idea of machines whose basic parts move and make contact with one another. These moving and bumping parts produce a predictable distribution of forces. The properties of the "model" can be worked out. Think of how one could use a tinker-toy model to explain to a child how a real building crane works. One would describe the model (articulate its properties) to the child and show the child the real crane. The model captures the basic idea of the real crane.

Scientists use models to capture the basic idea of what happens in nature. Sometimes the model does not quite fit with what we see and so the properties of the model are adjusted accordingly. Sometimes, though, the fit between the model and the world is so bad that the model is eventually rejected in favour of a better one.

Stephen Toulmin once gave a useful example:[4] We have always known that the shadows cast by walls are proportionate to the height of the wall and the angle of incidence of the light source. The scientific "discovery" was not of new facts, but of the development of a suitable model. If one asserts that light travels, the explanation becomes clear—i.e., we can understand what is going on by imagining particles of light moving from the light source toward the wall and being impeded by it.

8. What Newton Didn't Discover

Newton did not make discoveries about strange facts. (It was known that bodies fall, before the apple hit him on the head.) Rather, Newton rejected the older attempt to explain motion and developed a new model to use in physics. Newton's model assumes that bodies move at a uniform velocity in a uniform direction unless something interferes with them. What has to be explained is apparent "deviation" from Newton's laws of motion. Given the model, we can quite easily understand what is going on. Models are neither verified nor falsified. They are strengthened or weakened, and we change them when they become weak and extend them by deducing new properties from them when they are strong.

So Toulmin suggested that scientific theories are not really descriptions of the world, but rather like train-tickets that enable us to get about in the system. We want to move from one experience to another. The model suggests how it may be done. If we don't get there, we invest more energy and buy ourselves a different ticket. Toulmin emphasized the pragmatic features of the situation. But Thomas Kuhn and Mary Hesse emphasized the extent to which the models or paradigms that enter into "scientific explanations" reflect the cultures in which they arise. Our habits of thought make it likely that some explanations will be intelligible and thus satisfy us.

Mary Hesse stressed that some disputes, such as the one between science and religion, take on a different character if one grasps the role played by models, paradigms, or analogies. (Sometimes these terms are interchangeable but not always, or not completely. A model is a device within which some relations are clear and intelligible because, perhaps one built it that way. A paradigm is something that one takes as the most obvious or certain case from which to make one's inferences. An analogy is a relationship between two things that are alike in some clear respect but in which some properties of one of them remain unknown.) All these readings tend to emphasise the fact that science often works, like the law, somewhat by precedent, and so has a natural and built-in bias toward what is already intelligible.

There is, however, yet another possible account of the matter. One of the problems about scientific discourse is that it puts to work our ordinary observations but draws conclusions from them that seem quite far-fetched.

A Wilson cloud chamber is an ordinary perceptual object—an enclosure within which there is vapour. It is used to distinguish various sorts of basic particles, which, though not visible themselves, leave different kinds of trails in the vapour. These ordinary observations are used to support or weaken theories about those particles even though the particles never enter experience at all.

The theory that relates unobserved or "theoretical" entities to ordinary experiences is not, itself, a part of the science of physics. Physics "explains" ordinary experiences by showing us that vapour trails in the cloud chambers correlate rather well what the theories predict. When we expect certain kinds of particles according to the theory, we do in fact see the appropriate vapour trails.

9. Science and Reality

We are thus inclined to form the view that there is a reality, some theories about it, and some experiences—and that the three are quite different. It is this, in part, which creates the problems about scientific inference. It is assumed that many things exist that we have never experienced, that we have made some observations about, and that we infer the rest by developing techniques for making the "observations" yield the "theories."

On this view, science goes beyond the observations in many ways. General laws include more instances than can be observed. Theoretical entities lie below the threshold of experience. Observations are characterised in formal ways that do not conform exactly to what is observed. For instance, suppose that you observe a ball fall from the top of a building and hit the ground. "What did you see?" We ask. No doubt you would *characterize* your observation as follows, saying "I saw a ball fall from the top of a building until it hit the ground." But you could characterize your observation as follows, saying "At the top of the building I saw a ball which quickly vanished and another ball appeared slightly closer to the ground. This one vanished and another appeared still closer to the ground, and so on." The first characterization, the typical one, presupposes that there is a "continuous object" (i.e., the ball) underneath all the observations. The second characterization does not make this presupposition. Which characterization is correct? Observation alone cannot answer this question. We *choose* the "continuous object" hypothesis because it is simpler. We thus get all the problems we have examined and are left with the view that science is not designed to give us knowledge about the world but, perhaps, train-tickets for getting around in it.

It is, however, possible to take another view. It seems likely that what one sees does not have a univocal character. One may analyze one's perceptions either into constituent objects of perception, into "sense data," or into sequential appearances explained by theoretical entities. There is no reason to think that one of these is primary. The situation is like the one we face when we sit down to read a book. We try to make sense of the book though we often find that there are many alternative meanings available—a fact that provides a living to literary critics.

10. Reading What is There

Suppose we simply say that our immediate awareness is that of the symbol on the page. It has many possible meanings. Some meanings interest us and others don't. Some of the symbols make a story in which we can ourselves become actors—that gives us a wedge in the plot from which we can lever things to our desires. Other interpretations make this impossible.

Science, ideally, gives maximum coherence to certain features of the story to maximize the likelihood that some kinds of rational action will be effective. It is probably not the whole story or at least it does not include all the readings of experience that make sense of the whole story—i.e., all the interpretations of all the experiences with a strong claim on our attention. The best readings will also enable us to understand the significance of the other readings.

A good reading, on this view, would enable us to make sense of morality and religion as well as of the kinds of rationality which science uses in engineering. On this view, science, by itself, is not enough, although it is true that science can be held to be "about the world." For science is one of the reasonable interpretations of the world and the world is the most complete and coherent set of reasonable interpretations. It is also true, on this reading, that we need not hold that science goes beyond experience any more than one who reads a Dickens novel and has a mental picture of Oliver Twist goes beyond the experience given by the marks on the paper. When a given reading predicts future chapters in the story, its predictions are strong or weak depending upon the past coherence of the plot and the extent to which we think it likely that it will take a dramatically different turn. Outside that story there are other worlds—but they are other stories. The reality, perhaps, is in us as well as in the drama as we work it out with whatever plot-reading aids we choose.

We ought now, in the final part of this chapter, to return to our persistent concerns. Our theme throughout has been the use of logic in making us genuinely free. In some sense, science has always seemed to do just this. It has promoted the technology that—we suppose—has freed human beings, at least in the industrialized west, from much of the drudgery that plagued earlier generations of men and women. Steel mills, clothing factories, dish-washers and vacuum cleaners have all replaced labour that people previously performed for themselves.

Furthermore, science has freed us from the burden of many disabling diseases, extended the human life span and created conditions of comfort from which even philosophers benefit. Was it not harder to do philosophy in the steamy rooms heated with wet straw where Thomas Aquinas taught in the Paris of the thirteenth century? Did not even F.H. Bradley complain of the inconvenient cold of the lavatories in his Oxford college at the beginning of last century? Did not Marx have to give up reading at sunset because the light in the British Museum was so poor?

There is, of course, another side to this process. To make our economic system work we are required not so much to work hard and long as to keep busy consuming. Mass production requires mass consumption. In the end, the money for scientific research and development comes chiefly from the profits of such endeavours and the system would fail if its profits were not constantly re-invested. Constant expansion brings with it continuous frenetic activity.

Scientific research is closely linked to what such systems require. Much of it since World War II has been tied, too, to the needs of the armaments programs fostered by the Cold War and subsequent conflicts. The demand for atomic physicists was great in the post-war period. Until lasers were discovered the physics of optics languished.

To an important extent we have become prisoners of systems of expanding technology that many people believe will destroy the planet and eliminate us, if not through war, then through the destruction of the environment.

It is thus very important for us to assess what is going on in science and in technology if we are to be in any real sense free. And yet both become daily more and more specialized and complex. However, the topics we have been discussing here offer hope. It *is* possible to understand how scientific theorizing works, to explore its relations to the social order and to understand the standards that must be applied. In such ways it is possible to mount a critique of science.

The issues raised in this chapter, if followed far enough, can give intelligent men and women a genuine chance to make informed judgements. The start we have made here is, of course, only a start. But anyone intelligent enough to survive as an undergraduate at a major university can pursue it a good deal further.

QUICK QUIZ #3

1. What roles do models and analogies play in scientific theorizing?
2. Was Newton's most important achievement the discovery of important new facts?
3. Does science describe reality?
4. Is studying the world in important ways like reading a book? Why or why not?

Notes

1. This is named after Francis Bacon (1561–1626), who was perhaps the first systematizer of the notion of scientific induction. We will not be able to comment on the many detailed concerns about methodology included in Bacon's writings.
2. See his *Objective Knowledge,* Oxford: Clarendon Press, 1972 (revised 1979, 1981).
3. See Thomas Kuhn, *The Structure of Scientific Revolutions,* Chicago: The University Press, second edition, 1970; Mary B. Hesse, *Models and Analogies in Science,* London: Sheed and Ward, 1963; and Rom Harré, *The Principles of Scientific Thinking,* Chicago: The University Press, 1970.
4. For some early work along these lines see Toulmin's *Philosophy of Science,* London: Hutchinson, 1953.

Chapter 11

LOGIC AND HISTORICAL REASONING

1. History, Western Civilization And The Legacy Of René Descartes

The idea of history lies deep in Western culture. Judaism and Christianity alike are "historical" religions. They find their roots in what are claimed to be particular historical events—the captivity of the Jews, their exodus, the settlement in Israel, the lives of the prophets, the life, death and resurrection of Jesus. Moreover, they have always held that there is a meaning to history and that the point of human life, at least in part, is to be found in the history of human communities.

These religions promoted the study of history. But as history became more like a science, historical studies began to cast doubts on the authenticity of Scripture and even the existence of Jesus as a real person. In the seventeenth century the sciences began to support a world picture that excluded the human spirit, God and the afterlife. The idea of nature as a divine creation was replaced by the idea of nature as a self-explanatory machine. The rise of the sciences and the seventeenth century revolution in thought owed a large debt to the work of René Descartes.[1]

But Descartes' legacy is complex. He held that the human mind could directly "see" the rational order of the universe. This led to the use of mathematics in science to accurately describe the world. Descartes' theory of the mind and its ideas led to a long enquiry into the nature of ideas and fostered an interest in the psychology and physiology of perception. Descartes' certitude about self-knowledge as the foundation of all knowledge helped to give substance to individualism in politics, while his theory of common innate ideas encouraged, by contrast, communitarian politics. Descartes' theology preoccupied the thinkers involved in the Jansenist movement in France. But, above all, Cartesianism—or what passed for Cartesianism—split knowledge into two fundamental groups: the sciences and the humanities. Later, the newly-invented social sciences were subjected to the same fracture. Some, like econometrics, seemed allied to sciences. Others, like cultural anthropology, seemed linked to the humanities.

The sciences–humanities split took various forms. Sometimes the "hard sciences" were defined as those primarily concerned with Descartes' "primary qualities," like extension. These qualities were thought to characterise reality itself. Thus physics, wholly devoted to the study of such qualities, came to be *the* basic science. Other sciences involved secondary qualities (colours, sounds, tastes, smells and so forth), which were thought to result from the interaction of mind and matter. Since chemistry was sometimes concerned with colours and other sensorially testable secondary qualities of things, it was a "softer" science than physics. From there, the types of knowledge degenerated quickly toward the humanities, which were concerned with the reactions of human beings to things.

2. Vico's Objections

Nonetheless, Descartes himself worried and did not quite see the world in the simplistic terms, which we now know as "Cartesianism." Giambattista Vico (1668–1744), while accepting much that Descartes had to say, attempted to turn him on his head. Where Descartes had appeared as the champion of physics, Vico appeared as the champion of history. History, he argued, stood at the head of the list of things we can know,[2] for we *make* history. So we know history from the inside, not merely externally. Mathematics, too, we know with certainty, but the reason is the same: it is our own creation. As for physics, since we do not make the world ourselves, we can only know it from the outside and all the self-evident truths proposed by Cartesians may easily turn out to be false.

Compare Descartes' "tree of knowledge" with Vico's.[3] Descartes' tree has its roots in metaphysics (our most basic views about reality) and its trunk is physics. The tree's branches are all the sciences, but the chief ones are medicine, mechanics and morals.[4]

Vico's tree seems to have its roots in the human mind and its interactions with nature and myth. It has metaphysics for its trunk and two great branches, physics and poetry. Through poetry and "poetic logic," the imaginative human sciences are developed. For Vico, genuine knowledge is the result of the creative imagination. Indeed, it is *fantasy* that produces the break in the tree.

Descartes, perhaps, never reached the top of his own tree of knowledge. Late in his life his letters and other writings show an important concern with the "ethics of generosity" and with the concept of love. But he was still developing his theories when he died, though his first important work, the *Discourse on Method* of 1637, contains a good deal of moral advice, chiefly having to do with being reasonable as well as rational—i.e., with building one's life on a foundation of reason while refraining from bringing the house down upon one's head. The *Discourse* was written in French, not Latin, because it was directed to ordinary men and women.

Descartes and Vico alike remained faithful to the Socratic notion that the aim of knowledge is self-knowledge and that its ultimate purpose is to build genuine autonomy. For both writers are aware that one cannot be said to know unless one has been in a position to judge. Knowledge is at least *justified,* true belief. Descartes' hope was that individuals, by making use of what he called the doctrine of "clear and distinct ideas," would be able to master the pretenses of those who claim knowledge and thus will be able to see through the attempts to create illusion. Descartes thought that there was a simple and infallible mode of reasoning, mainly analysis, which leads to veridical claims to knowledge. Suppose that one (falsely) thinks that dragons exist. One thinks this because of a particular kind of confusion. That is, if there were not flying things, fires, and reptiles one could not come to imagine dragons. The person who thinks dragons exist simply confuses the elements.

The things one has clear and distinct ideas of—fire, wings, reptilian scales and so on—do exist. But many of our ideas, like the idea of "dragon," do not give us direct knowledge of reality because they frequently conjoin the elements wrongly or fail to make enough distinctions. By using Descartes' techniques for determining how ideas relate to reality,[5] and, above all, by analyzing all claims into their simplest, clearest components, one will separate the clear and distinct ideas from those unclear and indistinct. This enables one to achieve intellectual autonomy.

Vico was more sceptical of claims about physics. For the physical world is separated from us. We do not know *how* it was *made* despite what Vico thought of as Descartes' arrogance in supposing that he could demonstrate the existence of God and thus, by knowing what God was up to, learn something of the divine economy.

What we can do is to study history, which, since we make it, is open to us. We make it, that is, in the sense that it is composed of our actions. Vico conceded that we make it with some help from Divine Providence, pointing out that all societies achieve certain great ends, which they did not intend. They do so, as it were, despite themselves.[6] But this does not mean that we do not make history, only that divine providence is clever enough to act through us.

3. The Search for Pattern

Vico had in mind that Christianity also claimed a redemptive purpose to the world and suggested that the world would endure only as long as necessary to fulfil God's purpose for it.[7] Thus there must be a *pattern* to history. Vico found a pattern, based on the idea that history goes through repetitive cycles. Augustine found another pattern, based on the idea that the "city of man" must finally meet "the city of God" and that, in the long run, there is a kind of progress. In our own time, Arnold Toynbee combined these ideas.[8]

Eventually, a major theological preoccupation was to reconcile the providential pattern with human freedom. To find, understand and to attempt to master the pattern in history became a possible route to human autonomy. Mastering the pattern also came to seem as a necessary condition of autonomy, because if it is not mastered human beings become the mere creatures of history.

Thus the question of history became increasingly central to religion and by the nineteenth century, a near obsession. In 1835 David Strauss created a major crisis for Christianity with his *Das Leben Jesu*, which concluded that the historical evidence for the existence of Jesus was feeble. The religion that fostered the study of history was eventually threatened by it. But the passion for history was so great that no effort could stop the process.

Can there be an *objective* pattern to history? Does the fact that we learn that we can fit many patterns to history not create doubts about it? What kind of knowledge is really involved?

QUICK QUIZ #1

1. Why did the Cartesian philosophy produce a problem about history?
2. Vico thought that we could understand history because we made it. What does this mean? Was he right?
3. Judaism and Christianity involved notions of historical pattern. Why? How did history come to "turn on" religion?

---

4. Is All Knowledge Historical Knowledge?—Cassirer and Collingwood

Ernst Cassirer in *The Problem of Knowledge*[9] recounts Johann Gottfried Herder's struggles to establish a pattern of history, and then tells us about the efforts of Barthold Georg Niebuhr (1773–1831), Leopold von Ranke (1795–1886) and Wilhelm von Humboldt (1767–1835)[10] to create an objective history. The idea of an "objective history" may seem impossible in light of Vico's insistence that, since history is a human activity, it is something that we make, and we can and must see it from the inside. Herder, for instance, insisted on the need for an insight into the inner workings of the human mind, but Ranke, of course, thought that the idea of an objective history was possible if one attended strictly to the facts. Cassirer's story involves the inevitable wrestling with historical knowledge to develop the kind that gives us autonomy yet allows us to remain objective.

But for Cassirer, all knowledge can be turned into historical knowledge. That is, instead of studying physics, we can study the history of physics and we can follow the activities of the individuals who created physics. In this way we bring physics itself into the realm of history. This also applies to religious knowledge. In some cases (for example, the history of languages), as we see the thought processes involved, we inevitably bring unconscious creative processes into focus.

Indeed, in general, as we see how knowledge was acquired and pass through our own minds the processes of its recreation, we can bring under critical scrutiny the assumptions that lay behind the actions, and thus free ourselves from the prejudices brought into knowledge. This knowledge can be objective, as Collingwood insisted. Collingwood, a British philosopher and historian whose work on the logic of question and answer we met earlier, but who was above all a philosopher of history, insisted that, in so far as we learn to rethink the thoughts that went into the original processes,[11] we can have objective historical knowledge. But this raises fundamental questions about how to conceptualize historical knowledge and to these we must now turn.

5. Some Details of Historical Patterns and Some Problems about Imposing Patterns on History

If historical knowledge is possible and if it is essentially derived from the analysis of our symbols, we can form an understanding of what it is to "make one's own history." We make history in the sense of laying the foundations for historical knowledge by creating symbols and giving them a lasting structure of some kind so that they can be grasped later by others.[12]

If Vico had simply been content with the foundations that he had laid for such theories, his claim to have discovered a kind of knowledge consistent with human autonomy would have been vindicated. Even his ideas of Providence, which allowed the deity to use the unintended by-products of human action, would have remained consistent with the idea of autonomous human action. But Vico wanted a good deal more than this. He wanted an account of history that would enable us to understand the rise and fall of civilizations.[13] He thought that we begin as barbarians, and then focus our thoughts in the great mythological ages, which are peopled by gods. These are followed by heroic ages characterized by the dominance of the nobility. Finally the age of ordinary people dawns and civilization begins to decay again.

There are many readings of Vico's historical cycles, but one can at least notice in the successive phases increasing self-consciousness and rationality. We begin as barbarians and end as Cartesians. Vico didn't quite blame Descartes by name, but he certainly wanted to overturn Cartesianism. Put this way, an explanation for the historical process seems evident: as we begin to manipulate the world of symbols, we gradually gain control over our pasts and futures. At first the imagination fosters mythology and that in turn inspires great deeds. But reflection leads to caution and to the search for the orderly life of middle class citizens at all times and places. One might see Cartesian scepticism as a case of action paralyzed by reason, and Descartes' own apparent timidity (which many people believe led him to flee France when no one was hunting him)[14] might serve as an example of this.

Obviously, one could argue that, especially in our day, it is *not* rationalist timidity but romantic notions of heroic ages that threaten the survival of civilization. Many other criticisms could be levelled against Vico's speculations. Vico, however, inspired a succession of such schemes, all of which tended to create new problems for the notion of human autonomy. How can we be free if history determines in any case what will happen to us?

Johann Gottfried Herder attempted to develop an account of history based on human nature, but kept falling back on divine Providence in a way that again questioned human autonomy.[15] In his *Idea for a Universal History from a Cosmopolitan Point of View*,[16] Kant laid down the thesis that humans are creatures touched with "unsocial sociability." We seek to dominate others, but cannot live without them. The ebb and flow of such conflicts has led to endless adjustments as humans struggle up from the beast and, one hopes, toward "perpetual peace"—a phrase that forms the title of another of Kant's works.[17] Our progress is the result of the inevitable accidents of our freedom. Hegel advanced the notion in his *Lectures on the Philosophy of History*[18] that history is the inevitable unfolding of human freedom, for it is the idea of freedom that animates us. This creates a curious dialectic in which the idea of freedom frees us—a notion to which we will return a little further on. Hegel was followed by Marx, who believed that ideas free no one and that humans are prisoners of the economic forces that drive history. Marx held that we can only be free if we overturn the economic system that binds us and create one that frees us all.

Whether any of these claims could be substantiated is, of course, another matter, but it should be obvious that a theory like Marx's creates a paradox: We can only have real knowledge when we are free. For the economic system that controls us also binds and blinds us such that it is impossible for us to escape the illusions it produces. (This is just a particular form of the ancient claim that one cannot know unless one is free, for if one is not free, one cannot tell whether one is being forced to believe or not.) Marxists, however, face the dilemma of having to know what they ought to do now to free themselves and yet not being able to have real knowledge until they have achieved their ends.

Lenin forged the theory of the "Vanguard Party" out of notions like this by arguing that only a small minority of people are able to see through the economic illusions of their own time and they must, therefore, lead the others to freedom. They are entitled, indeed, to force the others to freedom.

6. Sir Karl Popper's Critique

Sir Karl Popper, whose views of science we saw in the last chapter, came to believe that positions like those of Marx and Lenin were dangerous nonsense. He set down his views in a succession of works: *The Logic of Scientific Discovery,* 1935, *The Open Society and Its Enemies,* 1945, and *The Poverty of Historicism,* 1957. More observations can be found in *Objective Knowledge*,[19] 1972, 1979. Popper came to believe a number of different but interlocking propositions to be true:

1. The overall pattern of the future cannot be predicted.[20] (If you could predict the overall pattern of history, you would know now what people will know in the future. But whatever you know now, they will have added something else by then.)
2. Theories about history that purport to reveal the overall pattern of history were put forward by Vico, Kant, Hegel and Marx. But they tend to involve categories so broad that almost anything confirms

them and they are rarely or never falsifiable. (If capitalism falls now, Marx is right; if it does not, the "historical process" of which he speaks is still going on, and capitalism is still building toward its final crisis.)

3. Such theories in fact persuade people to give up their autonomy to those who "know" where history will lead us. In fact such theories tend to lead us into dictatorships and to adopt a cruel tendency to sacrifice the present generation for future ones.

But in *Objective Knowledge*, Popper went further. He argued against the whole tendency toward the internalization of knowledge and mounts his critique of the notion that knowledge is a state of mind.

In Popper's view, we deal constantly with three "worlds": WORLD 1 consists of the objects in the physical order. WORLD 2 consists of our mental and/ or inner lives. WORLD 3 consists of logical entities—numbers, propositions, logical connectives and so forth. Popper's ultimate claim[21] was that knowledge is logical in kind and consists basically of theories, problems, problem situations and arguments, together with all the other apparatus associated with the possibility of critical judgements—logical systems, possibilities, mathematical entities and so forth. Popper was talking not about thinking but (as Frege[22] pointed out) about the "objective content" of thought. And he admitted that WORLD 3 has much in common with Plato's ideas and Hegel's objective spirit. Indeed, he said that he might have used Hegel's term himself, though he claimed that WORLD 3 is a *human creation*. It is like Plato's and Hegel's realms because it has a certain *autonomy*. Thus we create the series of integers but we cannot abolish the number 2, and we cannot write down or know the names of certain very large numbers that outrun the capacities of the human mind.

We use WORLD 3 even though we don't wholly control it. We use it because the way in which we come to know anything about reality is to find certain hypotheses (denizens of WORLD 3), and then we attempt to falsify them by applying them to WORLD 1, the physical world. We may make these applications by way of arguments (more denizens of WORLD 3) through which we derive certain characteristics that would hold if our hypotheses were true.

Knowledge is thus not a mental state but a logical relation that holds within WORLD 3 or between WORLD 3 and WORLD 1. The difficulty is that on this view we do not know anything that we originally wanted to know. We only know that some hypotheses have not been falsified and that some logical relations hold within the domain of WORLD 3.

It is not even necessarily clear when any hypothesis has been falsified: unfortunately, we can go on making it more and more complicated and broadening its concepts (as Popper said Marxists and Freudians, for instance, do in any case). However, so long as we do not do so to the point where nothing in principle falsifies the hypotheses, this seems fair game in Popper's system.

Popper certainly did provide a basis for individual autonomy in a world of propaganda: always ask what would falsify a proposition and then demand to know how such a falsifying instance could be found and whether the propounder is, in fact, busy looking for one. This is at least a small gain.

QUICK QUIZ #2

1. In what sense is it true that all knowledge is really historical knowledge?
2. Discuss some of the patterns that have been found in Western history.
3. Discuss Sir Karl Popper's critique of Marxists and others who thought they could predict the future.

---

7. The Idea of Idea

Let us return, for a moment, to Hegel.[23] Hegel's philosophy is very complex, so we will begin with some simple ideas that underlie his major works. They are as follows.

1. There is an objective world that imposes limiting conditions on what we can know at any one time.
2. Knowledge depends on our ability to grasp this order correctly.
3. The objective order tends to deceive us by imposing on us patterns whose origins and future we do not know, and, of course, by influencing the way we think.
4. The only way, therefore, in which the autonomy necessary for knowledge can be obtained is through a kind of re-enactment in our own minds of the processes of the natural order.

Thus nature begins with indeterminate states, discrete and externally related to one another—bits of matter, atomic particles—and passes through organic unity (life) to the higher kinds of unity that involve mental states. (Generally, material objects can be divided in a way that leaves us, after the division, with two material objects; usually living things, if divided, are not alive any more; one's consciousness at any moment is a unity that cannot be divided at all.)

We can reproduce this process in the dialectic of concepts by seeing that each effort to divide the world results in a contradiction. If one says "all that exists are bits of matter in space and time," one ends in a Kantian antinomy:[24] there must be a first moment in time and yet there cannot be. If there had been a first moment in time, how could the world have come from nothing? If there is not a first moment in time, then infinitely many moments have already elapsed. How can we have *traversed* an infinite series to be where we are?

There is a similar paradox about space: what would be on the other side of the last place? And yet an infinitely large universe would seem to create a causal problem about infinite series just like the paradox about time, for some events that influence us would be infinitely distant from us. Again, if one says "there are only bits of matter and living things," one is claiming to know that there are only such things. But one must admit that the world seems to be divided into discrete states so that no two things can form a real union. (All living things have parts; they all decay and die. Hence their parts are in some sense external to one another.) But then whatever passes for a mind in this world also cannot achieve a real union with what it knows.

The "contradictions" in things of which Hegel talks are *not*, of course, contradictions of the form "P and not-P" but tensions between concepts. These tensions, in Hegel's view, generate development in the outer world, and the logical progress of the world of knowledge. Knowledge is possible because we can repeat the process.

This process is driven by ideas, and that driving force is nowhere clearer than in history. Indeed, we become free and able to know precisely by developing the idea of freedom. Freedom began in the ancient despotisms of the Middle-East, where civilization replaced tribal societies with absolute monarchies, thereby increasing organizational efficiency, but, at the same time, making the despot perfectly free at the expense of everyone else. Once the idea of freedom is in the air, it quickly takes hold. Greek democracy arose out of the desire of everyone to be free in the way that the despot was free. Naturally this produced chaos; what we now call "interest group" politics became dominant and Greek society collapsed. The Romans reacted by creating the idea of a universal law, a system within which everyone acquired freedom by accepting certain restrictions. (Thus one is now free to walk down the street because the law inhibits people from hitting one another over the head with baseball bats.) This too is imperfect because the unity of the individuals is still imperfect, and each person renounces some things he or she wants to do in exchange for some arena of public freedom. Perfect freedom could only be attained if we all understood one another's aims and needs and wanted for ourselves what the others wanted for themselves. This would be the instantiation of the Absolute.

Short of this we can become internally (though imperfectly) free by grasping the idea of freedom for ourselves. Real knowledge, therefore, is essentially, knowledge of how such ideas work out. We could attain not only real knowledge of freedom by understanding how freedom works (and so becoming at least internally free), but equally real knowledge of redness by understanding all the ways in which redness enters into the world and shapes the surrounding ideas in politics, art, society and even physics. But this is a story to pursue later.

8. A Summary of Historical Reasoning

So it appears that if historical reasoning is to succeed, it requires a dialectical logic, or something very like one. Traditional formal logic poses special problems about the past. If all our evidence is in the present, then all the premises of our arguments refer to the present and all attempts to refer to the past are logically invalid.

For all we know, the world was created five minutes ago—complete with spurious memories and misleading "evidence" about the past. Traditional formal logic really gives us no handle on the past at all. Some historians have tried, by contrast, to use a Deweyite, pragmatic logic. They have even argued that one should believe about the past whatever is most useful in the present. But this was the doctrine of O'Brien, the dictator "Big Brother" of George Orwell's *1984*. O'Brien could control the present by controlling people's views of the past.

This is an obvious truth. Whether or not people supported one side or the other in the Iraq War depended largely on what they thought happened in the past—on what they thought Saddam Hussein did or could do, and on what they thought life was really like under Hussein's regime. Similarly, people will respond to the problems of the American economy in one way if they think the American Civil war was fought to enable the industrial north to dominate the agricultural south, and in another way if they think it was fought to free the slaves. But the position that is most "useful" depends on what one hopes to do, on what one's political aims are. In this case, does the pragmatic theory simply authorize political fraud?

If one adopts dialectical logic, one first seeks a general framework that will render human experience intelligible. Then one tries to balance off one's choice of intelligibility against the array of historical data presented. One knows that some of it is unreliable, and that one is not quite sure which parts are reliable and which are not. But one knows that some historical facts, verified by a wide array of documents and having withstood long probing— facts like the identity of the first prime minister of Canada or the manner in which Charles II died—could only be dislodged if we came to doubt nearly everything we believe about the past. Other facts, like who *really* fired the first shot in the Korean War, are not things that we can be sure of, and should not be given much weight in the overall picture.

One also knows that some general features of the pattern of human history are well enough established and fit what we have gathered from sociology, economics, anthropology, psychology and other disciplines that investigate human behaviour. But historical arguments always involve a search for a pattern that gives meaning to the whole human enterprise, and an attempt to render intelligible the historical facts that can only be disregarded if one becomes a sceptic about the whole notion of knowing the past.

A dialectical logic seeks to solve the problem of how to find the basic pattern of history as follows. We start with the simplest concepts, "pure being" and "nothingness." We can see, by the contradictions they generate and the concepts that we must add to prevent these contradictions, something about what is common to *all* patterns that can represent reality. Then, by applying these concepts to time, we can see something about how history must work.

9. Some Possible Laws of History

We can start with a simple example: all change, whether physical or social, requires the possibility of something that can take on a succession of forms. Aristotle thought that this something was ultimately "prime matter." One result of such a situation is that each change impresses itself on a material substructure and so creates a measure of resistance to further change. Each change therefore closes off some possibilities.

Jacques Maritain[25] called this "the law of two-fold contrasting progress." Its essence is this: though there is human progress, there is also evil. On the Aristotelian account, the evil, insofar as it is necessary, results from the passivity of matter. Matter can take on form but tends to keep it. It therefore accumulates effects that stand in the way of further change. Of course Maritain did not mean this merely in terms of the world in some sense external to us. No doubt our brains accumulate restrictive paths and patterns, too. However, so do organized systems of thought and this is, ideologically, much more interesting.

Every good that we achieve is somewhat counterbalanced by evil. But the wear and tear of time, as Maritain said, adds to this problem because things are "degraded" in this world. Everything wears out. People grow old. Machines rust. Even to keep the *Mona Lisa* in something like its "original" state requires constant cleaning and discreet repair.

Relieved of its Aristotelian implications, what this doctrine means is that every action closes off some existing possibilities even as it opens new ones, and at the same time, all actions in time take place in an unstable system whose generation is certain to produce unpredicted results. Maritain's law is a kind of social entropy.

In a sense this explains some of the failures of Marxism, once the hope of twentieth century reformers: the imposition of a vast all-embracing bureaucracy achieved certain obvious goods—the possibility, for instance, of organizing production for the public good. But the very size of that structure made it relatively impervious to small-scale pressures. Put bluntly, the individual had no real chance of making it respond.

What this suggests, though, is that we should look at history as a series of developments that seek to obtain goals by imposing patterns. However, these patterns create impediments to further change. Thus, old evils are replaced by new ones, which ultimately require major reorganizations. For instance, think of the internet. It has imposed a pattern upon us in that it has increased certain ways in which we communicate. We can quickly converse with friends in foreign countries. However, these "communication patterns" also have a dark side. As we sit conversing with others around the globe, we tend to cut ourselves off from our next-door neighbours. Basically, if one can understand the past in terms of new patterns imposed and impediments generated, one can begin to grasp the past in a way that will increase the options for the future. Planning has always to take account of the need to optimize freedom for change while creating techniques to counter the growing loss of community. In all these cases, we can see the "dialectic" of mutual trade-offs of advantages and disadvantages.

Other frameworks are likely to be useful, too. A different kind of law has to do with the human relation to space and time. All our experience, as Kant said, is bound to the orders of space and time. We need them, but we are disoriented by them. Indeed, experiences in space always terminate in an unknown shadow that human beings find threatening. Our temporal experiences prevent us from achieving the stability and permanence for which we yearn.

The great forces of human history have been aimed at conquering space and time. We hope to achieve communications systems that will open space to us so that nothing in our experience terminates in darkness. This has led to empire building, to the creation of communications networks and to our endless attempts to explore and conquer space. Our great civilizations derive from this impulse. But so do many disastrous wars.

The conquest of time has led to the search for mystical experiences that transcend time and tame it permanently. But it has also led to our desire for written records to render the past open to constant inspection, as well as to the search for knowledge. Thus will we be able to share in the experiences of the past and understand the future.

Nearly all historical explanation ultimately reverts to one of these impulses. If we can discover how we can effectively conceptualize these attempts, historical knowledge will become much more available. But notice that the process of dialectical logic, which leads from the known to the unknown by determining what is necessary to prevent contradictions, lies at the roots of such attempts.

Kant pointed out that we can grasp that space must extend infinitely and also that it cannot. We can put forward a simple argument to show this: every boundary has another side. Yet an infinity of spatial points would lead to a universe with infinitely many states of affairs, and, if we have infinitely many events, then everything possible will be actual. (If anything is possible it has a probability of greater than zero. It must therefore occur at least once in infinitely many chances, so any fraction multiplied by infinity will produce a number at least equal to one. Thus, in an infinite universe everything possible will be actual. Just what this infinity would be is arguable. Not everything is *com*possible, i.e., possible at the same time, but what the largest set of compossibles might be is difficult to say. Infinities include some things we might think impossible. Since Georg Cantor's smallest infinite number—aleph null—is unchanged by the addition or subtraction of finite quantities, a hotel with infinitely many rooms, all of which were occupied would still have a room available for the next guest. For aleph null + 1 is identical or equal to aleph null. This is so because infinities have odd properties. There are as many integers in the series 2, 4, 6, 8, 10, 12, 14... as there are in the series 1, 2, 3, 4,

5, 6, 7. So if you take away half the integers, you still have the same number of integers. If that is so, then the number of the integers minus 1 must be the same number as the number of the integers (namely aleph-null.) But in most cases things and their negations are probably not compossible. If the universe is infinitely large, it contains someone just like you except that he or she refused the extra helping of potatoes that you ate at dinner. But it cannot both contain and not contain Large Black English pigs.

These notions make us uneasy. To overcome them we need to introduce the notion of a space that lies within the control of our experience. Instead of space as a paradoxical object, therefore, we gradually form the notion of space as something that lies within our experience and which expands or contracts as our experience expands and contracts and does not extend beyond it.

This idea of a space within our experience is also the idea of a space within our control, and men and women have sought this control in the form of conquest and power. They have found, however, that it always escapes their grasp. Perhaps this brutal record would come to an end if we realized that it was only by controlling our own experiences and learning to share with others in a non-threatening way that experienced space will really be brought under control.

QUICK QUIZ #3

1. Could Hegel have answered Popper?
2. What are some key ingredients in Hegel's theory of history?
3. Does traditional formal logic make it difficult to make inferences about the past?
4. Does Dewey's logic do better than formal logic with respect to making inferences about the past?
5. Is it possible to make inferences about the past in a dialectical logic?
6. Is historical "progress" always mixed with new evils? What kind of argument suggests that it is?
7. What have the mastery of space and time to do with the patterns of history?

Notes

1. Descartes (1595–1650) is often called "the father of modern philosophy." It is certainly true that little in the modern world can be understood without reference to his work.
2. See especially his *Scienza Nuova,* 1725, ed. and tr. T.C. Bergin and M.H. Fisch, as *The New Science of Giambattista Vico,* Ithaca, NY: Cornell University Press, 1968. The best introduction to his work is Donald Phillip Verene, *Vico's Science of Imagination,* Ithaca, NY: Cornell University Press, 1981.
3. Verene, op. cit. p. 208.
4. See Descartes' *Principles of Philosophy* in *The Philosophical Works of Descartes,* ed. Elizabeth Haldane and G.R.T. Ross, Cambridge: The University Press, 1931,

p. 211. A more recent translation by John Cottingham, Robert Stoothoff, and Dugald Murdoch appears in *The Philosophical Writings of Descartes,* Cambridge: The University Press, 1985–1991.

5. Descartes distinguished between "objective" and "formal" reality as properties of ideas. Objective reality is the property of being able to refer to something real. For instance, the idea of "lionhood," is that of a "yellow-haired carnivorous, roaring quadruped." Notice that "lionhood" does *not* ensure that lions exist; American hunters may have wiped them out. "Lionhood" refers to reality by telling us how to distinguish between lions and non-lions. Formal reality is a stronger property in that it not only refers to something, but ensures that that something exists. For instance, the *numeral* "23" refers to the actual *number*, 23. The number 23 must exist; it cannot be brought into or put out of existence because of its form. Recall that lions have a form such that they *might* exist, but *need not* exist.

6. Think how the Sumerians changed civilization by developing writing, an activity in which they indulged mainly for commercial bookkeeping and political record keeping. Or think how Blaise Pascal changed civilization by developing the digital calculator, a device which, it seems, he intended only to help in his father's tax-collecting activities.

7. The announcements of the approaching end of the world around which various sects have been built are probably an inevitable by-product of religion, which combines this belief with the belief that God can achieve his ends whenever He wants to.

8. See *A Study of History,* 10 vols., Oxford: The University Press, 1934–1954.

9. Tr. by William Woglom and Charles Hendel, New Haven: Yale University Press, 1966, p. 216 ff.

10. He should not be confused with the great explorer and naturalist Alexander von Humboldt (1769–1859), though both Humboldts were wrestling with problems of objective knowledge.

11. When you work out Euclid's geometry, you rethink his thoughts, for only one procedure results in a "Euclidean proof." When you study a map that shows the successive positions of the ships and the various actions undertaken at the Battle of Trafalgar and understand them as an account of how Nelson hoped to win, you rethink Nelson's thoughts (assuming he intended to win and assuming that his ships followed his directions).

12. Vico himself meant that we could understand history from the inside because we made it. It consists of human acts and human acts can be understood in a way that objects cannot. But it seems altogether possible that we could make history and yet not grasp it, because, in fact, it belongs to the past.

13. There is always, of course, a certain ambiguity about the word "history" itself. Sometimes it means "what happened in the past" and sometimes it means "the knowledge of what happened in the past."

14. As far as we know, Descartes had no official enemies but he may well have had unofficial ones. The matter remains wrapped in obscurity.

15. Herder (1744–1803) was a German philosopher who was much interested in language and plurality of cultures. On the point at issue here, see Cassirer, *The Problem of Knowledge,* p. 217 ff.

16. First published in 1784 as an article in *Berlinische Monatsschrift,* translated by Lewis White Beck in *Kant on History,* Indianapolis: Bobbs-Merrill, 1963, p. 11–26. This volume also contains Kant's critique of Herder.

17. Also translated by Beck in *Kant On History*.
18. Successive German editions were published from Hegel's notes in 1837 and 1840. An English translation by J. Sibree was published in 1857 (New York: Collier, 1900).
19. See Popper's index references under "historicism," "historical explanation," and "Marxism."
20. Popper accepted the possibility of short-range predictions within limited systems of the sort referred to by economists (as he understood them).
21. *Objective Knowledge,* p. 106–107.
22. Gottlob Frege, 1848–1925, with Russell, one of the pioneers of modern mathematical logic.
23. See Chapter 5, Section 7 ff.
24. An "antinomy" in the Kantian sense is a situation in which there are or seem to be two equally valid arguments leading to contradictory conclusions. ("Antinomy" was originally a legal term referring to a contradiction between two equally binding laws.)
25. *The Philosophy of History,* ed. Joseph W. Evans, New York: Scribners, 1957, p. 43. The discussion extends to p. 52. (The book is based on four lectures at Notre Dame University, 1955.)

Chapter 12

LOGIC AND MORALITY

This chapter does not provide a complete survey of all the problems that arise out of attempts to reason about morality. Nonetheless, it will call attention to the range of problems and show how we might address the problems, revealing the difficulties but offering hope that reason *can* be brought to bear on moral problems.

1. Reasoning about Being Reasonable —The *First* Basic Issue

Although we do not always know what it is to be good, we know, at least in part, what it is to be reasonable. So, "reasoning about being reasonable" is our first and most natural topic. It is reasonable to determine standards for oneself in the same way that one determines them for others. Reasons are good or bad independently of the nature or stature of those who advance them. Hence what counts as a reason for one person must count as a reason for another in the same circumstances. But it is sometimes very difficult to determine what it is to be "in the same circumstances." So it is reasonable not to act on beliefs one is not willing to test or modify—for we have seen no manner or mode of reasoning that gives final certainty.

We have also discovered that the structure of one's logic might lead to substantive moral principles. If experience is a determinant of inference, and if inferences are designed to be self-correcting, then we have the following principle.

One ought never to act so as to restrict or reduce the horizons of relevance for oneself or any other sentient creature.

If one needs the reports of other observers as a minimal condition for self-correction, presumably it would be better to act out of benevolence than out of malice, for to act out of malice is to isolate oneself from what may be the truth.

Perhaps all this and much more counts as "being reasonable." Suppose that someone asks "why should I be reasonable?" Would we be able to give him or her *moral* reasons or would we find ourselves confined to merely prudential ones? It is *prudent* to be reasonable, but is it *good* to be reasonable?

Most likely there are connections between "reasonableness" and at least some high order values. We have seen that one function of logic is as a means to win our freedom and preserve our autonomy. Freedom is a value. But how does freedom rank with the other values? Perhaps we can go further. We depend upon reason for our self-identity and for our knowledge of others. In developing knowledge of ourselves, we engage in a kind of creation; we establish a web of meanings with which we link experience, reflection and action. Our personal identity is a central thread in that web—we do not find our identities in some simple introspection or in some dramatic act. (Recall our discussion of belief. Belief is a vital ingredient in self-identity and in our personal lives but it can only be explicated in a way that gives meaning to a pattern of action and reflection.) It takes reason to weave the web of action and reflection. Similarly, we learn about other people primarily by speaking to them. (One would not claim to "know" someone because one had watched him through a telescope, or checked his blood pressure, or watched the readings from his brain on an electroencephalograph.) Conversation establishes a community of meanings—a little world of its own, long or short in duration, important or trivial in its relation to the other worlds we encounter—that requires those common understandings and goals that make conversation possible. In this way reason is connected to the assignment of meaning, which in its turn is connected to values we apply or create. The commitment to reason is involved, in one way or another, in all such transactions.

Reasoning about being reasonable is thus the *first issue* in the logic of morality. Reasoning about right and wrong *is* thus tied to reasoning about reasoning. Still, there are serious questions that continue to be raised and that create serious difficulties for understanding how moral concepts relate to logic. One question concerns the *second issue*—reasoning about morality, about right and wrong, good and evil and what one ought to do. Another question concerns the *third issue*—the logic of moral discourse. These three are central to long-standing debates about morality.

2. Talking about Goodness and Morality—The *Second* Basic Issue

Let us now consider goodness and morality. We begin with what, after G.E. Moore, came to be called "the naturalistic fallacy."[1] Moore asked whether or not one could answer the question "is it good to be reasonable?" and whether one could give a moral answer to the question or only a prudential one.

Some people have thought that one could define moral terms by providing substitutes for them. Some of these people have thought that happiness is "the good," that is, "happiness = goodness." But Moore claimed that "good" is really an indefinable term since, logically, the substitution could never be made. If someone says "2 + 2 = 4" we agree that what is one side of the equation is the same as what is on the other side. So one could be substituted for the other. But Moore claimed that if one says "happiness is good," someone could still *always* reasonably ask "But is happiness really *the* good?" When someone says "happiness is good," the statement still refers to *two* properties, "happiness" and "goodness." (When someone says that "2 + 2 = 4," the property on each side of the equation is called "fourness," for "2 + 2" is another way of *writing* "4.")[2] Are "happiness" and "goodness" identical in the same sense as "2 + 2" and "4"? If one could be substituted for the other, one would not have said anything. If "happiness" = "goodness" then to say "happiness is good" is to say "happiness is happiness" and "goodness is goodness." (If "7 + 5 = 12," then "12" is the same as "7 + 5," and "7 + 5 = 12" is the same as "12 = 12," or "7 + 5 = 7 + 5.") The confusion may be about "good," an adjective, and "goodness," a noun that means *the good.* For "the good" is not something you meet on the street. It always appears through something else—there are good people, good books, good acts and so on. But there can be, one would think, good and bad happiness too. Seeing your competitor lose may make you happy, but it is not good to be happy because someone ends up with a broken neck when her horse trips on the fence.

Moore thought one could raise such objections in terms of indefinability about all the kinds of things that philosophers have most commonly maintained about goodness. Some, like John Stuart Mill, tended to equate a certain sense of happiness (essentially, as he said, sensory pleasure) with goodness.[3] We can clarify things by pursuing the questions: Is pleasure good? Is happiness good? Mill himself realized that one can certainly ask: Are some pleasures better than others? The question itself is a clue to the problem. For if one thinks, as Mill did, that some pleasures are better than others, then the nature of goodness is given by whatever principle enables one to order pleasures from best to worst. This makes goodness different from pleasure. When Mill argued that one should choose the pleasures that would appeal to the person with the widest range of relevant experience and basic understandings, he apparently was moving from his original theory toward a self-realization theory, or perhaps, an "ideal observer" theory.

Others, like T.H. Green and F.H. Bradley associated goodness, indeed, with self-realization.[4] But, one may say, self-realization is good if and only if the self to be realized is good. One may think, like Kant, that one ought to act on a principle of rational Universalization, that is, to act so that one could rationally will that one's acts be the acts that all other human beings (all others so placed?) should perform.[5] Still, one may ask whether the rational will itself is good.

Like Hume before him, Moore deduced from his discussion of good the principle that one may not derive conclusions about values from premises that contain no value statements. In other words, one cannot derive an "ought" from an "is" Facts and values, according to Hume and Moore, are forever separate. To show that pleasure is good, one needs a premise containing a statement about goodness. But then pleasure would not be *the good* but an *instance of goodness.*

3. In What Way are Value Terms Special?

The claim, here, about the indefinability of "good" is of some interest to us in this discussion, not merely because it may represent a "principle" that was widely held by philosophers for nearly fifty years, but also because it poses a logical question. But in fact, it is not clear what the principle is. Moore states as a principle that "good" cannot be defined by terms that denote something other than goodness itself. So value terms, which concern what is good, what one ought to do and so on, are unique. One needs value terms in the premises in order to get them in the conclusion of a valid argument.

But if one puts it this way, it seems not to be a special claim about "good" or about values; rather, it is just a statement of the inference principle of the Aristotelian syllogism, the principle that what is in the conclusion must, in some sense, be included in the premises. Evidently, a form of *this* (Aristotelian) principle holds for *all* arguments structured so as to be, or to resemble (in logical type) a syllogism. The syllogism, amongst other things, represents a rule against drawing rabbits out of hats. Every case of an illicit substitution of a term of one sort for a term of a different sort is a case of smuggling something in.

The seeming force of Moore's use of this inference principle *may*, therefore derive from a confusion of two issues. One is about *all* inferences of a certain sort—namely, that since they depend upon inclusion and exclusion relations expressed as something like class membership, there is an absolute prohibition against information turning up in the conclusion that was not, somehow or other, represented by the premises. But what gave Moore's argument its popularity was that it was believed to address a different and more specialized issue. This second issue is less clear but it is evidently about whether or not reasons of a certain sort could lead us to conclusions about *morality. Can we use premises about the facts of the world to sustain moral claims? And can we legitimately connect goodness with any of the facts about the world?*

Surely we must accept the principle that one should found one's inferences on some connection between the premises and the conclusions. But we need not read this in the Aristotelian way. We have seen alternative modes of inference. It is the issue about goodness and the facts about the world that is pressing and important.

QUICK QUIZ #1

1. Is it good to be reasonable? How is being reasonable related to establishing one's self-identity?
2. Is "goodness" indefinable?
3. Should we simply accept that "facts" and "values" are ultimately distinct?
4. Is there a "naturalistic fallacy"?

(*Give your own answers to the last three of these questions and then* read on through the next several sections. *Did you change your mind about anything?*)

---

4. Is it a "Fact" that Spitting at People is Rude?

Let us imagine a very simple argument. Suppose we say "While at a concert, you ought not to stamp on the foot or spit in the eye of the person next to you," and you say "Why not?" We might answer, Because it's rude." Now it is a matter of fact that it is rude to do such things. We might argue about other cases, such as whether or not it is rude to swear in front of senior citizens or to smoke while being introduced to the Queen, and the answer may be "yes" or "no," for it may depend on the circumstances. If one is performing a play that contains coarse language and there are seniors in the audience, it is not rude— whatever else it is—to utter them as the script demands. Most likely no one would say that, if you meet the Queen while out riding your horse, you must necessarily extinguish your pipe before saying "Hello." But no doubt, rudeness, whatever else it includes, includes the concert case. If it didn't, the word "rudeness" would cease to have any meaning.

Now "rudeness" is like many other expressions—it expresses matters of fact and matters of value all together. It is a fact that some things are rude, and it is also a fact that it would be unreasonable to advocate rudeness as a policy. It would be unreasonable because rudeness seems to consist of giving unnecessary and unjustifiable offence to others. Rudeness can be excused; we excuse the rudeness of someone mentally ill. But we recognize that rudeness *needs* to be excused. So it seems to follow that to understand rudeness is to understand that one should not be rude. It is unusual to argue that one should be rude for it makes no particular sense. However, it *is* usual, in every generation, to argue over what *counts* as rudeness. But these arguments take the form, as a rule, of debates over whether or not a given act is sufficiently like the cases that everyone counts as rude. We could not argue unless we had some case in mind.[6]

If one moves to larger issues, the same rule applies, though other kinds of reasoning may come into play. It is "evident" that murder is wrong because values are associated with people in such a way that values emerge from human acts and thoughts. In principle, a person is a source of value. A dead person ceases to be such a source, and her loss, *potentially*, is a loss of some important value that diminishes all of us along with her. It is not common, therefore, to argue in favour of murder. One who did so would have to hold that (s)he acted in the name of some transcendent value, which, probably, none of us could understand.

What *is* common *is* to argue about what *counts* as murder. Is bombing people in a war murder? Is killing another while one is insane murder? Is luring another into a risky adventure that takes that person's life murder? Eventually, we get a legal definition such as: "One who unlawfully, with intent and premeditation, takes the life of another is guilty of (first degree) murder"; but this is only a kind of framework into which we try to fit the arguments as they come up. In this case, one who advocated murder would be advocating a state of affairs within which we could no longer readily understand our own or anyone else's values. One would be denying, that is, the *prima facie* value of persons and so denying us the opportunity ever to understand persons through the understanding of values.

Now it does not seem that these arguments—be they good or bad as arguments—commit any fallacy. They simply insist that value terms have a context, that this context supplies reasons and that the reasons are adequate to the making of some value decisions. None of them *smuggles* in any value terms, none of them makes reference to ultimate "goodness," none of them seems to fit a context in which one might ask "but is it good to be polite?" or "is it good to protect the lives of others?" for they give reasons for thinking we already know what the answers are.

5. The Logic of Moral Discourse—The *Third* Basic Issue

Nonetheless, G.E. Moore's claim that "goodness" is somehow a "unique, unanalyzable" property that cannot be defined by other terms, raised several philosophical issues. Moore decided that, since one could not grasp "good-ness" in any of the kinds of argument that Moore was prepared to accept, our knowledge of goodness must depend upon a direct intuition of goodness itself. Here "intuition" is like a special kind of vision. Other British moralists—Sir David Ross[7] and A. C. Ewing[8] amongst them—followed Moore's approach and devoted themselves to an attempt to organize their moral intuitions in a consistent and coherent way. Reason, for them, played its part in moral theory by working on moral intuitions in somewhat the way reason works on percep-tions to form scientific theories.

But there was a group of philosophers, the logical positivists, who denied this. The positivists rejected the idea that humans had "moral intuitions" analogous to perceptions. So, the positivists held that moral language is not about matters of fact. Consider the following sentences:

> "Hitler is a bad man."
> "Spitting in church is rude."
> "Women are valuable human beings."

The positivists admit that these look like they are about matters of fact. But they really are not. For instance, "Hitler is a bad man" just means "I don't like Hitler and I wish you didn't like him." Hence, "Hitler is a bad man" is not about the facts in the external world; it is really just about emotions, attitudes and so on. So, we have moral feelings or attitudes or sentiments but we don't have any moral intuitions. In a refined form, Charles Stevenson put forward the "emotive theory" that moral statements are really mixtures of fact and attitude.[9]

Let us use the emotive theory to analyze what happens when Joe says, "Apartheid is wrong." The emotive theory says that Joe is questioning the supposed "facts" used to support the policy of apartheid and expresses an attitude–disdain—toward those who argue in favour of apartheid. But, as Ewing argued, there is something logically curious about the emotive theory.

The logical curiosity is two fold. First, the emotive theory tells us that the sentences "Hitler was bad" and "Hitler was not bad" do not really contradict each other. Second, the emotive theory tells us that if we properly interpret these sentences they are *both true.*

6. Is it Absurd to Make the Statement "Hitler was not a Bad Man" a Logically Necessary Truth?

The logical curiosity of the claim grows, perhaps, if we notice that the oddity may extend to the claim that Hitler was not *bad.* If the analysis that purports to show that "Hitler was bad" and "Hitler was not bad" are not contradictory statements is correct, then anyone who says "Hitler is bad" is involved in the wrong logical analysis of such claims. Such a person has made a logical mistake. But this seems to imply that Hitler was *not* bad. In fact it seems to make it a necessary truth that Hitler was not bad, for no one could be bad.

One can see what happens if in response to Ewing's point that the two original statements *do* contradict one another, a Stevensonian claim that "Hitler was bad" and "Hitler was not bad" only *seem* to contradict one another. We would see that if we carried out the analysis in which the word "bad" disappears along with its relative "not bad." I say, really, "I don't like Hitler" and you say, at least, "I don't dislike Hitler"—then we don't contradict one another. But something very odd follows from the proposition that one *ought to* perform this analysis: Hitler *could not possibly* have been "bad." For if nothing *is* bad, the word "bad" ought never to be used without the addition of its correct analysis. Is there still something left?

Though moral theorists disagree with one another about many things, it will follow from very many moral theories that what Hitler did was bad and that one who does what he did *is* bad. More seriously, perhaps, it ought to be a test of a moral theory that it should not authorize putting millions of people into gas chambers. For it is likely that we know more certainly what one shouldn't do than that we know any moral theory or analysis of moral language to be correct.

7. Morality and Human Experience

Gradually, the point emerges. We have experiences such as friendship, love, benevolence and so on that provide a context to moral language and so make sense of it. How to analyze these experiences is, indeed, a difficult question. But one who says, "nothing is 'really' bad" seems to imply things like "it is not better to love than to hate, or to make friends than to make enemies." That is, one implies that the experiences that give moral language its meaning do not have to be reckoned with. Now this is quite different from questioning how one may theorize about these experiences, or how one may test such theories, or how one may make sense of moral language.

To analyze it all away goes too far, in a very special sense: it leaves us no longer able to understand why there was a problem in the first place. But of course there is a problem, and it is caused by the fact that we seem to know a few things—it is good to give water to thirsty dogs, love is not evil and so on—and we are greatly puzzled by many more moral issues. The problem of moral theory, in large part, is to explain our certainties and our puzzles.

However, the "emotive" theory of value however was not the only attempt to reconstruct moral language. From much the same considerations, other philosophers concluded that moral statements were really statements in the imperative mood, or that, like R. M. Hare, moral statements included imperative ingredients along with ingredients that simply describe alleged facts.[10]

On this view one who says, "Hitler was a bad man" is saying, in part, "Dislike Hitler!" or "Act so as to frustrate Hitler," and, expresses, in part, ordinary ideas that imply classifications of Hitler's behaviour.

Now this is probably sometimes true. Moral statements are meant to influence behaviour in some way or another. They may be commands or they may be reasons for acting in certain ways and not others. Some of them, probably, are commands.

This in itself gives rise to a problem with the logic of some kinds of moral discourse. Commands are not true or false, but they do have implications. One must respond in some way, by obeying them, disobeying them or ignoring them. How is a command related to the proper response and what can one say about that relation?

One could, of course, say that moral language ought to be purged of imperatives as quickly as possible. But you will recall that when we talked about arguments from authority, we suggested that some alleged authorities do have moral authority. Those with moral authority are those established as authorities—arbitrators, for instance.

8. Morality and Commands

Hence, we need to look at this matter. It will turn out not so baffling as it seems at first sight. Commands are not true or false—but they are sensible or foolish. Foolish ones should be voided; sensible ones should be weighed. Thus in reasoning about commands we could use "sensible" and "foolish" as logical devices like "true" and "false," pairs of predicates, one of which must be assigned to every relevant assertion. Then we could do "truth table" inferences. Moreover, predicates like "sensible" and "foolish" have connections to matters of fact. It is foolish to order the passengers to jump if the ship is going down in icy waters. It is foolish to order someone to learn Latin if his I.Q. is 66. These factual connections provide fact/value links and also make it possible to align the new predicates with the old—to associate what is foolish and sensible with what is true and false by new inferences.

Furthermore, most obviously, commands may be justified or unjustified, and this gives us a further set of available predicates for constructing inference rules and linking them to the "logic of assertions." (One will have to give meanings to "justified" and "unjustified," but one can do that by analyzing how authorities become established, the acts performed by *us*, and which of them do or do not license authorities.)

Perhaps, as we have suggested, this is a branch of moral theory but not the central branch. But even if a proper analysis showed that moral language did consist mainly of imperatives, it would not follow that moral theories could not be developed or justified. It would only follow, as we have seen, that there would be a good deal of new, interesting work for logicians—which, indeed, has been going on in recent years.[11]

9. A Final Argument for an Objective Moral Theory

But let us notice a pair of points. First, it *is* possible to produce an argument in defence of a moral theory that involves only "rational" considerations, given, at least, one seemingly harmless admission. The admission is that it is logically possible that there are some true statements about what it is your duty to do that are not contradictions. That is, statements of the form, "You ought to do X" (where X is some action) are logically consistent. Now, if these statements are logically consistent then it is logically possible that you have duties. But *if* it is possible that you have duties, then it is *one* of your duties to conduct enquiries to determine whether or not you actually do have other duties and to find out what they are. For, if you do have other duties and you could have found out about them but failed to do so, you are certainly culpable.

It is, therefore, your duty to make or *try* to make correct ethical judgements. If this is your duty then you must accept, also, that it is the duty of everyone else who might have duties to conduct the same search, and you ought to try to further their attempts to make correct ethical judgements. They may find the truth that you are looking for. To help them, you must try to keep them free, alive, and in cheerful psychological condition so they will recognize the truths when and if they find them.

This sounds like a prescription for a democratic society that provides a good deal of public welfare. Nonetheless, we must remember that actual reasoning about what to do is *practical* reasoning, and we have seen throughout our discussions that practical reasoning differs from theoretical reasoning in at least one respect: practical reasoning involves argument forms that may be invalidated by the addition of new premises. All the facts about everyone are relevant to what anyone should do when it comes down to matters of detail.

It is a universal truth—if the argument we just advanced is sound—that you shouldn't kill anyone and that you should do your best to keep everyone healthy and cheerful. It is not a universal truth that you ought to give up your life in Winnipeg and go to fight the AIDS epidemic in Tanzania, though it may be that you should. To know if you should, we need to know a good deal about you and about the people in Tanzania. Still, there is hope for a rational basis for reasoning about right conduct and public policy. But we are moving toward the subject matter of our final chapter—the logic of politics and the politics of logic.

10. What is to be Judged?

The argument we have just outlined raises, obliquely, an issue at the centre of disputes over moral theory: when we make moral judgements, what do we judge and what should we judge?

The argument in Section 9 maintains that we have certain duties, that these involve moral enquiry, moral judgements and moral truth. It suggests that it is always our duty to try to find out the moral truth and that part of the reason for this is that wrongs might be committed—or good opportunities for good deeds missed—if the requisite moral knowledge is not forthcoming.

The argument suggests that what we are concerned with first of all is the quality of our moral judgements themselves and the search for moral truths. Obviously, however, the suggestion is that there are some rules of conduct involved, and that what ultimately concerns us is the quality of our moral actions themselves. Almost as obviously, we are concerned with the results; for our arguments seem to suggest that the world would be a worse place if people habitually made wrong moral judgements or avoided moral judgements altogether. Moral theorists have differed over the object of moral judgements and their disagreements have given rise to the main lines of rival moral theories.

One group, whose principal philosopher is surely Immanuel Kant, has argued that what is to be judged is the rational will.[12] What we expect of people is that they should *will rationally*, that is, according to rules. In Kant's view, these rules are universal and the test of a moral rule is whether or not one can will it rationally to be a universal rule. Accordingly, one judges one's acts by conformity to these acts. The will is judged. The standard is the availability of universal rules. Thus the ultimate object of judgement is the rational will, but the immediate object of judgement is a proposed moral rule.

Others have argued that we should judge the moral act itself—not the intangible will and not the rarely universal moral rules. That is, what a person *does* is what counts. After all, we do not know what others will and perhaps not even what we ourselves will. They would also argue that there are exceptions to all proposed moral rules: you should lie if it will save someone's life, steal if your child is starving, and cheat at poker if you need to buy your way out of slavery. But the judging of acts is equally problematic. What you do may depend on all sorts of things. You may be insane, you may not have understood what you were doing, you may have acted under duress. There are often good excuses for bad acts. (Excuses are often treated with contempt. But they are serious matters.)

The next obvious proposal—and this one, too, has attracted a phalanx of philosophers led by John Stuart Mill[13]—insists that *neither* the will *nor* the act should be judged. We should judge the consequences of the acts because results are what matters. In particular, Mill thought that what matters is whether more people are happier if a given course of action is adopted or if more are happier if it is rejected.

One judges happiness, which, according to Mill, is associated with pleasure. Of course, as we saw earlier, he admitted that there are better and worse (or higher and lower) pleasures and that one ought to seek the best kind, consulting those with wide experience before making up our minds.[14] But Mill's proposals are problematic, too.

How can we know what the consequences of our actions really are? How far into the future must we look? How do we know who is happy? If we equate happiness with pleasure, then shouldn't we just have the pleasure centres of our brains wired up and live forever in ecstasy? If, like Mill, himself, we insist that there are higher and lower pleasures, haven't we issued a new standard? And how do we justify this new standard? Is it really true that those who have experienced both prefer the higher?

There are many paradoxes in such a view. If we look to the long-range consequences of our acts, then the elderly and physically challenged should be last into the lifeboats because they are less likely to survive and have long and happy lives. Are those who are most likely to be happy most worthy to survive? If we could make 40 million people happy by exterminating four million, should we do it?

In fact, one might argue, as did F.H. Bradley in *Ethical Studies*,[15] that all moral theories are paradoxical. Bradley thought that all moral theory was just a prelude to some higher metaphysical understanding in which we might see how to transcend our self-interest, and ourselves, and so pass beyond the normal realm of moral discourse.

If we look at the argument in Section 9 again, however, we may be able to clarify the issue. On that view what is to be judged, if you like, is your moral posture. Do you try to find out the truth about morals? Do you try to act on the best approximation of truth that you can find? Do you weigh the consequences against the formulation of any rule proposed to you to see if this occasion might be an exception to the rule? It is not the act or the will or the consequences that are judged. Rather one asks whether the person concerned has reviewed all the relevant kinds of reasons and then done his or her best to act on them.

11. Must There be Only One Rule?

There is, though, a further logical difficulty to be faced. Obviously one must act on the most certain rule one can find. And the most certain rule, probably, is that one should try to make correct moral judgements and try to create conditions under which others can do so too. Every act ought to be oriented toward creating the conditions under which others can adopt an acceptable moral posture. Poverty, war, ignorance, pain and prejudice, for instance, all make it difficult for people to adopt an acceptable moral posture. But avoiding these evils involves disparate values and the values involved can and sometimes do clash.

Indeed, one must try to find some overriding rule, for if there is a plurality of rules, logically they will conflict at one time or another. The duty to tell the truth sometimes conflicts with the duty to save lives. And sometimes one must risk one's life to prevent a war. Poverty is evil. But sometimes one must endure it for a time to avoid the kind of social chaos in which lives are lost and misery increased.

An overriding rule, if it exists, must be guided by what Plato called the form of the good itself: that is, it must relate all the good things to one another. Could there be such a rule? Perhaps there could. Kant[16] saw the complications in his own theory and sought to develop further the idea of a universal rule. One of his suggestions was that the idea of a universal moral rule is not "a rule to which there are no exceptions," but also the idea of what he called a "Kingdom of Ends."[17] One might call it a "Monarchy of Ends" to use non-sexist language. For Kant included us all in his scheme.

In a "Kingdom of Ends" we treat others as an end in themselves—never merely as a means to an end. But Kant does not clearly explain this. Essentially, this is a community in which decisions are made by consensus (because each individual understands the interdependency of everyone) and every person's ends have the same weight.

There is a duty in such a "Kingdom" to continue the argument when disputes arise until some agreement is reached.[18] This duty follows, as well, from the argument put forward in Section 9. It derives from the fact that the moral truth or some new moral truth may be just around the corner. But such a "Kingdom" also demands a community within which there are conditions for the creation of an adequate moral posture: it demands, that is, that people be free to make serious judgements and not be compelled to act from hunger, or to avoid pain, or under the morally impossible conditions of a full-scale war.[19] In the "Monarchy of Ends" everyone is a king or queen and must adjust to the fact that all others have equal rights. The ultimate rule is complex and is precisely about how all the values fit together. It is difficult to express, but not impossible to talk about.

QUICK QUIZ #2

1. If it is not a "fact" that spitting at people at symphony concerts is rude, what is it?
2. Is there a special "logic of moral discourse"?
3. Can moral judgements contradict each other?
4. Could it be a logically necessary truth that Mussolini was not a bad man?
5. Are there experiences on which morality might be founded?
6. Is there any moral theory that is more certain than propositions like

"love is not evil" and "boiling dogs alive is bad"?

7. Is there a "logic of commands"?
8. Is there, despite all the objections, a conclusive argument in favour of an objective moral theory?
9. Is it better to judge acts or consequences? Should one judge neither?
10. Can one judge the rational will of which Kant speaks?
11. Should there, in the end, be only one moral rule?

Notes

1. G.E. Moore, *Principia Ethica,* Cambridge: The University Press, 1903, Chapter 1. Moore (1873–1958) was a Cambridge philosopher, a friend of Russell, McTaggart and Whitehead. His ethics greatly influenced the "Bloomsbury group" of writers including Virginia Woolf.
2. The expression "2 + 2" does contain the additional notion of "plus." It is also true that "3 + 1 = 4," something that made Kant think that "2 + 2 = 4" is not so simple a notion as one might think. The identity here is just the identity of substitutability.
3. See his *On Utilitarianism.* There are many editions. One with useful commentary by James M. Smith and Ernest Sosa is published as *Mill's Utilitarianism*, Belmont, CA: Wadsworth, 1969.
4. Thomas Hill Green, *Prolegomena to Ethics,* Oxford: Clarendon Press, Fourth Edition, 1899; Francis Herbert Bradley, *Ethical Studies,* Oxford: Clarendon Press, 1876, second edition, 1927.
5. Immanuel Kant, *Fundamental Principles of the Metaphysics of Morals,* tr. T.K. Abbott, London: Longmans Green, 1907.
6. Such questions, especially those to do with limits to the possibility of questioning all moral issues, have been raised by Philippa Foot in *Virtues and Vices,* Berkeley: University of California Press, 1978. There has been a great deal of moral theorizing of late about questions of this kind, often in the context of doctrines attributed to Ludwig Wittgenstein to the effect that not everything, after all, can be questioned because the language that we need to pose such questions becomes debased. The rudeness example indicates how one can end up talking nonsense if one is not careful. Most of these issues have been raised and explored by Robert L. Arrington in *Rationalism, Realism and Relativism,* Ithaca, NY: Cornell University Press, 1989.
7. *The Right and the Good,* Oxford: Clarendon Press, 1930.
8. Especially *The Definition of Good,* London: Macmillan, 1947; and *Second Thoughts in Moral Philosophy,* London: Routledge and Kegan Paul, 1959.
9. Charles L. Stevenson, *Ethics and Language,* New Haven: Yale University Press, 1944, and *Facts and Values,* New Haven: Yale University Press, 1963.
10. *The Language of Morals,* Oxford: Clarendon Press, 1952.
11. See, for instance, some of the material in Peter Geach, *Logic Matters,* Oxford: Basil Blackwell, 1972, second edition, 1981.
12. Immanuel Kant's basic moral theory is found in his *Grundlegung zur Metaphysik der Sitten,* Riga, 1785, *Werke,* Prussian Academy Edition, Vol. IV, p. 394; tr. as *Fundamental Principles of the Metaphysic of Ethics* by Otto Manthey-Zorn, New York: Appleton-Century, 1938. He says (p. 8), "It is impossible to conceive of anything in the world or even out of it that can without qualification be called good,

except a Good Will." It quickly emerges that what is good, however, is the will subordinated to the principles of pure practical reason, the rational will.

13. John Stuart Mill's *On Utilitarianism* was first published in *Fraser's Magazine*, October-December 1861. A good modern edition with explanatory notes is James M. Smith and Ernest Sosa, *Mill's Utilitarianism,* Belmont, CA: Wadsworth, 1969.

14. This is a sticky matter. Does the notion of a hierarchy of pleasures introduce the idea of a moral distinction between pleasures or is the distinction merely a matter of fact, like the distinction between a BMW and a Chevrolet? (One is "better" than the other in that it will probably last longer, accelerate more quickly and so forth.) Mill is not very clear. For instance, he talks about people and pigs being different and about pleasures suited to human "faculties." But then he says "human beings have appetites more elevated than the animal appetites." (Smith and Sosa edition, Belmont: California, Wadsworth, 1969, p.37.) "Elevated" suggests a moral distinction. If Mill means this, he has introduced a moral theory that adds to and is not much like the theories he has been appealing to.

15. Oxford: Clarendon Press, 1876, second edition 1927.

16. See note 12.

17. See note 12.

18. For a discussion of a kind of moral based on this notion see Leslie Armour, "The Duty to Seek Agreement," *Journal of Philosophy,* December 3, 1959.

19. For more about this question, see Leslie Armour and Chhatrapati Singh, "The Kingdom of Ends in Morals and Law," *Indian Philosophical Quarterly*, Jan–March, 1986, p. 13–27.

Chapter 13

LOGIC AND POLITICS

We come now to a difficult—and final—issue. We have seen that one can reason about morals and about public policy. Our investigations into the justification of persuasion and the traditional fallacies revealed that arguments always presuppose a framework. We direct arguments to each other and suppose an orderly process for the giving and taking of reasons in which the argument can progress to a conclusion. The possibilities of public debate and of developing the parliamentary "rules of order" are necessarily related, as is our legal system, to the notions that reasons can be given and taken and there are good and bad reasons. We will see that adopting certain kinds of logic makes it difficult or even impossible to state and argue certain political positions. As logicians we are concerned with the nature of reasons, and in the context of this book, with the use of logic to set us free. Thus we want to make it possible to state and argue for the widest possible array of political positions and not to preclude the possibility of certain positions whether or not, as political philosophers or ethicists, we like these positions.

1. Russell's Logic and "Individualism"

We have so far hinted at but not explored the problems posed by the structures of logic itself. Both Aristotelian and Russell-Frege logic suppose that the world was made up of collections of distinct things, which can be identified as individuals and assembled into classes or otherwise clustered so that they can be referred to collectively. These logics assumed that the world is composed of things with clear boundaries or sharp edges to them. Indeed, the classes to which they are committed are, themselves, abstract individuals.[1]

To get at the roots of any subject matter, one must first identify the classes involved and then come to specify the individuals within them. Sentences like "All doctors provide health care" and "If anyone is a doctor he or she provides health care" express basic features of Aristotelian and Russell-Frege logics respectively. Each assumes that doctors can be assembled into a class so that there is a single statement about them. "Some doctors are socialists" and "there is someone such that he or she is a doctor and a socialist" express the possibilities that such classes can be broken down into individuals and, indeed, are abstract individuals themselves. There are classes and there are members of classes. Classes are assembled from members.

It seems that such logics have an "individualistic bias." This has troubled those who insist that we need some other kind of logic—these include dialectical logicians (Hegelians and Marxists of various sorts) as well as those who assume a "holistic" viewpoint. It is certainly true that, in the United States, when logic is taught, it is overwhelmingly either Russell-Frege or Aristotelean logic. In the former Soviet Union interest in dialectic logic was quite considerable, as it is now in China. There is also a strong interest in it nowadays amongst environmentalists and others who, as they say, want to see things "whole."[2]

But let us consider whether there is such an "anti-holistic" bias in the Russell-Frege logics, and how it affects one's choice of logics. We will begin with a non-political example that elucidates what is at issue. Consider two cases that do not involve the *nature* of one's logic, but ways in which it is used.

Sentences like "P and Q know X" suggest that there are two true sentences:

P knows X.
Q knows X.

But this is often false. For instance, it is true that "The Boeing Aircraft Company knows how to make airplanes." So there is a long sentence naming its workers that reads "P and Q and S and R and T... know how to make airplanes." But it is virtually certain that no one person in the company knows how to make an airplane. The knowledge of a great many people is required.[3]

So it is sometimes argued that when we say "Denmark is a peaceful country," we infer, if not that all Danes are peaceful, at least that by and large Danes are peaceful—perhaps that a majority of Danes are peaceful. This is probably true but it need not be. (Denmark has its share of biker gangs these days.) Much of the time, Canada, like Denmark, has been a peaceful country. But anyone who has seen Canadians in a hockey arena will doubt whether Canadians, as a whole, are peaceful.

What makes for a peaceful country is not necessarily an assembly of peaceful people but a whole social context—a set of shared beliefs about public order, a legal system, and various traditions. The individuals, if removed from this context or put in another one, might turn out quite differently. In two world wars many people were surprised by the behaviour of Canadian regiments like the Princess Patricia's Canadian Light Infantry and the Royal 22nd Regiment. (The Danes did not get a chance to show *their* ferocity.)

2. What is an Individual?

The difficulty in the two previous cases is that we make mistakes in deciding what counts as an analyzable individual. Consider "P and Q know X." "P and Q" may name a group that we can think of as composed of individuals and each knows X. For instance, if it is true that "Joe and Ted know how to skate," it is true that "Joe knows how to skate" and "Ted knows how to skate." But "P and Q" may name something that has to be taken as a whole, a single individual. That is, sometimes "P and Q" has to be taken as a unit and so the *unit* knows X. Similarly, sometimes "Denmark" and "Canada" name *collections* that can analyzed into individuals. However, sometimes "Denmark" and "Canada" name "*unanalyzable collections*," that is, a collection that must be treated as though it were an individual.

It is very important for political analysis to remember this. Indeed, it is sometimes assumed in political discussions that all interests, for instance, are the interests of individuals (in the common sense of individual persons) and that there is no such thing as a "community interest" which is anything other than the sum of the interests of individual persons. This would seem to be a dangerous assumption.

For instance, it may well be that we have duties to future generations and that the community that owes so much to the past can be said to owe just as much to the future. But this concern—which is surely legitimate whatever priority you give it—cannot be analyzed out into the interest of any existing individual or group of individuals. We will all be dead when the long-range future arrives.

There are other, much more difficult questions. Some of them demand— or seem to—that we look at the world in ways that do not require us merely to be more careful about how we use our logics but also to think about things in ways that the traditional logics make very difficult, indeed.

All the traditional logics *do* require us to look at things in terms of individuals and classes (or whatever we want to substitute for classes to designate what are essentially clusters of things, or names of ways to cluster things). But this supposes that one can draw lines between things.

3. Aspects or Individuals? A Different Way of Looking at the World

In the discussion of dialectical logic, we used the example of the rabbit. We think we know where the rabbit ends and the world begins. But without food to eat, grass and carrots and whatever else, the rabbit dies. If there is a little too much of the wrong kind of radiation from a distant star, the rabbit dies. If people use too many of the wrong kinds of spray deodorants and damage the ozone layer of the atmosphere, the rabbit may also die.

The rabbit depends as much for its existence on these distant elements as on the continued good functioning of its stomach. If we really are concerned about rabbits we have to think of the whole world as "rabbit-and-environment."

Things get even more puzzling if we pursue what we know as ordinary objects in the world. Over there is a motor car. It weighs, let us say, a little more than a tonne. But we can only express its weight as a relation between it and a weighing machine. How much would it weigh if it were the only object in the world? Moreover, It is 4.36 metres long. But that is a relation between it and what physicists define as "the metre."[4] Could the car have "length" if it were the only object in existence? If the definition of the standard metre changed, would that change the length of the car?

When we come to distinguish ourselves from the rest of the world, the situation may become more puzzling. Can you draw boundaries around yourself? Can you say just where you end and the rest of the world begins? Everything you know is within your own experience. You could think of yourself as co-extensive with the whole universe. Perhaps all the other apparent people are only figments of *your* imagination. At the other extreme, you could think of yourself only as a kind of spectator, aware of but not really involved in the world. You are not, after all, literally identical with your body or with any other object or state of affairs in the world. Blaise Pascal remarked that to be human is to be both *"infini"* and *"rien"*—everything and nothing.[5]

You can only talk about yourself in a certain context. You divide the world when you use the concept of "responsibility" to connect yourself to certain events. When you know what you and others are responsible for, you know how you fit into the world. "Responsibility" is a difficult concept to use, but the point is that only within a certain context do we know what rabbits are, what motor cars are, and what people are.

Otherwise put: there are no individuals of any particular kind except in the context of a scheme within which individuals can be individuated from one another. Given that there are systems of material objects, we can measure them. Given that there is a whole environment, we can see how rabbits represent one possible focus of it. Given systems of responsibility, we can distinguish one person from another.

4. Politics and Ways of Dividing the World

In political arguments this is very important, and the way in which it is important poses interesting logical issues. People only become effectively individuated within social contexts. It is thus of the utmost importance to maintain those contexts in a healthy condition. We become genuinely distinct when we have a chance to individuate ourselves and to become responsible beings. For this we need education, companionship and the basic necessities of a physical life. If we assume that society is simply a collection of entities competing for various spoils, we may well miss the need for these arrangements.

But the *conditions* necessary for the creation of individuals are *not* other "individuals" in any intelligible logical sense. If we fail to notice this, the state may become a sort of super-individual, which is a mythical creature. Nonetheless, the idea of the state as super-individual played an important part in the creation of the illusions that made possible Hitler and Stalin, and such illusions still play a major part in world politics.

5. Logic and Social Reality

The problem created by logics that recognize only individuals and assemblies of individuals is precisely this: Either they ignore the social realities that make individuality genuinely possible and so create individualist societies altogether too much like Thomas Hobbes' imaginary war of "all against all,"[6] or they recognize these social realities but mistake them for additional individuals, sometimes super-individuals. Both mistakes are ultimately disastrous. But what is the alternative?

QUICK QUIZ #1

1. Russell's logic has often been related to "methodological individualism." Is it also related to political individualism? Explain your answer.
2. Is it difficult to say what an individual is? Why or why not?
3. Would it make a difference to our political discourse if we regarded the world as a single unity with many different aspects?
4. Can we still talk about ordinary things if we are not committed to the ultimate existence of logical individuals?
5. Do we need to talk about social realities? What logical problems does this question pose?

---

6. The Need to Find Alternative Propositional Forms

Obviously we need to find alternatives to propositional forms like "For any x, if x is F then x is G" or "all F's are G's" to express collections, and some alternatives to forms like "Some F's are G's" and "there is an x such that x is F and x is G." We need some way of getting referential objects into discourse without supposing them to be either individuals or collections of individuals. There are a number of ways of achieving this, two of which can be discussed here. One is to follow out some of the implications of John Dewey's program. The second is to develop an appropriate kind of dialectical logic.

There was a latent issue in the discussion of Dewey's program, which we can now bring to the surface. We do not quite know how Dewey himself would have developed it as a logical issue, but recall that we presented his system as involving initial assumptions about the probabilities of propositions. Such assumptions have to do with the context of the discussion. Suppose, for instance, that we want to predict the behaviour of a group of people.

7. A Deweyite Analysis

Suppose there is a city, Megalopolis, which has a high rate of violent crime and that there are good reasons to believe that about eighty percent of the violent crime relates to the drug trade. People meet to predict the future and to take steps to control the situation. One might say that (as Nancy Reagan once did) drug users cause society's drug problems. So, urge people not to consume illegal drugs. If people voluntarily stop using illegal drugs, the demand for them drops and so will all drug-related violence. If people do not voluntarily stop, then prosecute them. (Nancy Reagan once suggested the death penalty for drug dealers.)

Although it is true that the dead neither sell nor use drugs, on the basis of past experience, a Deweyite would assign quite a low probability to the success of any such program. Very likely continued experience would suggest lower and lower probabilities of success for any project directed solely at users and dealers.

Instead of addressing the individuals, we could ask why we assign a low probability to the success of such a program. Have we made a mistake about human nature? Is it false to claim that people are free to decide *not* to take drugs? Did we make a mistake about human rationality? Are people not able to see that taking drugs is bad for them, or that a complex technological society—one in which people fly airplanes, drive automobiles, and operate dangerous and complex machinery—needs to have most of its citizens, most of the time, in their right minds?

Neither of these assumptions seems very plausible. But it does seem likely that there is a social context that is not to be understood simply in terms of the behaviour of the persons addressed by Mrs. Reagan. This context, quite likely, has something to do with it. Why do people want to "escape" their normal experiences and find new ones? Why are people attracted to the amounts of money that can be made quickly by dealing in drugs? What kinds of social arrangements make the illegal drug industry feasible? Drug users do not make the social conditions that lead to the need for escape. The social fabric involved is no doubt very complex. Boredom is a factor. Another is the pressure people face in competitive societies, not all of whom succeed. Finally, there is the question as to whether or not human beings can physically or psychologically adapt to the kinds of societies in which they live.

Drug dealers are sometimes just drug takers who need the money to supply their own needs. Sometimes they are relatively poor people who are denied access to the more attractive jobs that our society has to offer. And so on. But notice that these propositions about the social structure do not refer to individuals—they refer, rather, to the conditions under which it is appropriate to assign probabilities to events. Just as not all propositions about horse racing are about race-horses, so not all propositions about the social order are about individuals. To know what odds to give on a particular horse in a steeple chase, you do need to know how fast it can run and how high it can jump with a rider on board, but you also have to know about the track, about how the horse reacts to the other horses (and they to it), about how this race fits into its whole schedule of races and so on.

You need to establish a context. The context is given in such "Deweyite" logics by asking what information you need to assign the initial probabilities.

Notice there are different levels of analysis. Some are about the individuals, the horses, while others are about the context of the event. This context is not a super individual; rather, it is the conditions under which individuals are expected to behave in one way or another. Looked at this way, the state, the social order, one's social class or whatever are unlikely to become new objects of hero-worship.

Of course a social context, say a state, may function as an individual at another level of analysis. Sometimes we want to know how states will behave, and the context for estimating this is the world order, the system of international law, the United Nations, the pressure of world trade and so on.

But there are always two sorts of questions: what individuals are involved and what is the context in which they function? Generally—though this is not a certain and universal truth, either—both questions need to be addressed.

One advantage of the "Deweyite" analysis is that one does not have to take the things one talks about as ultimately real in themselves. Is there really such a thing as Canada or Belgium in the sense that there is such a person as Susie Smith? That question has resulted in much spilled ink. But it may not even be a sensible question. Canada cannot be an entity like Susie Smith. It has neither a body nor a mother. Nor can it literally suffer or rejoice. But Canada is a very real social context.

Susie Smith can suffer and can rejoice; though, as we saw, it requires a social context to identify her. She and her social context are not ultimately separate except in the sense that she can move from one context to another. But even then she will take a lot of her existing social context with her.

There is a relation between this account (which derives from some of Dewey's notions) and the dialectical thesis. As we have seen repeatedly, our "standard" logics conceive of the world as a collection of bits and pieces of things. But now, let us think about the idea of "totality." Is the totality another thing? Surely not. If it were, there would have to be still another thing: it and the totality it sums. Is it not-another-thing? But then how can we talk about it? To talk about it is just to talk about all the individuals.

It is so with any totality. Is the United States something over and above all the people in the United States? If it is, shouldn't it have a vote too? But if it is not, then we can only talk about various groups of individuals—and various kinds of individual interests? This not only seems odd but of course breeds "interest-group" politics and all that such politics imply.

8. A Dialectical Analysis

The dialectician maintains that the problem is that certain issues have been buried. What has been buried, basically, is the fact that conceiving of the world as a collection of bits and pieces is itself a framework that biases the outcome. We are always involved with some way of conceptualizing the totality. But whatever way we choose, it always excludes something. But what is excluded from the bits-and-pieces conception is the very idea of totality itself.

The Russell-Frege and Aristotelian logics are very useful within the domain of what Hegel called "determinate being." But they exclude whatever reality cannot be conceptualized in that way. The obvious alternative is a picture that we called Systematic Unity.[7]

It is not that one of these pictures is right and the other is wrong. It is that each captures some aspects of reality and excludes others. This is clear when we look at the propositional forms appropriate to each viewpoint. Compare:

> "There is an x such that x is F and x is G" *and* "For any x if x is F, then x is G"

with

> "Reality manifests itself at some time and some place as x and does so through F and G"

and

> "Whenever reality manifests itself as x through F, it also manifests itself as x through G."

So as not to mystify ourselves, we can give meanings or values to the various variables "x," "F," "G," "reality" and "manifests."

To do this, we must first say a little about each of them.

"x": Russell usually meant by "the class of all x's" "the world," that is, he saw the world as a collection of denotable things, each one of which would be an x.

"F" and "G": These are usually the names of characteristics—qualities and relations—or properties. Whether, apart from their instantiations in things, they have any "being" is a matter of dispute. Philosophers like Quine say they don't; Platonists say they do.

"Reality": In this (for the moment purely logical) context, reality just means the background unity within which things are distinguished, differentiated or individuated (i.e., depends on your choice of terminology.)

"Manifests": The relation between the background reality and the individuated particular. (The individuated particular is often, but not necessarily, a concrete individual. The number two is, however, quite likely an individuated particular, too. Whether "justice" can be an individuated particular is a matter of dispute. In ordinary speech, at least, only concrete particulars are normally called individuals.)

Now we can notice the difference between the propositional forms we have distinguished. The first group—which has only x's and F's and G's in it—says nothing about the background conditions. Russell sometimes believed that one should spell it out, however, and thought that an x might be anything "in space and time."

This begins to give the game away. Canada is not in space and time in the same way that Susie Smith is. Canada has a history but Canada is not an actor on the stage of history. In fact, before we can make sense of history we have to create a structure to give it meaning. Can we write a meaningful history of Susie Smith, or only of the Smith family, or only of Manitoba (in which they live), or only of Canada as a whole? Do we need, really, to see Canada in the context of the British Commonwealth, or the English-speaking nations, or the whole of Western civilization? Or is all history really world history? Before historians can tackle it, space and time have to be shaped by some background.

The reality of Susie Smith may be expressed through the history of Canada (or whatever), and it may be that we have to see Susie Smith as one of the manifestations of that history. Of course, she influences it just as it influences her, and the relation of "manifestation" is probably very complex.

The dialectician wants to say that when this background has been spelled out, the propositions may have very different meanings, and what is more, new kinds of inferences may develop. If we know that Sally Jones and Richard Wagner are both Australians, and if we know something about how Australian culture is shaped, we may be able to make inferences about them. Probably both will be able to tell a kangaroo from a wallaby, for instance, whereas if they were Belgians they might be more likely to get them wrong.

These inferences will only be probabilistic, of course (some Australians will surely get them mixed up), but there is nothing wrong with probability if one does not confuse it with certainty. However, the dialectician claims that all propositions have buried background structures to them.

Sometimes we do not want to be bothered by any of the unifying structures and only want to count the individuals. This is true if one is counting ten euro pieces or dollar coins. Of course, if one wants to do something with the money (like start an auto factory), one will want to know about the background—the French or the Canadian economy within which the currency is a "manifestation" of an underlying reality (which is the difference between *Monopoly* money and the real thing). It is not, of course, just whole and part relations which give rise to these problems.

9. Problems of Process

The concept of process, for instance, can be equally puzzling. Henri Bergson (who developed the first useful concept of process)[8] noticed that biology textbooks seem to falsify reality. They paint the development of the butterfly as passing from egg to caterpillar, to pupa and to moth as if each stage were a distinct jump. Reality, by contrast, he said, is a seamless process. This unfolding background cannot be described effectively as a series of distinct jumps. But it can be regarded as a background reality, that manifests itself in different ways, and propositional forms can be developed—meanings given to the "reality" in question and to the "process of manifestation."

Processes are tricky in human affairs and politics as well as in biology. A human being is a continuous thread running through time. If the world stopped tomorrow, we could tell little about Susie Smith or Heinrich Waldheim or Gaston Laforge—or anyone—from the slice of reality that would be left. (Indeed, physical theory suggests that much of the world would simply not be there. Perhaps there could be no world at all in a single moment of time.)

We can make the mistake in politics of looking for "punctiform" solutions when none are available. Consider the case of those Canadians who wanted something called the *Meech Lake Accord*, which would have defined for a good while into the future certain basic relations between French and English Canada. It would have frozen the situation—or tried to freeze it—at a particular point in time.

But if we think of constitutions not just as pieces of paper but as sets of background, governing principles that limit what can and cannot be done in political life, we will see that they are not really like that. They can come into being only when there is a consensus, and their legal interpretation over time tends to give shape to that broad consensus. At a certain moment in June 1990, no such consensus existed in Canada that was broad enough to include women, French Canadians, Aboriginal peoples and all ethnic minorities. No constitution could have come into existence. Only a gradual process within which such an agreement could grow could possibly do the work that the *Meech Lake Accord* was supposed to achieve. (Despite the efforts of their historians to set them straight, many Americans have been misled as to how their constitution came into being. Their revolution was fought by people who demanded the common law rights of Englishmen, which had been denied to them as colonists. Their constitution did not create a new instant agreement but tried to render an existing consensus incarnate. Even this proved difficult enough.) Clearly, simple, individual, events are not enough.

10. Logical Structures with Two Levels of Analysis

The propositions that emphasize background reality and its manifestations provide ways to avoid being frozen into a doctrine of individual events. They propose various kinds of two-level analysis to circumvent the problems posed for logical analysis by the denial that all reality is punctiform. One level of such an analysis spells out a background unity and the other specifies the individuals concerned. The propositional forms with "reality" and "manifests" in them have the further merit of demanding that we specify some of the relations between the levels.

The dialectical schema tend to emphasize the different ways of conceptualizing the backgrounds, and the "Deweyite" schema have the merit of emphasizing the elements of probability involved. But they can be combined in various ways. The issue is whether or not one seems to have grounds for saying something that one logic or another prevents one from saying.

Since the first account of dialectical principles appeared in the work of Proclus[9] in the fifth century, philosophers have been looking for ways to clarify these structures. Proclus laid down three general principles: everything begins in unity; develops by some process into particularity; and returns to unity. All true propositions have a place within one of these phases. We are far from having a finished dialectical logic and yet we have made a good deal of progress.[10]

One final question remains, however, though it will turn out to have some connections to the issues already raised. It has to do with the tricky matter that most clearly divided Russell from the Aristotelian tradition.

Aristotelians had thought that one could infer validly from propositions of the form:

> "All doctors live by assault."

to propositions of the form:

> "Some doctors live by assault."

Philosophers like Russell argued that, in fact,

> "All doctors live by assault"

really means something hypothetical:

> "If anyone is a doctor, then he lives by assault."

But he believed that

> "Some doctors live by assault"

means:

> "Someone (at least one person) is a doctor and he lives by assault."

11. The Ideology behind Russellian Logic

Now there might not be any doctors in one of several senses. It might be that if we define doctors as "persons who provide health care and who live by assault," we shall find that there are not any. Or even if we mean by doctors only "licensed dispensers of general health care," there really aren't any, anyhow. But such a world is at least imaginable.

For several decades after what amounted to a fairly widespread revolution in logic, Catholic universities generally continued to teach Aristotelian logic and to resist the logics of philosophers like Russell partly because of the important philosophical and ideological issue involved. As we shall see, this issue not only has some possible religious significance, but may also have political significance. And it is by no means so obvious as one might think that the Russellians were right. Indeed, this dispute is not easy to settle. Yet, however we finally do settle it, discovering why the answer is not obvious will tell us something important about the nature of logic and its relation to various ideological disputes.

12. St. Thomas Aquinas and the Proofs for the Existence of God

We can see why this might be of *religious* interest if we look at the way our decision might affect certain arguments used, for instance, by St. Thomas Aquinas in the *Summa Theologica*.[11] We can then see why there might be political implications to the problem. In the *Summa*, Aquinas presents five "ways" to God. The third way goes like this:

> Some things in the world are contingent (i.e., they are merely possible elements in any world and do not exist necessarily).
>
> But not everything can be contingent (i.e., not everything can be merely possible).
>
> Everything that is contingent depends on something else for its existence (otherwise it would be necessary).
>
> Thus if everything were merely contingent, the chain of causal events would go back infinitely in time.
>
> But if any thing is contingent, there will be some time in any infinite series when it does not exist.
>
> This is true for each and every contingent thing.
>
> If time goes back infinitely, there would have been a time when no contingent things exist.
>
> Therefore, there would be a time when nothing existed.
>
> But if it is true that there was a time when nothing existed, then there would still be nothing, for out of nothing nothing comes.
>
> There is something that does exist.
>
> Therefore some *necessary being* exists.
>
> (In Aquinas' view this necessary being is God.)

Now notice that this argument depends on there being a certain relation between hypothetical assertions and what are called categorical assertions— i.e. assertions that state something to be the case. The argument goes from premises like "For any x if x is F then x is G," to a conclusion of the form "there is an x such that x is a necessary being." One premise is "If anything is a merely possible event, then it has a cause." The conclusion is "a necessary being exists."

Thus stated, the argument has two premises of the sort Russell thought to be "existentially quantified," that is, premises from which one could infer something about the actual world. One asserts that "something exists" (to say that there *are* some contingent things is to say that some—at least one—exists. Another premise asserts that "some things are merely possible." (If some things are contingent and not all of them exist at once, then some things are just possible things some of the time.)

Each of these assertions is a little odd. Russell admitted that there must be at least one x to make his system work, but the assertion that something exists sounds strange when it is translated into a form like "there is an x such that it exists." It is doubtful that anything will follow from such an assertion, in any case.

The assertions that "not everything is actual" and that "some things are merely possible" are also somewhat odd since they involve what are sometimes thought to be "modal operators." They appear to be expressed in sentences that are used, in part, to distinguish between *necessary* and *contingent* truths. Logicians are inclined to say that statements like "All red balls are red" express necessary truths, while statements like "Some red balls have black spots on them" express contingent truths. There is no way, that is, that a factual investigation could falsify "All red balls are red," but we could look at all the red balls in the world and find out that none of them have black spots on them. But necessary truths, many logicians would say, tell us nothing about the world, and, in fact, expressions like "necessary" and "contingent" distinguish only between kinds of propositions and not between states of affairs in the world. Thus it is not so clear what the premises in question actually say about the world. If all truths about the world are contingent, then a statement like "Some things are merely contingent" tells us nothing except that there is a world, for *all* the truths about it will be contingent. The difficulty in settling these questions makes the premises suspect.

Indeed, the argument seems to refer to possibilities—contingent events are sometimes merely possible. But Willard Quine in his famous essay "On What There Is" spoke darkly of "the slum of possibles," which is a "breeding ground for disorderly elements." He wondered how we can we talk about possibilities as real things? "How many possible fat men are there in that doorway? Are there more possible thin ones than fat ones?"[12]

We could, however, avoid this difficulty by simply defining the "merely possible" as something that needs to have a cause to exist. Then we can quite easily produce an argument that is valid in Aristotle's logic, though *not* in Russell's or in Quine's. It would go like this:

> Whatever is merely possible has a cause.
> Whatever has a cause is part of a causal chain.
> If nothing were necessary, the chain of causes would be infinitely long.
> If one had an infinite chain of contingent events, there would be a time when nothing existed.
> If the whole truth about reality were ever that nothing existed, nothing could ever exist.
> If nothing ever existed, propositions about the existence of something could not be made.
> If propositions could not be made, this argument could not be stated.
> This argument has been stated.
> Therefore something exists and is necessary.

In this form, it is clear that all the premises except the last are hypothetical, and the conclusion is categorical. The last premise merely refers to the argument and not to the world, and its force depends entirely on the hypothetical arguments.

The reason that this argument is valid in one logic and not in the other is that, in Aristotelian terms, the premises are all universal affirmatives and the conclusion is a particular affirmative. This inference, as we saw when we talked about Aristotle and Russell, is valid in Aristotle's system and not in Russell's because Russell believed that universal affirmative propositions were all hypothetical. "If anything is an x then it is a y" is his translation of Aristotle's "All x's are y's" and this argument is stated in the Russellian way. From the merely hypothetical, nothing about the real world follows.

But the question is: What justifies the translation? Let us restate the argument in more nearly Aristotelian terms and then ask some more questions:

> All events that are contingent have causes.
> All events that have causes are parts of causal chains.
> All causal chains that contain no necessary events are infinitely long.
> All infinitely long causal chains that contain no necessary events contain an element that is a moment in time at which nothing exists.
> All moments at which nothing exists are followed only by moments at which nothing exists.
> All instances of nothingness are states of affairs in which no arguments can be stated.
> We have stated an argument.
> Therefore a necessary event has occurred.

Allowing, perhaps, for a few oddities of expression, this is a valid Aristotelian syllogism of the sort called a "sorites."[13] It is true that it concedes to the Russellian that some matter of fact (i.e., that an argument has been stated) is admitted; but a Russellian would not want to admit that "arguments can be stated" is a sufficiently powerful matter of fact to be the only one needed to prove that God exists. (Russell was a self-professed atheist.)

St. Thomas Aquinas himself, certainly, always insisted that some matter of fact must enter into all the sound arguments for the existence of God and that all knowledge begins in sensory experience. But he tended to regard propositions of the form "some events are contingent" as expressing matters of fact and as dependent, in some sense, on experience.

The dispute between the mediaeval and modern Aristotelians (or some of them) and the Russellians, and perhaps between Aristotle himself and logicians who want to restrict what can be said about the world to what can be said in certain existentially quantified propositions, amounts to this: one side really wants to talk about certain necessary organizing features of the world. These universal propositions can only be expressed in sentences like "All cases of F are cases of G" or "If anything is an F, then it is a G." If one cannot claim that these propositions are about the world, then one cannot talk about these general organizing features.

Such notions are expressed in the assertions that we saw earlier about how contingent events are related to causes and about whether something can come from nothing. Our concern here is not with the soundness of our sample argument,[14] but simply with the logical issues involved. This may be another case like the one which we saw in Chapter 12, in which one might be reluctant to allow one's choice of logic to decide what one can and cannot talk about. But the issues, as I said, are not so easy to settle in these terms.

13. The Political Implications of Logical Ideologies

Notice, that there are political implications. They arise when one begins to talk about human rights, which are usually enshrined in documents like the United Nations' "Universal Declaration of Human Rights" or in the fundamental clauses of national constitutions. Their essence is that, without exception, they apply to *all human beings.*

But on the Russellian analysis, statements beginning "All x's" or "For any x" express hypothetical propositions, which are not about facts of the world but how concepts are related. They cannot be given existential quantifiers (or should not be), and so cannot be made to refer to states of affairs in the world. Russell himself was a strong supporter of human rights. But he thought that these rights had to be supported on emotional rather than rational grounds. And when emotions collide the victory tends to go to the side with the most force at its disposal.

Universal sentences or propositions seem to be about how certain organizing principles in the universe function. They suggest certain necessary connections between properties of things, for instance that all potentially rational human beings are entitled to be protected against cruel punishments, or to have their lives safeguarded, or to exercise freedom of speech.

In a world picture like that of St. Thomas Aquinas, these ideas had a natural place. For it was supposed that, if God existed (and St.Thomas believed that he had proved that God did exist), then God would have created the world in such a way as to instantiate his own goodness. He could not create another God but he could create a world in which each object possessed at least one divine property, but no single object possesses all the divine properties. All the properties, taken together, would form "a great chain of being," which, as a whole, would contain as much of the goodness of God as God deemed possible or suitable for any world.

One could therefore suppose that there would be various kinds of things— inanimate entities, animate beings, beings that were not alive but could reason, and purely rational beings. Each thing would play its part in the whole. Now when you ask what part humans are fitted to play, it becomes clear that we are animals who reason and therefore can play the part of rational animals. There is no need for humans to behave like pigs since pigs do that very well. We cannot behave like angels because we are not *purely* rational creatures.[15] It follows, reasonably, that we should have the rights appropriate to the part we have to play—i.e., the natural rights of rational animals.

This picture depends on information about the general organizing features of the universe. If we do not have this knowledge, it will not be possible to argue in this way for universal human rights. Notice that the argument is not that we are rational but that the part we can best play is that of rational animals and that we live in a universe in which every creature is expected to play its part. (This has profound implications for the environmental movement, the animal rights movement and nearly every major contemporary cause.)

One can certainly look at the universe in other ways and get other arguments, but they, too, depend on the claim that we can use the general organizing properties of the universe as premises in important arguments about rights. For instance, one can argue that the universe, as we know it, comes in three parts: "nature," "knowledge," and "art." A slow, evolutionary process organized matter so that sentience can be expressed, and thereby "knowledge" enters into the world. "Knowledge," however, has many different forms. It can be the capacity to accomplish something. Aristotle recognized that bees "know" how to build nests.[16] Marx observed that beavers "know" how to build dams (productive skills not tied to capitalist wage-slavery!). But no great bees and beaver architects show themselves.[17] Beavers only build the same kind of dam and bees only the same kind of nest. Art, however, is a human product. We can therefore regard nature as a process in which nature is transformed into knowledge and knowledge into art. Values—even our most fundamental ideas of the good—arise at the level of creativity. The lion that eats the lamb acts only according to his nature and earns no blame. The human being who eats another is indulging in an innovation that must be justified. If value and art are conceptually linked in this way, then we can regard the process of nature transforming into knowledge and knowledge into art as necessary to all values, and therefore valuable in itself. If so, again, the participants have the right to be considered creators of value, but so do the systems of nature and those of the sentient creatures on which our transformations depend. In such a way we can defend human rights and the rights of nature. But this can only be done by drawing on arguments about the organizing properties of nature and making use of universal propositions of the kind that can justify existential conclusions in Aristotelian (but not Russellian) arguments.

Once again the issue is not the soundness of the arguments. Very many questions can and ought to be raised about the nature, knowledge and art argument just sketched. The question is whether or not we want to use our choice of logics to determine what sorts of things can be discussed.

It seems likely that if we want the human race to survive into the next century we should be careful about such things. But, again, let us return to our original theme: logic and human freedom. In the end, freedom consists of being able to see beyond the horizons of every enclosing system—of being able to ask every kind of question. And this is the ultimate reason for being careful about the politics of logic. One should not let one's choice of logic impose restrictions on one's freedom—provided of course that one can see rational alternatives. Where that line is drawn readers must decide for themselves.

QUICK QUIZ #2

1. Do we need alternatives to the propositional forms in addition to those proposed by logicians in the Russellian tradition?
2. How would a Deweyite analyze the problems discussed in this chapter?
3. How would a dialectical logician's answers to the problems posed in this chapter differ from those of a Deweyite?
4. Why does the idea of process pose logical problems?
5. Does it help to introduce two-level analyses of problems about process?
6. How would you characterize the ideology behind Russellian logic?
7. To argue for the existence of God in the way that St. Thomas Aquinas did, does one need to take issue with Russell's logic and with all similar logics?
8. In order to argue for the existence of universal human rights, does one need to take issue with Russellian logic and with all similar logics?

Notes

1. The view that the world consists of concrete and abstract *individuals* is quite widely held. For instance Hector-Neri Castañeda, in a recent and very sophisticated attempt to build a contemporary world view, makes use of a wide array of contemporary logical devices and discusses in detail many possible world views. But all the views he takes to be worthy of detailed analysis are world pictures in which the existents are individuals of various kinds. See his *Thinking, Language and Experience,* Minneapolis: University of Minnesota Press, 1989.
2. See E.V. Ilyenkov, *Dialectical Logic, Essays on Its History and Theory,* Moscow: Progress Publishers, 1977; D.P. Gorsky, *Definition,* Moscow; Progress Publishers, 1974. For a history of the whole issue, see A. Makovelski, *Histoire de la logique,* Moscow: Progress Publishers, 1978. For a non-Marxist account, see Leslie Armour, *Logic and Reality,* Assen: Royal Vangorcum; and New York: Humanities Press, 1972.
3. There is a good discussion of this and related issues in Gerald J. Massey, "Are There Any Good Arguments that Bad Arguments Are Bad?" *Philosophy in Context,* Volume 4, 1975, p. 61–77.
4. Physicists define the "metre" as "the length of path traversed by light during the interval of 1/299,792,458 of a second." A "second" is defined as 9,192,631,770 vibrations of a cesium atom (when it is vibrating in a particular manner.)
5. Blaise Pascal, *Pensées*, ed. Louis Lafuma (Paris: Delmas, 1960). (The numbering from this edition is used in the English translation of John Warrington, London: Dent, 1960, [Everyman Vol. 874]. The words occur in *Pensées* #343 [#233 in the

numbering of Léon Brunschsvicg, which is often used].)

6. *Leviathan* was first published 1651. See Part I, Chapter 13, "Of the Natural Condition of Mankind..."

7. See chapter 5 of our text as well as *Logic and Reality,* Assen: Royal Vangorcum; and New York: Humanities Press, 1972.

8. See *L'Évolution créatrice,* Paris: Presses Universitaires de France, 1907, tr. as *Creative Evolution* by Arthur Mitchell, New York: Henry Holt, 1911.

9. For an account of Proclus (411–85) and his relation to later dialecticians—including Hegel and Marx—see Alexander Philipov, *Logic and Dialectic in the Soviet Union,* New York: Research Program on the U.S.S.R., 1952, p. 10 ff.

10. For recent work see Howard P. Kainz, *Paradox, Dialectic, and System*, University Park, Pennsylvania: Pennsylvania State University Press, 1988.

11. Part I, Question 2, Article 3.

12. *From a Logical Point of View,* Cambridge, MA: Harvard University Press, revised edition, 1961, New York: Harper, 1963, Chapter 1, p. 4 There actually is an answer to Quine. One cannot say how many possible fat men will fit into a doorway. But if one asks a slightly different question, "For how many fat men does this doorway provide a possible shelter?" the answer is usually "one or at most two" and it is usually obvious that this is so. By asking about "possibilities for fat men" instead of about "possible fat men," we may well solve the problem. Quine insists that we can't identify them because they don't exist. "No identity without entity" is one of his slogans. But our strategy is to not talk about "possible fat men" but only about "possibilities *for* fat men."

13. In chapter three we noted that the syllogism can be extended by adding more premises. As long as the relations of class inclusion and exclusion continue to hold the argument remains valid. Such extended arguments are called "sorites."

14. We did not raise questions like: Is it really true that something cannot come from nothing? or: Is it really true that all contingent events have causes? Answering these questions is very difficult and demands inquiry into what the world needs to be intelligible, amenable to reason and so forth. The answers to such questions form part of the subject matter of metaphysics, a branch of philosophy that, in recent years, has been increasingly active and has regained some of its relations with scientific cosmology. (See John Leslie, ed., *Physical Cosmology and Philosophy,* London: Collier Macmillan, 1990; and his *Universes,* London: Routledge 1989.)

15. It is sometimes thought that the purely spiritual nature of angels is associated with *their* pure rationality. Having a body is associated with lacking perfect rationality. (The belief that women were less rational than men was derived from the allegation that women were more deeply connected to their bodies.) The basis of the association of the body with a lack of rationality was originally, we think, in the notion that bodies have appetites—for food, water and so on. But reason does not control appetites. So the more that one is connected to one's body, the more one is controlled by appetites and the less that one is controlled by reason.

16. Beekeepers construct "hives." Bees, however, build "nests."

17. It may well be that they already have the perfect design. For evolution has adapted the bee to an environment in which the nest plays a very large part. Almost any change would leave the bee less well adapted. Any change from nest to hive would require a change in the bee, but bees do not control their own environment. When we breed dogs we change their natures so that they are less well adapted to the natural environment from which they come. Whether we succeed in better adapting

them to the human environment in which we force them to live is open to question. After all, many serious canine diseases result from breeding. Human beings can create new environments for themselves and even influence their own biology. So they are not like bees and can afford architects. (Dogs fall somewhere between bees and human beings. They can exert some pressure on human beings, but they can't draw blueprints or directly hire architects to build them new environments.)

INDEX